Greta Michie, 1905–85.

GLENESK

THE HISTORY AND CULTURE OF
AN ANGUS COMMUNITY

by

Margaret Fairweather Michie

compiled and edited by

Alexander Fenton and John Beech

with a chapter by

Christina Mackenzie

EUROPEAN ETHNOLOGICAL RESEARCH CENTRE

First published in Great Britain in 2000
Reprinted 2001 by
Tuckwell Press Ltd
Phantassie
East Linton
East Lothian EH40 3DG
Scotland

ISBN 1 86232 181 7

British Library Cataloguing-in-Publication Data
A catalogue record for this book is available from the British Library

Typeset by Initial Typesetting Services, Edinburgh
Printed and bound by Cromwell Press, Trowbridge

CONTENTS

FOREWORD

I was born at the farm of Cairncross in Glenesk and had the benefit of kind parents and a good home. I had one brother, Duncan. My parents had been late in marrying, but we had many happy times, and my father was a great fiddler. Both parents were interested in antiquities. My ancestry is not a real Glenesk one, although my grandparents on the Michie side first set up house at the Drum of Lochlee in 1839. They were Aberdonian, from Corgarff. My grandfather, Duncan Michie, was a gamekeeper with Lord Panmure, later Earl of Dalhousie, and in 1854 he became Ground Officer. Eventually, he farmed Cairncross, and my father, George Michie, his fifth son, followed in his footsteps, becoming purely a farmer when no ground officer was required. My brother, Duncan, succeeded him in the tenancy adding to his ground the farms of Glentennet and Shinfur, another portion of the medieval davach of Cairncross. My mother, Alexina Fairweather, was not a native of the Glen. She brought into our lives contacts with the wider area of the low country and town. I attended Tarfside School until I was eleven and a half, and then went to stay with relatives of my mother, first attending Kirkcaldy High School and then Edinburgh Ladies' College, but thereafter both my brother and I went to Montrose Academy where we stayed in lodgings. During my last years at Montrose, after my brother had left school, I was lucky in contacting a cousin of my father, and I went to stay with her. Aunt Barbara, as I called her, taught me to appreciate Glen life. She had been brought up in Glen Lethnot, and there had been much coming and going between the two families. She spoke of the days when they thought nothing of walking across the hill to dances at Tarfside and returning by the light of the moon. She was full of tales of Queen Victoria, for several of our relatives were in the Royal service.

From Montrose I went to the University of St Andrews and lastly to Dundee College of Education. My first teaching post was in Brechin, which meant that I could go home for the weekends and on holidays. It was then that I discovered how much Glenesk meant to me, and started consciously to think of its past. One cold, winter's day, I looked out on the hills opposite Cairncross, observed the path to Lethnot outlined against the snow, and wondered about those who had gone that way. This was the start of my searches, and at that time I was particularly interested in prehistory. After six years I went to Monifieth to teach English and History. During this time I started working on a thesis on the depopulation of the Angus Glens, research which would turn into the Glenesk Museum. It was then I started collecting documentary material at the Register House in Edinburgh. By 1947, the post of teacher at Tarfside School was advertised. I got the job and stayed for fifteen years. There I found that history in depth was certainly my line and that nothing quite equalled the atmosphere of a one-teacher school. Before I went to Monifieth I had started collecting objects of historical interest. Indeed, I had asked an old friend, the late John Porter, if he would keep a cruisie mould from the Midtown Smiddy for me until I came back. The day after I moved into the schoolhouse he returned it to me.

During my stay at Tarfside there was much about what could be done for such places as Glenesk. With the enlargement of farms following mechanisation, the people were drifting out. Meantime we were interested in crafts, and I was trying to record local history. One day, encouraged by friends, I wrote to Lady Dalhousie asking for accommodation for a small local collection of museum material. Her delightful letter of consent from Lord Dalhousie and herself was the first step towards the creation of the Museum at the Retreat as part of the Glenesk Trust founded in 1955 by Lord and Lady Dalhousie for the good of the locality. Early in the year they called a meeting at Tarfside, and the Glenesk Trust was formed. The Retreat Shooting Lodge was made available to house activities consisting of a shop, tearoom and museum, and also craft classes during the winter. All departments were staffed by local people, including Davina Skene, Marion Campbell, Jessie Scott and Nancy Skene. In 1961 I gave up Tarfside School and stayed at the Retreat flat, teaching English and History at Edzell until I retired from teaching in 1965. I continued at the Retreat until 1973, and relinquished the curatorship in 1975, becoming Consultant Curator thereafter.

The Museum attempts to represent the past of this upland rural community in which it exists, mainly from the mid-eighteenth century. Practically every Glen family has contributed to the display. Yet the collection cannot be described as purely local, for descendants of Glen families from all over the world take an interest in it, and have even contributed objects once used locally. The Museum could never have existed had it not been for the people who valued their inheritance and wished it to be recorded. The Retreat itself is a pleasant place, admirably suited, both outside and in, for housing a community centre.

The scope of the museum depends on available accommodation and on the donations received. Nothing could have been more suitable so far as atmosphere is concerned than the rooms we were allotted. Except for the handsome front room, once the dining room, the museum is housed in the older part of the building, part of it built by Captain Wemyss in the mid 1840s and part of it by George Inglis, the 'Silver King', in 1879. The front room contains straight displays on such subjects as prehistory, the Church, sport, minerals, snuff, the dram, coins and tokens. There is also a collection of archival Guard Books for visitors to see. The rest of the museum, although it also contains displays in cases, is set out in rooms: the kitchen, milkhouse, best room, costume room, children's room, and farmer's room. The passageways are similarly displayed. Outside can be seen prehistoric gravestones, cheese presses, remains of querns, millstones and such like.

I have worked on documents for many years, and it was this interest that enabled me to start the Museum with some certainty of what it should contain. It took years to establish anything like a comprehensive collection. Although I have gleaned a great deal from the Register House, a tremendous amount of important material has come direct from the Glen people themselves. Eventually this accumulated material has been contained in Guard Books, each dealing with a certain subject.

The tales of our collecting adventures would take a long time to record completely. There are close on a thousand pieces from the late Miss Lindsay's house at Tarfside. There are the entire contents of the Tarfside Smithy. There are gifts from the Skenes of Turnabrane, notably an eighteenth century box bed, brought across the river by a tractor and bogey, except for the glass which I took across the 'shaky brig'. There is the head of a whisky still found near the head of Craig Soales by the late James Moir during a grouse drive, no doubt deposited by a fleet-footed fellow evading the gauger by running uphill. Its site had been marked with white stones. There is the Scandinavian-type wooden graip found in the thatch of the old house at Buskhead. There is the beautiful plough made by one of the Stephens. There are dresses, one of which, dated 1853, was the wedding dress of Mary Falconer, a relation of Robert Burns. She became Mrs Welsh of Gleneffock. The dress comes from the Skene family.

I could never have done what I did without help. It was a great experience to work with so many wonderful friends. If I started naming them the list would be as long as a chapter.

MF. Michie

Greta Michie

MARGARET FAIRWEATHER MICHIE
1905–85: A MEMOIR*

RONALD G. CANT

Greta Michie – to use the family name by which she was generally known throughout her life – was born at Cairncross in Glenesk on 29 November 1905. Her father, George Simpson Michie, had succeeded his father Duncan Michie in the tenancy of this grouping of two hill farms (Upper and Mid Cairncross near Tarfside) which formed part of the Dalhousie estates in the Glen. It was indeed as a gamekeeper to the Dalhousies that this Duncan Michie – after whom Greta's own brother was named – had come to Glenesk from Corgarff on Donside in 1839, serving later as ground officer and acquiring a farm tenancy. This association with the Dalhousie lairds, continuing into Greta's own lifetime, was characterised by a mutual respect and understanding on the basis of which her greatest achievement, the Glenesk Folk Museum, would be established in 1955.

George Michie's wife was Alexina Whyte Fairweather, daughter of a prosperous and much respected shoemaker at Carmyllie in Angus. Her brothers included three distinguished ministers of the Free and United Free Church and she brought to her home in Glenesk an appreciation of literature, art, and music, the last shared in part with her husband even if his tastes inclined to the vernacular and hers to the classical. Family life at Cairncross was active, stable, and affectionate. Both Greta and Duncan (two years her junior but her constant and cherished companion) began their schooling at Tarfside and came together again for part of their later education at Montrose. When he left to join his father in the work of the farm Greta was taken into the household of a cousin of her father, herself the mother of two girls also attending the Academy. By this kindly arrangement not only was Greta spared the loneliness she had known at Kirkcaldy and Edinburgh but introduced to whole new aspects of traditional country life through the lively reminiscences of 'Aunt Barbara' of her own girlhood in Glen Lethnot.

In 1924 Greta entered St Andrews University to begin the four-year course of study for the MA Honours degree in Modern History and English. She was

From:– *Review of Scottish Culture*, 3 (1987), of European Ethnological Research Centre, Edinburgh, 1987.

happy in the companionship of her fellow-students in what was then a quite small community of three to four hundred, many becoming lifelong friends. She was notably successful in her class work but was prevented by illness from doing herself justice in the final examinations, and after teacher training in Dundee took up an appointment in a primary school at Brechin in 1929.

If her professional career thus assumed a form somewhat different from what she herself may have envisaged, her imaginative enterprise enabled her to achieve results uniquely influential in their scope and character. With her young pupils she established an immediate rapport, persuading them that learning could be a joyous as well as an endlessly interesting affair. Furthermore, as Brechin was less than twenty miles from Cairncross she was able to spend a good deal of time at home and to enlarge her already well-developed interest in the history of the Glen community. This continued after she moved from Brechin to Montfieth where she remained (teaching both History and English to junior secondary standard) from 1935 to 1947 and being accepted in 1946 as a research student in her old university, working on the topic of 'The Depopulation of the Glens of Angus'.

In 1947 Greta came back to Glenesk to take charge of the now single-teacher school at Tarfside. If this involved some loss of professional status and emoluments, it had the compensation of reduced commitments for someone of rather uneven health and the attraction of becoming for the next fourteen years more deeply involved than ever before in the life of the glen folk. These years were of crucial importance to rural communities of this kind, characterised as they were by changes in farming methods that involved a yet more drastic reduction of population. More fundamentally, however, they marked the final disappearance of the old self-sufficient country life that had existed since men first settled in the glens. On previous homecomings Greta had noted the traces of early dwellings, cultivation, and tracks on the hillsides and pondered on the factors that had produced such change. She had also begun to collect old artefacts and, in her research, documentary evidence on all aspects of glen life in earlier days. Now, while continuing and extending these activities, she began to record, and wherever possible to preserve, every evidence of the past life of the community.

From these endeavours emerged the Glenesk Folk Museum of 1955. Its creation came at a relatively late stage in the development of 'folk studies' and Greta was well aware of the debt which it owed to the pioneer work of Artur Hazelius in Scandinavia and Isabel Grant in Scotland. Nevertheless her conception of its character and function was very much her own. On a visit to Norway some twenty years before she had been greatly impressed by the way in which certain smaller ventures of the kind were related to the everyday life of the communities in which they were set, integrating the present with the past and providing a historical perspective for the ongoing activities of the whole social group. She was also in her way a pioneer of what would come to be known as 'total history', not through any theoretical preconceptions but in the innate width and warmth of her understanding.

Thus the museum grew quite naturally out of the work of a good teacher with her pupils and the community from which they were drawn. It was indeed in recognition of her 'services to rural education' that she would receive the award of MBE in 1956. Outside the school Greta encouraged the continuation or recording of local crafts and customs so that when she came to write to Lady Dalhousie for help in finding accommodation for her growing collection of objects and information illustrating life in the Glen she was in a position to guarantee that this would be no mere assemblage of antiquities but a living portrayal of a community with an unusually interesting past and some prospect of a future in continuity with what had gone before.

The response of Lord and Lady Dalhousie to Greta's request was all that could have been hoped for. Early in 1955 they called a meeting in Tarfside and with an assurance of active local support arranged to form the Glenesk Trust for the general wellbeing of the community. As a centre for its activities they made over the shooting lodge at The Retreat just below Tarfside. Here accommodation would be provided for the museum collections, also a craft shop and a tearoom, with space for future extension if required. These would be staffed by local people during the summer season and it was hoped that at other times there would be craft classes and a variety of activities to associate the historical collections with the current life of the Glen. For the post of Honorary Curator Greta was the inevitable choice.

In these early days the arrangement of the museum was necessarily simple and in part frankly makeshift. Yet it embodied from the outset the principles that its creator had developed in her own approach to the history of the glen community. Exhibits were rarely shown in isolation but in association with their context, whether by means of a photograph of a vanished building or bygone craft, a tradesman's bill or the inventory of a displenishing roup, family letters or reminiscences. Many of these were bound into large volumes which visitors were encouraged to study for themselves, a daring innovation this when it was first introduced and difficult to continue in its original form, yet justified by the way in which it involved the reader in past life and customs as no enclosed exhibit could. Enclosed displays there undoubtedly were for objects of special value, and the curator did not hesitate to include among them items of external provenance such as fine china and furnishings where these had formed part of family life in the Glen.

In her work at the school and the museum Greta was always alert to make use of any opportunity that might come to enlarge their ambience – as on the occasion when a quite casual visit by Helen Cruickshank (known to Greta since her Montrose days but not yet a close friend) ended in her writing a set of character sketches to be acted by the children. She also agreed, with other authors, to the inclusion of several of her poems in the remarkable *Glen Anthology* produced by Greta for the Glenesk Trust in 1958 and in an extended form in 1961. As the unusual merit of the museum became more widely known it attracted visits by individual scholars in its field together with a wide variety of cultural organisations. At times indeed it formed the centrepiece of special conferences and study-courses on the locality. These contacts encouraged Greta to publish articles, often in partnership, on aspects of life in Glenesk, together with a general survey of the parish of Lochlee for the Angus volume of *The Third Statistical Account of Scotland.* She also gave radio talks though all her friends wished that she could have found the time and energy to do even more.

In 1961 Greta gave up Tarfside school and moved into a flat at The Retreat. From here she travelled to Edzell where she taught History and English at the Junior Secondary School. Although successful and happy in her work here and at the museum, she was greatly shocked and saddened by the sudden death of her brother Duncan in October 1963. Two years later she retired from teaching to concentrate on what would be the concluding phase of her curatorship, guiding the collections into new areas of interest and improved methods of presentation while still retaining their pristine simplicity and integrity. In 1973 she left The Retreat for her own little house of Burnside in Edzell and in 1975 relinquished the active direction of the museum for which she had been responsible since its inception twenty years before. At the request of the committee, however, she agreed to continue in an advisory capacity as 'Consultative Curator' and in 1977 was awarded the Queen's Jubilee Medal in recognition of her work.

Although Greta was now advanced in years and often far from well, she was sustained through successive crises by the care of her friend Mary Findlay and the skill of her doctor Wilfred Dally who had become closely involved in the work of the Glenesk Trust and its museum. And despite failing energy she worked heroically on her accumulation of research material to make it available for publication in book form. But the winter of 1984–5 left her, though still cheerful and mentally alert, much reduced in physical vigour. On 5 April 1985 she suffered a severe stroke necessitating her removal to Brechin Infirmary and there, after a second stroke, she died peacefully on 27 June. Five days later, on a singularly beautiful summer afternoon, a great congregation of glen folk and friends from further afield that completely filled her own beloved church at Tarfside took its leave of one who would be remembered with deep affection as a person and enduring respect as a scholar and interpreter of country life.

INTRODUCTION

Glenesk has been described as 'the glen of glens'. It is one of the most beautiful in Angus, rising from a height of 300 feet at its mouth to over 3,000 feet in the peaks at its upper end. It is a crescent shaped valley, through which the North Esk flows, taking a rather straighter course than the road that twists and turns and falls and rises like the music of a song alongside. From Gannochy, the river flows through well-tilled, productive Angus land, past Edzell and on through Marykirk till it gains the sea at North Water Bridge a little above Montrose. It is a source of sport for fishermen, and of danger to those who cross it carelessly at times of flood.

To the motorist, Glenesk is a dead end; but on foot or on horseback, travellers can pass to and from the Aberdeenshire lands that lie further north. To judge the accessibility of the glen through the windscreen of a car gives wrong perspectives. Because of the hill that passes through the Mounth to the north, and contact with the low country to the east through the opening of the valley, the people of Glenesk were probably less insulated from the world than their neighbours in Glen Clova and Glen Prosen to the south, or in any areas without through traffic. This is one reason why the glen is so rich in the relics of the life and work of the people who have lived there and who have passed through it from early times onwards.

Because and in spite of links with the north and east, the people of Glenesk developed their own distinctive character, traditions and ways of thinking and speaking. The story of the Glen and its people is here recorded and interpreted. It is time that this work should be done, for the ways of life have been changing rapidly, with fast transport, mechanisation and amalgamation of farms, and the introduction of modern amenities. Depopulation has probably been going on since the wars and famines of the seventeenth century, and certainly since the middle of the eighteenth century. An analysis of population patterns over the last two centuries shows a great difference between the hill-set parish of Lochlee, and its lower parts in the parish of Edzell and part of Kincardineshire, which have the same number of inhabitants now as they had in 1755, though this is due to the growth of the town of Edzell. In Lochlee or

Upper Glenesk, the story is one of steady decline, except for a brief increase in the 1840s and 1850s. Since then, almost four-fifths of the total population have gone. By the 1970s, there were only 126 permanent residences in an area of over 90 square miles, the second largest parish in the county of Angus. There are about 47 permanently occupied houses and 49 other dwellings, of which 34 are occupied only in summer or at weekends. Of 128 houses mentioned in 1841, many are empty ruins, and whole valleys are silent where once was the sound of human activity. Berryhill is an almost forgotten waste. Glentennet and Arsallary are empty except for occasional weekend visitors. Glencat and Kedloch have been deserted for over a century. Glenlee has only ruins to tell that, when the nineteenth century began, over a score of families were dwelling there. In many places are rickles of stones marking the former homes of sub-tenants and cotters, lost to memory except for the chance tale or reference in a document. And the number of farms continues to decrease also.

The steady outward flow of men from about 1850 was accompanied by the spread of sheep and amalgamation of holdings. Lime-burning ceased about then, as grazing rather than arable needs began to prevail. The whole of the north-west part of Glenesk was thrown into a deer-forest, uniting the extensive reserves of Prince Albert and the Earl of Airlie on the north and west, and those of the Marquis of Huntly on the north-east, to make one of the finest and most extensive sporting fields in Great Britain. Deer and grouse became more important than people. Much cultivated land went out of use, leaving rigs and furrows and worn out field dykes as memorials. Only in the 1960s was there something of a reversal, through ploughing and re-seeding, on farms like Blackcraigs (entered by James Skene in 1927 when it had no arable at all), Dalbog (David Myles), Keenie and Dalhestnie (John Main), the Hillock (Andrew Scott), Auchronie (Robert Littlejohn and son), and Cairncross (the late Duncan Michie). Though these activities put farm-stock on to the hills, they do not bring more men about the farms.

This 'glen of glens' has been so called, not out of romantic sentimentalism, but because it is composed of many side glens that join the main valley. Far above Loch Lee stretch the Glens of Unich and Lee, and, beyond Invermark, Glen Mark reaches deep into the hills. There is Glen Effock, with its East and West grains, Glen Cat, Glen Tennet, Arsallary, the Aucheen area, the great stretches of ground beyond Keenie and Dalbog, and, at the mouth of the Glen itself, the Newdosk or Balfour area. Apart from the latter, the outlying parts are now largely empty, though at one time the Kirk of Lochlee, now a ruin at the lower edge of the loch, stood near the heart of the main settlement in the parish of Lochlee. On 6 December 1730, the minister undertook four 'Dyats of Visitation and Examination'. The first began at the Bridge of Lee and ended in the Drum; the second was from Glenmark to Droustie; the third from Auchronie to Achlachie; the fourth from the Haugh to Gleneffock. He would find the circuit much less of an effort nowadays, for only six permanently occupied houses remain in this large district, and the settlement lies principally in the main Glen, near the River North Esk or its tributary, the Tarf. Glenesk is no longer known for the large numbers of small tenants it could support. It is a place of rich and varied scenery, from the wild beauty of Glen Mark and the hills beyond Lochlee, to the soft beauty of the birch woods and the waterside. It is a couthy glen, where people like to live. This record of its story may help to add a little to its strength for future survival. A goodly number of those who left must have gone unwillingly.

The book of Glenesk can be aptly described as an *histoire total*, and it is inevitable in a work with such a time span that it should have some areas that could have been more fully covered. But we have tried to make the best use of the material that Greta gathered and left behind. This book will stand as an enduring testament to Greta's love of the Glen and to her never flagging industry in collecting evidence of the past. We hope she would approve.

Greta Michie, as she was known to her friends, died on 27 June 1985. We have added an appreciation of her life and work by the late Ronald G. Cant, of the University of St Andrews. This was first published in *The Review of Scottish Culture*, 3 (1987), 1–3. One of the Editors, Alexander Fenton, had been helping her with her book during her lifetime, and on her death he was entrusted with the relevant papers and undertook the task of seeing it through to completion. He is responsible for chapters 1–2 and 4–9. In October 1997, John Beech was appointed to help on a part-time basis, and is responsible for chapters 3 and 10–17. Chapter 18 is by Christina Mackenzie, a graduate of the School of Scottish Studies of the University of Edinburgh, who was sponsored to carry out this research in the Glen.

The book was completed in December 1999. It was sent to Robert Smart, former archivist at St Andrews University, for final approval, and we are grateful to him for his comments. Robert showed the typescripts to Ronald Cant, who had been a great supporter of Greta and her work, and to whom the production of this book is indebted, just a few days before he himself died on 31 December 1999. We also see the book as a tribute, through the Scotland Inheritance Fund, to Ronald's kindly generosity.

The Editors

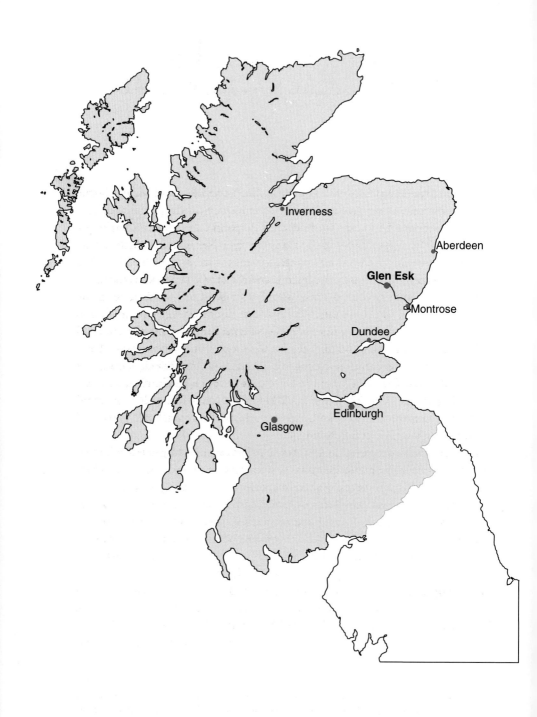

1

SHAPING THE GLEN:
THE PHYSICAL BACKGROUND

Glenesk, bounded on the north by the Aberdeenshire parishes of Birse, Aboyne and Glenmuick, covers the parish of Lochlee and part of the parish of Edzell. Lochlee extends to 58,382 acres and the Edzell part to 19,126 acres, making a total of 77,508 acres. Through it flows the river North Esk, which has its source in a number of small streams that coalesce into the Unich and the Lee (which join about a mile above Loch Lee), and the Mark, which joins the Lee at Invermark, about a mile below the loch. The combination of these form the North Esk, which continues through a broader valley reaching widths of up to half a mile, with cultivated land interspersed with heathy or marshy land and strips and patches of woodland. The two main tributaries on the north bank are the Tarf and the Turret, and those on the south are the Effock, the Keenie and the Mooran. The woods that mask the river are chiefly of birch and rowan. According to the Rev. Mr Roger in 1794, the North Esk rolled 'its rapid stream for 15 miles eastward through the deep and dreary valley of Glen-Esk' a description which is certainly unjust.[1]

Because of its geography, Glenesk has a dual character. The pattern of human settlement is affected by its geology and soils, geomorphology and climate. These factors form the backcloth for the human actors, and in many ways influence and control human actions. The inter-relationships are numerous and varied.

The sixteen mile long Glen slopes form the broad plateau of the eastern Grampians and sweep down to the lower-lying lands of Strathmore east of the Highland Boundary Fault, which extends from Stonehaven on the east coast to Loch Lomond and the Clyde in the west. The effects of glacial action and continuing erosion are everywhere apparent. Lochlee is itself a mile-long glacial trough, filling the whole 500 yards, width of the valley, and receiving two of the North-Esk's head-streams, the Water of Unich and the Water of Lee. At each side of the North Esk are ice-shaped hanging valleys from which issue numerous

---

[1] Reverend James Roger. *General View of the Agriculture of Angus or Forfar Drawn up under the Direction of George Dempster of Dunnichen; for the Consideration of the Board of Agriculture and Internal Improvement*, John Paterson, Edinburgh, 1794, 2.

tributary streams. Below Invermark, the distinct flood-plain left by the river, with well-marked gravel terraces, dates from immediately post-glacial times.

There appear to have been three movements of ice during the last glacial period which left their mark on the metamorphic schists, grits and gneisses of the Upper Glen and on the igneous rocks that penetrated these, leaving up-standing relief features like Mount Keen (3,077 feet). In the Glen itself, the river cuts through a series of schists, grits and gneisses. In Strathmore, the underlying rock is Old Red Sandstone, seen exposed in the spectacular gorge at Gannochy Bridge. However, this once overlay the Highland part also, though the circumstances that created the main Highland Boundary Fault exposed

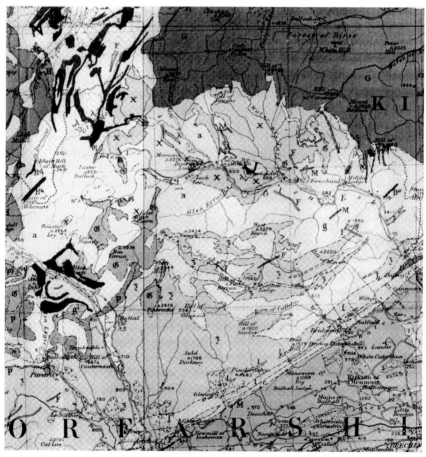

Geological formations in Glenesk. Code:- a= Gneisses, partly of igneous origin; g= Mica schist; F= Felsite Quartz-porphyry; M= Basalt & Dolerite; G= Granite; X= Quartzite & Quartz Schist; 3= Altered Grits; BG= Hornblende-Schist, Hornblende-Gneiss, Epidiorite; λ= Limestone. IPR/2-101 British Geological Survey. Copyright © NERC. All rights reserved.

the higher lying sandstone formations to powerful erosion forces which eventually led to their disappearance. The north-west to south-east flow of the North Esk is contrary to the general trend of the Highlands, and must reflect the direction of flow when the river ran through sandstone.

In the highland areas metamorphic rock has been penetrated by granites and other igneous rocks. At the time this happened, mineral veins containing lead ores such as galena were laid down in the Glenesk district. This was exploited at two periods in the later history of the Glen. The whole Glen was probably under ice which smoothed the hills, stripped them of soil, established hanging valleys tributary to the main glen and left a great deal of moraine. The first movement, from the north-west, brought deposits that are grey in colour, with cobbles and boulders of granite and metamorphic material. Over this lie deposits from the second ice-movement from the south-west, which brought clay from Old Red Sandstone formations. The boulder clay is reddish as a result, and contains sandstones, conglomerates and some quartzites and other metamorphic rocks. Lochs were formed at this period, and fluvio-glacial deposits were laid down which now appear as terraces, as a result of later erosion.

The third movement, however, had the major effect on the geography of the region.[2] In the hills it has left lateral moraines, and there are several melt-water channels and a good deal of ground moraine and other deposits. The lateral moraines are often associated with water-laid deposits in the tributary valleys, as in the Tarf and Turret catchment areas, where the valleys are crossed by a series of conical kame-like deposits of sand and gravel. An overflow channel connects these glens at about 800 feet, between Craig Soales and Craig Crane, which suggests that the ice had blocked their narrow outlets. There is another high channel between the Hill of Rowan and Cairn Robie, connecting part of the main glen to the valley of the Tarf, and others can be seen farther down the Glen, south of the Craig of Dalhestnie and also between The Crannel and Hill of Corathro. The final re-advance of this glacier is marked by the terminal moraine that crosses the valley at Migvie. To the west of this the landscape is one of fresh-looking ground moraines, especially between the Hill of the Rowan and Invermark. Here the valley has widened, probably as a result of a slowing down of the glacier's movement, with consequent depositing of moraines. These remain as irregular hummocks, with numerous traces of former cultivation now reverting to heather and birch scrub.

Another geomorphological feature of note is the way in which the Glen, east of Invermark, has rounded hills and gentle slopes, as in the Southern Uplands. This is partly due to the great volume of material, which has obscured the mother rock itself, even at high levels, and partly also to scree

[2] J.B. Simpson, The Late Glacial Re-Advance Moraines of the Highland Border, West of the River Tay, *Transactions of the Royal Society of Edinburgh,* LVII (1933), 633.

development. Some slopes have marked kinks in them which are likely to be due to the stabilisation of screes below the indentations.

Glenesk can, therefore, be described as having three broad zones: one of highland character, one of lowland character, and one of intermediate 'upland' character. The highland and lowland extremes differ climatically. In the upper reaches of the Glen, the annual precipitation can reach 55 to over 60 inches, though in Strathmore the figure is only 35 inches. The maximum is in November to January, due mainly to heavy snowfall. First falls usually occur in early October and falls may continue well into April, lasting nearly a third of the year. Melting snow may cause flooding of the haugh-land on the flood plain of the river, and lambing is affected if the melt comes late.

In terms of farming rhythms, July and August have a higher average rainfall than May and June, with an October maximum, and September is often drier than August and November. There is rain on an average of 200 days a year, though with great variation from year to year. In July and August, the summer warmth encourages growth, but showers can delay work in the fields, especially for the July hay crop. They may also disturb potato lifting in October. Ploughing and manuring usually go ahead in September after the crops have been taken, though manuring may be delayed until October.

The coldest month is January, and the warmest, July. June to September have uniformly high, and December to February uniformly low temperatures. The usual pattern, therefore, is of two levels linked by a uniform rise and fall, though in the upper Glen, the Spring rise and Autumn fall of temperature slightly precede the comparable fluctuations lower down.

The prevailing winds from the south-west are associated with the warm fronts of depressions. Glenesk is so aligned, however, that the warming effect of the south westerlies is restricted. Nevertheless, the same alignment reduces the bite of the strong east winds of spring and early summer, though agriculture suffers in exposed parts through retarded crop growth, especially when the winds are at their strongest in May. The earlier period of gales, December to February, does not affect farming other than by limiting the period of intense frosts. Autumn gales may damage unharvested crops, though after the completion of harvest they are viewed as favourable drying winds. The Rev. David Inglis clearly appreciated the 'rainbow halo, and particularly the polar lights', the aurora borealis, that sometimes made the sky bright in the Glen.[3]

Temperatures are in general lowest where rainfall is highest, with consequent effects on soil, vegetation and land use. The soils in Glenesk derive from the underlying geology, and the effects of erosion. The higher-lying areas have a relatively thin soil sheet, whilst the deeper accumulations of soil are in the

[3] *New Statistical Account of Scotland*, Forfar. Kincardine, XI, Wm. Blackwood and Sons, Edinburgh, 1845,192.

valleys. Peat cover in some areas can reach a depth of fifteen feet, but this is not so much a true soil as a clothing of decaying mosses, heather and grasses. The lower hill slopes have soil that, in part, derives from debris from higher levels. It is light and sandy, and has been cultivated for crops in the past, though now reversion to grass is more or less general.

The valley floor provides the best soil for cultivation. Alluvium brought down by the river and its tributaries has given the floor a generally flat appearance, through which glacial deposits peer at intervals. At some points terraces have been carved by the river. On the gentle slopes above the alluvium there are glacial deposits that weather to a light, sandy loam, in which there are frequent pockets of clay that make it cold and somewhat stiff to plough. An intermixture of vegetable matter can produce good soils, though the ground may be too steep for cultivation. The river alluvium is fertile and quite easy to work. The slightly sloping terraces drain freely, but the more level areas can be damp and prone to flooding.

These are characteristic highland glen conditions. Lower down the soils of Strathmore, formed from glacial drift or from the underlying Old Red Sandstone, generally constitute a fertile loam, with sandier soils in the more upland parts, and a greater clay content towards the east. The loamy soil, dark and fertile, is well suited to the growth of permanent grass. In general, natural drainage is good.

Peat, which is common, was a valuable resource as fuel, and blown peat dust collecting in hollows could help to provide a basis for fertile soil. Eroded peat appears as great, dark scars on the hill tops. The soils of the highland and lowland parts of Glenesk create a variety of differences that affect settlement pattern and land use. Roots and stumps of trees found in the peat bogs on the plateau areas are part of an original widespread forest cover. No trees now grow at such high levels. The nearest is a plantation of Scots pine and larch in Glen Lee, lying between 1,250 and 1,760 feet. In the 1840s there were no plantations, but about 100 acres of natural birchwood, with a few ash trees, mountain ash and alders.[4]

The heather moors of the hill tops and upper slopes contain patches of grasses, Nardus, Molinia, Agrostis and Festuca, in more favoured areas. Spring burning of older heather growth, at about two feet in length, is done by the gamekeepers to encourage fresh shoots on which the grouse feed. Burning also gives rise to the spread of coarse grasses.

Somewhat lower down is a moorland type that can be classed as rough pasture, where grasses predominate, and bracken stands ready to invade. Here arable farming had once been carried on, though grazing is the only use nowadays. Bracken is spreading, in spite of strenuous efforts to check its advance, and is reducing the quality and extent of the sheep pastures.

[4] ibid, 193.

In the valleys the sandy and gravelly deposits islanded amongst the fertile alluvium support clumps of birchwood, rowan, blaeberries or heather, but do not repay the cost of clearing. Such birch and scrub vegetation is mainly found on the valley floors and on the slopes below 750 feet. The islands are numerous enough to give the upper glen the appearance of quite a well-wooded valley, even though it is by no means a single extent of woodland. In the 1790s, natural birches and alders were described as fringing the banks of the North Esk.[5]

Many of the Glen farms have plantations of trees near them, providing shelter from the prevailing winds. A plantation of about 50 acres in Glen Lee was intended to shelter deer in times of storm and snow. It consists of pine, spruce and larch. Around Invermark Lodge where the Lee and the Mark come together, there is a stretch of woodland, mostly silver birch, planted for its scenic effect. Lower down in Strathmore there is beech forest, planted in the age of agricultural improvement by lairds eager to embellish their homes and land.[6]

The valley floor of the Mark and the alluvial flat stretching west of Lochlee are covered by grass from side to side. The former shows no traces of farm buildings, though the latter is former agricultural land that has reverted to pasture and remained as such for 80 years or more. Sheep and rabbits crop the grass of Glenmark, and cattle graze in Glen Lee. It is against this background of geography and geology that the picture of human life and activity has to be seen.

[5] Roger, op. cit. 5.
[6] E.B. Dobson. Angus. In L. Dudley Stamp, ed. *The Land of Britain*, Part 27, London 1946, 483 ff; Kenneth D. Collins. *A Thesis on the Parishes of Lochlee and Edzell*, Department of Geography, University of Glasgow, 1963.

2

PREHISTORIC SITES AND WAYS

It is almost impossible to produce a complete list of sites of habitation in Glenesk, though an attempt was made in 1977 (see Appendix). Some are locally known to have been occupied, others are mentioned in records, but many more are lost to memory, their locations covered by grass and heather, hidden in woods, or obliterated by land clearance. Yet enough can be discovered to bring the past and the present nearer to each other.

The hill paths act as a link between now and earlier times, leading as they often do to sites of prehistoric occupation, and crossing the Mounth that separates Aberdeenshire from North Angus and the Mearns. Several pass through Glenesk. Indeed, it was only in the 1790s, with the growth of a system of turnpike roads, that these old north-south routes began to decline, though they were given a slightly longer lease of life following the erection of bridges at Ballater (1809), Alford (1811) and Potarch (1817). These enabled the droving of cattle to continue with greater ease than when the animals had to be ferried and driven over the rivers.[1] No doubt it was along these that the first signs of human occupation came – the tiny microliths and flint artifacts used by man thousands of years ago, mostly of the dull amber shade of flint from the northeast, for Glenesk is not a flint area. Flint artifacts have been found around the Kirkton of Lochlee, and appear to have been specially numerous in the vicinity of the Monks' Pool, near which is a mound worthy of examination. Others have come from the Hill of Rowan, behind Glentennet, in the wood beside Tarfside Schoolhouse, in front of Waterside Cottage and nearby in the manse garden, at Fernybank, and elsewhere. Larger flints of a reddish-brown colour, possibly scrapers, were found below Corhairncross in the Keenie area. One is of a cloudy grey colour, similar to a beautifully made flint knife excavated at the long barrow at Dalladies in 1971, and it is razor sharp.

Objects found in the Glen could come from even farther afield than North-East Scotland. An axe-head found by William Reid, Auchmull, in a turnip-pit at Dowan Dreich in the Doulie area, proved to be of a kind of stone not

---

[1] S. Wood. *The Shaping of 19th Century Aberdeenshire*, SPA Books, Stevenage, 1985, 19, 22.

found in Britain, but common in Switzerland. It has been dated to around 2,000 BC.

There are a number of stone circles in the Glen, which often lie on a small rise in fertile ground. The stones are not particularly high and are uneven in size. The circles include a recumbent slab with fairly prominent stone flankers at each side. At Colmeallie (Culindie) there were originally two circles and what was described at the end of the eighteenth century as a 'sort of portico', but now all that remains is one circle, measuring approximately 40ft in diameter. It may have originally consisted of twelve stones, the rest having been destroyed by the farmer in the mid nineteenth century, when he needed stones to build dykes.[2] A bronze axe-head with a herring-bone pattern was found between the dyke and the house in 1849.

The remains of one of the most southerly examples of such recumbent stone circles is at Newbigging in Lethnot. Though now much destroyed, it was still recognisable in 1862, when the circle was assessed at 40 feet in diameter. In the 1820s, 20 to 30 large stones enclosed an even wider area. In the nineteenth century it was reported that a cairn, now removed, was surrounded by a double width of what may have been kerb-stones.[3] A single stone still stood, five feet four inches high. It is said that 400 cart loads were taken from the circle by the farmer. There was also a stone nearly three feet high, known as the Priest's Stone, which has now been removed.[4]

Possible Bronze Age burial sites may include two at Dalbog. The Hillock of Tornacloch was the site of some sort of circle which has disappeared. What may have been a clay-luted cist containing an inhumation was found behind the house.[5] At the kiln hillock of Dalforth, on the way to the ruined township of the same name, a burial was found at a depth of three or four feet in the gravel. The bones were more or less complete, but there was no trace of a coffin. When seen in the early 1850s, some hair was still attached to the skull.[6] Under these circumstances, a prehistoric date may be unlikely. The Muckle Cairn, on the Lang Howe on the Hill of Rowan not far from the Lochies, is among the numerous land-gatherings that are a marked feature of the area. Among these, a multiple burial was discovered in a gravel hillock near East Migvie during the construction of the new road in the 1850s.

On Cairn Robie, beside the pathway from Westbank to Milton, is the Chief's Cairn, in which a grave was discovered in 1861, by a gamekeeper looking for his dog. In fact a child called Mary Agnes Birse (later Mrs Charles Skene) had

[2] R. Oram. *Angus and the Mearns. A Historical Guide*, Birlinn, Edinburgh, 1996, 13.

[3] J.R. Sherriff. *The Archaeological Sites and Monuments of Scotland* 18, Central Angus, RCAHMS, Edinburgh, 1983,12.

[4] ibid, 25.

[5] ibid, 9.

[6] A. Jervise. *Land of the Lindsays*, Edinburgh. 1853, 90.

found it earlier. She had run off in fear, partly of what she had seen and partly because she was illegally trying to catch a rabbit. The grave contained a skeleton that was taken to Townhead of Cairncross by a day-labourer called Herald, who was so afraid it would be destroyed that he kept it under his bed. The pottery food-vessel found in the cist is now in the National Museums of Scotland. The cist of this early Bronze Age burial remained, and a tale is told of it by James Skene. As a young man he was caught in a blizzard on Cairn Robie, and crawled into the cist for shelter, remaining for half-an-hour till the weather calmed down. Since it was a short cist, he had to hunch up his legs. He said he had been 'awfu fine and cosy'.

There is another cairn of similar type on Glentennet road, not far from the Docken Well. In Aucheen there are several burial sites. Two cinerary urns were found in 1830 in an arable field about 220 yards south of the farmhouse of the Mill of Aucheen, and about 430 yards north of Damside. A stone cist was found east of the Mill of Aucheen in 1792, beneath a cairn of stones several feet deep. The finder, William Dunn, carved his initials and date on the lid, which is now at the Glenesk Museum by the dyke at the bottom of the garden along with some Bronze Age burial stones from Dalladies. A large cairn on the site of the steading of Auchmull was demolished for its stones during World War I.

A short cist was observed over 150 years ago near the Shank in the bog of Allrey. The late Miss Minnie Lindsay, a descendant of the Caithnesses, tenants of the Shank, described what happened. Fear had prevented investigation. They 'bedded the moss right away, for the rowers said they would never row anither peat if the grave was opened'. And the granny, who told the story, said: 'To tell ye the truth, lassie, I was just as feard's the lave'.

There is a badly damaged cairn in Glenmark at the bridge near the Cowiehillock Plantation. Across the Mark are land gatherings generally found with muckle cairns in what is now uncultivated ground, as on much of the surface of the Hill of Rowan, most of the lower slopes of Craig Soales, above the Burnfoot of Glen Cat, between Eastertown and the Crosspits Burn above it, above the Burn of Cleary, between the Tennet and Easter Burn, between Blackcraigs and Blackhills, up the Burn of Allrey above the Shank at the parish boundary, with the Red Castle at the other side of the Turret in the parish of Edzell, and elsewhere. Lethnot also had cairns at Blairno and Craigendowie, with land gatherings beside them. It is not known if the Parson's Prap (Cairn) on the north side of Loch Lee is in the same category, but a fine bronze spearhead was found there by David Stormonth. In the school grounds beside Dalhousie Cottages there are the remains of the Blue Cairn. It was in excellent condition in 1862, but was partly destroyed when a house was built on the site. The stones and earth were deposited below the road. It was built of large stones, with rubble above. A loom weight was found nearby in 1971. On the south side a section of the boulder kerb can still be seen.[7] At Cornescorn, just west of the farmhouse road, are to be found more than one hundred small cairns, and a further dozen or so, along with some clearance heaps, are situated just west of the farmhouse.[8]

Near the burial cairns and land gatherings may be seen foundations of circular form, of varying sizes up to about 40 feet in diameter. They are mostly in well-chosen sheltered places. Some may be the remains of circular huts, others enclosures of some kind. Two of the larger size can be seen above East Migvie on the south side of the Rowan, one complete and the other broken by a pathway. Another is on the old road to Westbank, among large heaps of stones. There are several of varying sizes beside the ruins of the Chapel of the Rowan, at least five above the present cultivation level on the Craig of Dalhestnie and one in the wood behind Tarfside over the fence among scrub, near the top of the school wood. An unenclosed settlement, consisting of four hut circles situated within a group of small cairns, can be found on the south side of the Craig of Cornescorn.[9] There is a long story of occupation to be revealed in such areas, even if only through surface surveying and plotting of the sites of clearance heaps.

Some later historical practices may go back to early times also. One such is the movement of stock to summer shielings, traces of which can still be seen up the Unich, the Lee, the Mark, and on marginal areas that later became farms above Corhairncross and Cornescorn, on the Rowan and elsewhere in the Glen. The grass on the plateau between Glenesk and Clova provided useful pasturage. In one such area, the Burnt Hill on the south side of Loch Lee, five jet buttons were found 'by the side of a moss hummock' by Douglas Middleton and George Crockett in 1901. These Bronze Age buttons lay about four inches apart, partly embedded in the moss, apparently marking the position of a vanished garment. The largest button, no doubt from the neck, is two-and-a-quarter inches in diameter. The others vary between $1^1/_4$ to 1 plus $^1/_{16}$ inches. The originals are now in the National Museums of Scotland, but the Glenesk Museum holds exact replicas.[10]

A number of querns for grinding cereals have been found in Glenesk. A prehistoric saddle quern was found near the old well beside the ruins of Cosie Howe, adjoining the gamekeeper's house next to the Glenesk Museum. The quern is on view at the Museum, along with fragments of two later rotary querns. Parts of querns and a complete one were found at Drumore, adjoining

[7] R. Oram, op. cit. 33.

[8] Sherriff, op. cit. 13–14.

[9] ibid, 28.

[10] R. Munro, Notes on a Set of Five Jet Buttons found on a Hill in Forfarshire. *Proceedings of the Society of Antiquaries of Scotland* XII (1901–2), 464–7.

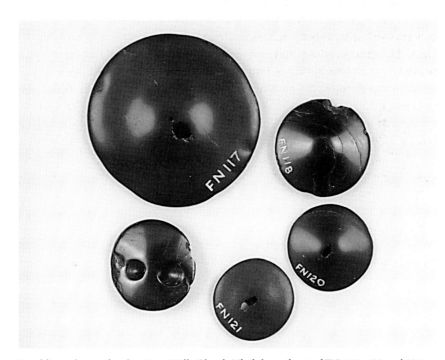

Set of five jet buttons found at Burnt Hill, Glenesk. The holes in the top of FN 117, 120 and 121 are
from the borehole going too close to the top of the button. The buttons had seen some wear before burial.
© *Trustees of the National Museums of Scotland.*

Edzell Castle. This hill, now covered with trees, was cultivated as recently as the nineteenth century, and seems to have a long history of occupation.

On the side of the Hill of Rowan, just west of Tarfside, stands a cross-slab. One side of the stone has been flattened and bears an incised cross. The stone may have served as a boundary marker or, possibly, as a wayside marker, indicating the position of a path which could have led to Lochlee Church.[11] (Local legend says that the stone was put there to commemorate the place where a local minister was killed after falling from his horse; the stone was allegedly taken from another unidentified location in the Glen.)

As yet, no hill-forts have been identified within Glenesk itself, though there are sites in the surrounding area. Two of the most outstanding are the forts on Brown and White Caterthun above Menmuir, the latter recognised as one of the best examples of a hill-fort in Britain.[12] So far, no evidence of Roman activity has been found within the Glen. However, the campaigns of Agricola in AD 84 and the Emperor Septimius Severus in the early part of the third century AD, saw forts and temporary camps established along Strathmore, no doubt to guard the mouths of the Glens leading to the hill country beyond.

Although we may not be able to interpret the evidence of these antiquities clearly, they do point to continuity of settlement and activity from prehistoric times, including movement into and through the Glen from the north and east, and cultivation of fields from which stones have been cleared in great quantities. Cropping has probably been going on from prehistoric till medieval times, even in places like the Rowan which have long lain above the levels of tolerance permitted by the present climate. All of these things lie in the period before history, but all are, nevertheless, part of Glenesk's history.

[11] F.C. Eeles. Undescribed Sculptured Stones and Crosses at Old Luce, Farnell, Edzell, Lochlee and Kirkmichael, With Some Late Medieval Monuments at Parton, Maryton and Wick, *Proceedings of the Society of Antiquaries of Scotland*, XLIV, 1910–11, 360.
[12] R. Oram, op. cit. 27.

3

LORDS OF THE GLEN

The ruins of the once magnificent Edzell Castle stand as testimony to the power and wealth of its builders, the Lindsay lairds of Edzell and Glenesk. But its crumbling stones also bear witness to the downfall of that family, who had been masters of their domain for nearly 360 years.[1] Edzell is strategically situated near the southern end of the Cairn-o-Mount Pass, the most important crossing on the eastern section of the Mounth, where a route branches off west up into Glenesk, from where the Forest of Birse Mounth, Fir Mounth and Mount Keen crossings are reached.[2] In a site of such strategic importance, it is no surprise that the remains of an earlier Norman motte and bailey castle are to be found approximately one quarter of a mile south of the house of Edzell.[3]

Very little is known about the early Norman or Normanised lords of Glenesk and Edzell. In the earliest records they are simply styled as 'de Glenesk'.[4] The first record of the name is John de Glenesk, knight, who witnessed a charter by Christian Vallognes in 1256.[5] Black thought that they may have been a Normanised native family, on the grounds that one of them, Morgund, had a Celtic name.[6]

The de Glenesks may have been descended from a family by the name of Abbe, who are on record as disposing of lands in the early thirteenth century. John Abbe in 1204, with the consent of his son Morgund, granted the Abbots of Aberbrothoc the right to cut and burn charcoal in their wood of Edale.[7] The Abbe family, in turn, may have taken its origin from the lay Abbots of the Celtic Monastery of Deer which, tradition says, was founded by St Drostan,

[1] 1. E. Cruickshank. *Navar and Lethnot*, Black & Johnston, Edinburgh, 1899, 274.

[2] W. Douglas Simpson. Edzell Castle, *Proceedings of the Society of Antiquaries of Scotland*, LXV 1930–1, 117.

[3] ibid, 117.

[4] G.F. Black. *The Surnames of Scotland*, Birlinn, Edinburgh, 1993, 314.

[5] A. Jervise. *Memorials of Angus and the Mearns*. Vol 2, David Douglas, 2nd edn, Edinburgh, 1885, 89.

[6] Black, op. cit. 314.

[7] A. Jervise. *The Land of the Lindsays*, Sutherland & Knox, Edinburgh, 1853, 23.

who may have been a contemporary of Columba.[8] The Breviary of Aberdeen contains a life of St Drostan in which it is written that he built a church in Glenesk: 'ubi vitam eremiticam ducens in loco qui dicitur Glenu Eske ecclesiam construxit.'[9] Another train of thought argues that Deer probably reflects the cult of the later Pictish Drostan, dating from the eighth century or later. Place-names allegedly commemorating the saint in Glenesk and the surrounding area include Drousty's Well, which is to the west of the House of Mark, and St Drostan's Well near Newdosk.[10] Saint Drostan is reputed to have died in Glenesk and his body taken over the hills to be buried at Aberdour in Aberdeenshire.[11]

The Abbes and de Glenesks seem to have been lords of considerable influence as John of Glenesk was one of the signatories of the letter of the Community of Scotland to Edward I of England, assenting to the marriage of that monarch's son, Prince Edward, to Princess Margaret, Maid of Norway, in 1289.[12] Incidentally, the name 'Glenesk' survived as a surname, and there were still Glenesks living in Aberdeenshire in the twentieth century. In the cemetery of Lumphanan Parish Church, Lumphanan, there is a gravestone commemorating one John Glenesk, who died aged 92, at the 'Firs', Torphins, in 1936.

Another family mentioned in early records was that of Adzell, a name which survived in Angus until past the middle of the fifteenth century.[13] There is no surviving evidence which indicates that they were lords of Edzell, whence their surname is taken, but the fact that John Adzell witnessed a charter in 1451, granting some lands to Alexander, son of the Earl of Crawford, suggests that they must have been of some standing in the district.[14] The name Adzell is of doubtful origin. At the beginning of the thirteenth century the parish name is written as 'Edale' and 'Adel', names which Jervise believes signify 'plain or meadow ground.'[15] The Reverend David Inglis, in the *New Statistical Account of Scotland* in 1845, writes that Edzell, pronounced Aigle or Eagle, is supposed to be a Gaelic word which signifies 'the cleft' or 'dividing the waters'.[16] It has been suggested that Aigle or Eagle is a corruption of the Gaelic 'Eaglais', meaning 'church', perhaps in reference to that established by St Drostan in Glenesk.[17] There are many 'eccles' (church) names throughout

[8] Simpson, 118.

[9] A.C. Lawrie. 1930–1, *Early Scottish Charters*, James Maclehose and Sons, Glasgow, 1905, 221.

[10] M.F.M. Michie. Typescript notes.

[11] D. Fraser. *Discovering Angus and Mearns*, Standard Press, Montrose, 1966, 149.

[12] Black, op. cit. 314.

[13] 13. ibid, 9.

[14] Black, ibid, 9.

[15] Jervise, 1853, 1.

[16] *New Statistical Account of Scotland,* Forfar. Kincardine, XI, William Blackwood and Sons, Edinburgh, 1865, 621.

[17] A. Watson & E. Allan. *The Place-names of Upper Deeside*, Aberdeen University Press, Aberdeen, 1984, 75.

Scotland, and sometimes they took the form 'Eigle'. One example is Falkirk, which is written as 'Eiglebrec' in its Gaelic form in the 'Holyrood Liber' in 1164.[18] While none of these suggestions is without foundation, the etymology of the name remains uncertain. In contrast, there is little doubt that the name Esk, in Gaelic, 'uisge', 'easg', simply means 'water'.[19]

The name 'de Glenesk' disappears from the records and they seem to have been replaced by the Stirlings or de Strivelyns as the next ruling family. It is not known how the Stirlings acquired Glenesk, but they held sway there until the middle of the fourteenth century when the lands passed, through marriage, to Alexander Lindsay. Lindsay was a descendant of Walter de Lindsay, an Anglo-Norman who came to Scotland around 1116.[20] Alexander Lindsay, third son of Sir David Lindsay of Crawford, acquired Glenesk, Edzell and Lethnot, by marrying Katherine Stirling, daughter and co-heiress of Sir John de Stirling, in 1357. Local tradition records that a son of John de Stirling, known as Jackie Stirlin, was also heir to the estates but he was assassinated on the orders of Alexander Lindsay, who saw him as a threat to his own ambitions.[21]

Alexander Lindsay and Katherine Stirling had a son, Sir David Lindsay of Glenesk, who also succeeded to the title 7th Lord of Crawford, when the line of the Crawfords of Clydesdale failed without male issue.[22] Sir David married a daughter of Robert II, a union which would fuel his descendants' claim to be of royal blood. In 1390 this valiant knight successfully represented the chivalry of Scotland in a tournament at London Bridge on St George's Day, and in 1398 he was created the first Earl of Crawford.[23] Earl David and his father spent most of their lives in Angus, with Sir Alexander living in the Norman castle at Edzell and his son residing at Finavon Castle, now in Oathlaw parish.[24] The first Earl is credited with building the castle at Finavon, which then became the principal residence of the Glenesk line of the Earls of Crawford.[25] It was not until the beginning of the sixteenth century that the Lindsay lairds abandoned the ancient motte of their predecessors and built another castle a quarter of a mile to the north in a more sheltered position. While waiting for the new residence to be completed, it is believed that Dalbog was the principal messuage of the Lindsays in the early part of the sixteenth century. The new structure, known as the Stirling Tower, was traditionally thought to have

[18] W.F.H. Nicolaisen. *Scottish Place-Names*, B.T. Batsford, London, 1976, 8.

[19] Watson and Allan, op. cit. 75.

[20] D.H. Edwards. *Historical Guide to Edzell, Fettercairn and Glenesk*, Brechin Advertiser, Brechin, 1915, 29.

[21] J.G. Low. *Edzell Castle, Past and Present,* William Jolly, Montrose, 1897, 11.

[22] Jervise, 1853, 28.

[23] ibid, 28.

[24] A.J. Warden. *Angus or Forfarshire. The Land and the People*, I, Charles Alexander & Co, Dundee, 1880, 316.

[25] Jervise, 1853, 140.

been built by the Stirling family, but this is unlikely as the square keep dates from around 1500, over 140 years after the Lindsays had succeeded to the estate in 1357.[26]

By the mid fifteenth century, the Earls of Crawford had become one of the most powerful noble houses in Scotland and, as such, they were involved in many of the major political events of the period. This involvement in affairs of state meant that the impact of the outside world often had disastrous consequences for the Angus vassals of the Earls of Crawford. David Lindsay, 3rd Earl of Crawford, entered into a bond of association and friendship with the Earl of Douglas in a bid to overthrow the government.[27] He was killed while trying to avert a battle at Arbroath in 1445–6, between his son Alexander, Master of Crawford, and Alexander Ogilvy of Inverquharity who had replaced the ousted master as chief justiciar of the Benedictine Abbey of Aberbrothoc.[28] Enraged at the unchivalrous nature of the Earl's death, the Lindsays attacked and slaughtered the Ogilvies. The dead Earl's body lay unburied for four days as his family waited for an excommunication order to be lifted, which had been put upon him for attacking the lands of the Bishop of St Andrews one year earlier.[29]

Alexander Lindsay, who succeeded his father as 4th Earl of Crawford, was known alternately as 'Earl Beardie', because of his beard, and the 'Tiger Earl' because of his fierce temper.[30] The fourth Earl immediately formed a new bond with the Earls of Douglas and Ross, probably the most powerful nobles in Scotland.[31] These Earls were devising a plot, aimed at reducing the King's status to that of a figurehead. They were determined to prevent James II from meddling in the localities, which the nobility regarded as their domain, and to stop him from making attacks on their landed inheritance.[32] However, such ambitious and treasonable plans may have been considered as beyond the pale by the other Scottish magnates, who, in the main, were very loyal to the institution of the monarchy.

The bond came to an end with the murder of the Earl of Douglas by King James II at Stirling. Although the Black Douglasses marshalled their forces and sacked Stirling in revenge for the murdered Earl, and despite having some powerful allies, it was the King who took the initiative. Crawford was defeated at Brechin by a royalist force led by the Earl of Huntly. Meanwhile, the King held a parliament which cleared him of the murder of the Earl of Douglas and proceeded to raise a force which harried Douglas lands in the

[26] Low, op. cit. 16. See also Jervise, 1853, 140. Warden, *Angus*, 316.
[27] R. Nicholson. *Scotland. The Later Middle Ages*, Mercat Press, Edinburgh, 1993, 338.
[28] Lindsay, 1849, 128.
[29] Nicholson, op. cit. 345.
[30] Jervise, 1853, 145.
[31] Lindsay, 1849, 135.
[32] Nicholson, op. cit. 358.

south.[33] After the battle of Brechin, Crawford was put to the horn as a rebel and his lands were forfeited. Although defeated, the 4th Earl exacted his revenge on those Angus barons who had opposed or not supported him, by harrying and devastating their lands.[34] Predictably, after suffering much destruction of lands and property at the hands of royalist forces, the Earl of Douglas submitted to the King, and Crawford, feeling deserted and realising that he was in no position to fight on alone, did likewise.[35] He humbly submitted to the King and had his estates and titles restored.[36]

Alexander, 4th Earl of Crawford, died within six months of being accepted back into the King's peace, and his son, David, succeeded to the estates and titles in 1453.[37] Walter Lindsay of Beaufort, younger brother of the 4th Earl, was tutor and guardian of the 5th Earl during his minority. Because of his influence on the young Crawford, Lindsay of Beaufort was able to persuade the Earl to grant the mills and lands of Invereskandye and the lands of Edzell and Knocknay to him, in exchange for his own northern estates.[38] The lands of Edzell now no longer formed part of the earldom of Crawford. Walter Lindsay's son, David, succeeded to the Angus estates and was the first to style himself 'of Edzell', and he became the progenitor of the Lindsay Lairds of Edzell.[39] On 15 August 1511, a Royal Charter, 'erected Glenesk of new in a free and entire barony', and in the same year, James IV presented these lands to Sir David Lindsay of Edzell. The Earl of Crawford as immediate tenant ratified the agreement with Sir David. Although the boundaries have altered, since that time the Laird of Edzell has also been Laird of Glenesk.

David of Edzell's eldest son, Walter, was killed at Flodden, leaving four children, the oldest of whom would be the new heir to the estates. However, David Lindsay of Edzell re-married and attempted to alter the succession, so that the estates would go to his oldest son from his second marriage, effectively by-passing the legitimate heir.[40] James V intervened in the matter, forcing Edzell to re-convey the estates and titles back to the rightful heir, thus preventing a serious miscarriage of justice.[41]

Walter Lindsay's son, David, succeeded as the next laird of Edzell. Moreover, he also succeeded to the title of 9th Earl of Crawford, when his cousin, the 8th Earl, disinherited his son and heir, Alexander, known also as the 'Wicked Master'. Alexander Lindsay, time and again, terrorised and extorted illegal

---

[33] ibid, 363.
[34] Lindsay, 1849, 140.
[35] ibid, 141.
[36] Jervise, 1853, 150.
[37] Lindsay, 1849, 141.
[38] Jervise, 1853, 30.
[39] Lindsay, 1853, 146.
[40] ibid, 192.
[41] ibid, 193.

payments from the inhabitants of Glenesk and Edzell, ravaged the surrounding countryside, and even imprisoned his own father, the 8th Earl, in the dungeon of his castle of Finavon.[42] Tried for his crimes at a Justice Ayre held in Dundee and presided over by the King, the Wicked Master had to forfeit his succession of his own free will as punishment for his wrongdoings.[43] He met his end one year later, 'Stickit by ane souter of Dundee'.[44] The 8th Earl presented David Lindsay of Edzell to James V as his rightful heir, and the King executed a special charter of entail in 1541, whereby the whole Earldom was conveyed to David Lindsay. In 1546, Lindsay of Edzell, the 9th Earl of Crawford, restored the earldom to the son of the Wicked Master as the rightful heir, while his own son from his second marriage succeeded to the estates and baronies of Edzell and Glenesk.[45]

Edzell Castle had by now become the principal residence of the Lindsay Lairds of Glenesk.[46] David Lindsay, 9th Earl of Crawford, was responsible for much of the expansion work done on the castle, with the building of the castle hall being accredited to him.[47] His son David, who later became Lord Edzell from his appointment as a Lord of Session, was even more ambitious. A Privy Councillor, well-travelled and a man of culture, he was caught up in the spirit of the renaissance, as his many projects demonstrate. He completed the building work on Edzell that had been started by his father. It was he who added the Pleasance and the garden wall, the latter being considered one of the most outstanding examples of architectural decoration and renaissance art in Scotland.[48] There are sculptured panels on three sides of the garden wall. The panels consist on the south side of the Liberal Arts, on the east side of the Planetary Deities, and on the west side of the Cardinal Virtues. All are thought to be copies of engravings by the Nuremberg 'Kleinmeister', whose work is identified by his signature, 'Meister I.B'.[49] The castle of Edzell was described by Ochterlony in 1684–5: 'It is ane excellent dwelling, a great house, delicate gardens with walls, sumptuously built of hewn stone polished, with pictures and coats of arms in the walls, with a fyne summerhouse, with a house for a bath on the south corners thereof, far exceeding any new work of their tymes, excellent kitchen garden and orchards; new park with fallow deer; it has ane excellent court, so large and level that they used to play at football there'.[50]

[42] ibid, 194.
[43] ibid, 195.
[44] ibid, 195.
[45] Jervise, 1853, 34.
[46] Low, op. cit. 42.
[47] Lindsay, 1849, 346.
[48] Fraser, op. cit. 139.
[49] Simpson. 1930–1, 140.
[50] John Ochterlony. *Account of the Shyre of Forfar 1682–1722*, J. Maidment, ed., 2 Vols, Edinburgh, 1845.

Lord Edzell also took a keen interest in forestry, and his replanting schemes saw Glenesk develop into a nursery for the local countryside, from where Lord Ogilvie was supplied with one thousand young birch trees.[51] A replanting movement had been launched in Scotland towards the end of the sixteenth century, and it would have been in Lindsay of Edzell's character to embrace such a scheme.[52] Angus had formerly been heavily forested but much had been cleared from the Middle Ages onwards, first to rid the woods of wolves, and then to provide charcoal and timber.[53] It is also possible that the trees were intended to be used as furnace fuel for future mining operations in the Glen.

The discovery of lead, copper, iron and limestone in Glenesk led to large sums being invested in mining enterprises, but it is not known if these ventures were ultimately profitable to the Lindsays.[54] The more profitable option seemed to be to lease the mines out for others to work. In 1592, quarries were leased to Henrie Lok for 21 years, and in 1593 Bernard Fechtenburg from Nuremberg was involved in mining operations in the Glen.[55] Workers from the continent were approached because of their expertise in mining, and in 1602 another German, Hans Ziegler, leased local mines for 25 years. Signs of his activity are still visible on Craig Soales and disused limestone quarries still exist in the Glen. It was reported in 1678 on Gilfamman in Glenmark that, 'miners were digging deeper every day.'[56] No vast amounts of metal were ever extracted from Glenesk, and the foreign mining experts probably realised that no rich seams existed.[57] It may be that David Lindsay wanted to explore the possibilities of mining in Glenesk in order to pay off his debts. Lord Edzell's brother, John, later Lord Menmuir, shared his enthusiasm for mining, and during a very successful public career he was appointed 'Master of Metals within Scotland', a post which he held for life.[58] Although all Lord Edzell's projects had been carried out with exceptional taste, the costs were high and he incurred very heavy debts. His generosity towards his wife only compounded matters.[59] Realising how much she had contributed to her husband's indebtedness, she made over her holdings which were used to pay off some of those

[51] Lindsay, 1849, 345.
[52] E.B. Dobson. Angus. Part 27, in L. Dudley Stamp. *The Land of Britain. The Report of the Land Utilisation Survey of Britain*, Geographical Distributions Ltd, London, 1946.
[53] ibid, 538.
[54] Low, op. cit. 46.
[55] M.F.M. Michie. in *The Third Statistical Account of Scotland. The County of Angus*, Scottish Council of Social Service, 1977, 170.
[56] ibid, 170.
[57] Greta Michie & Bruce Lenman. The Miners of Glenesk, *Scots Magazine* 98, 2 (1972), 113.
[58] 58. M.F.M. Michie. *Studies in the History of Glenesk. Guard Book 1:The Parish of Lochlee*, (unpublished). Lord Menmuir was also founder of the House of Balcarres. See Lindsay, 1849.
[59] Low, op. cit. 52.

debts a few days after his death in 1610, on condition that she be allowed to reside in Edzell Castle.[60]

The Lindsays lived a very extravagant, carefree lifestyle, which earned them the title 'Lichtsome Lindsays', and the castle of Edzell was dubbed the 'Kitchen of Angus', where 'Oxen were roasted whole and everything was conducted in a correspondingly sumptuous style'. After the family had dined, the poor of the parish would gather in the castle courtyard, where they would be fed by the lady or daughters of the house.[61] This extravagance brought the estate to the brink of financial ruin. Interestingly, Lord Edzell sold to James Allan in Arbirlot, for 5,000 merks, the woods of 'Auchnintowl, Cornescorne, and Dalbog, and all the growand treis in thame bayth crukit and evin lyand within the barony of Glenesk'. This sale could have been an attempt to muster funds to pay off his debts which, by this time, were quite substantial.

Further financial burden followed in the wake of the Lord Spynie affair. Lord Edzell's son and heir, David, was accused of the murder of his kinsman, Lord Spynie, in 1607. Wishing to avenge the death of his kinsman Sir Walter Lindsay of Balgavies at the hands of the Master of Crawford, David Lindsay ambushed that nobleman and two of his companions in an Edinburgh street. In the ensuing struggle, Lord Spynie was, by accident, fatally wounded.[62] Young Edzell fled into hiding up into the farthest recesses of Glenesk. The Master of Crawford, later the 11th Earl, continually harassed Lord Edzell, holding him accountable for his son's actions, and seeking some form of retribution or reparation for the murderous act. Young Edzell took refuge at Invermark and the castle of Auchmull. The latter was reputedly built in 1607 by Lord Edzell who wrote that he is building '... ane little house in Auchmull of thre hous heicht and threttie fuitt of lenthe, seventeen fuit of breid, with ane jamb of tuelf fuittis always' (Lord Lindsay, *Lives of the Lindsays*). The matter was only finally resolved in 1617, when Young Edzell, by now the Laird, paid Lord Spynie's heirs the sum of 10,000 merks plus the lands of Garlobank by Kirriemuir, as compensation for the slaying of their kinsman.[63] Despite such outlays, strict control of finances saw the House of Edzell partially overcome the extravagances of previous lairds. However, the political upheavals of the mid seventeenth century would bring it to its knees.

Lord Edzell had also been prone to hot-headed and reckless actions. When younger he aided and abetted his cousin, Alexander Lindsay of Vane, in harassing John Campbell, Bishop of the Isles, incurring the wrath of the Earls of Argyll and Montrose to such an extent that there was 'ane enterprise devisit to harry and spoil all Glenesk be the moyen of MacGregor.' This action was avoided

[60] ibid, 52.
[61] Jervise, 1853, 55.
[62] Jervise, 1853, 40.
[63] ibid, 42.

only because of the good counsel given to Edzell by his brother Lord Menmuir, and because of the latter's influence with Argyll and Montrose.[64] The Glen has been frequently harried and burned. It has already been noted how the Tiger Earl and the Wicked Master spread desolation throughout the region. In 1543, the Wicked Master's son attacked and spoiled Glenesk at the head of 600 men, horse and foot, carrying away 84 oxen and 69 kye, and otherwise ravaging the country. In 1692, a ballad describes how a great discord fell between Sir David Lindsay of Glenesk and the Highlanders, 300 or more of whom had ravaged the glens. Sir David valiantly opposed them until he was sorely wounded.[65]

Invermark Castle, standing between two converging streams, the Water of Mark and the Water of Lee, was an outpost of Edzell Castle. Built in the sixteenth century, Invermark was strategically sited to control the movement of caterans who tried to cross the Mounth from Aberdeenshire into Angus.[66] In the second quarter of the seventeenth century, there was great need for such control. The castle was, however, not altogether successful in checking the incursions of caterans from the north, as one raid carried off almost half the cattle and sheep in the glen, with five Glenesk men being killed in the ensuing struggle to recover their stock. Almost another dozen were taken prisoner and were released only after payment of a heavy ransom.[67] Ochterlony of Guynd in 1684, describes Invermark thus: 'In Lochlie is the great and strong castle of Innermark, upon the water of Northesk. It is very well peopled; and upon any incursions of the Highland katranes, for so those Highland robbers are called, the Laird can, upon very short advertisement, raise a good number of weill armed prettie men, who seldom suffer any prey to goe out of their bounds unrecovered'.[68]

Some inkling of the scale of the problem can be got from the *Acts of the Parliaments of Scotland*. In 1641, at the time of Charles I, Parliament heard of two supplications that David Lindsay of Edzell had made on behalf of himself and his tenants in his lands and baronies of Glenesk, Edzell and Newdosk. He complained about the depredations caused by 'great nomberes of brokine Hielandmen (i.e. men without a proper feudal superior or chief, living by violence and robbery) carieing away great quantities of horss nolt sheepe and other plenishing fra him and his saidis tennentis'. This was because he had subscribed to the National Covenant and had shown 'forwardnes in the guid caus' of his country.[69]

[64] Low, op. cit. 60.

[65] Michie, *Studies, Guard Book* 1.

[66] W. Douglas, Simpson. Invermark Castle, *Proceedings of the Society of Antiquaries of Scotland*, Edinburgh, LXVIII 1933–4, 41.

[67] Edwards, op. cit. 123.

[68] Michie. *Studies, Guard Book 1*.

[69] T. Thomson, ed. *The Acts of the Parliaments of Scotland, 1625–1641*, V (1625–41), London, 1817, 482.

Invermark Castle. John Beech, 1999.

Inevitably, the matter was referred to a committee. Lindsay was still appeal-
ing to Parliament in 1647, when losses sustained were estimated at
£99,895.13.4 Scots. He also asked to be exempted from all public duties. This
time action was taken to the extent that Parliament agreed to grant him repara-
tions of £20,000. The money was to come out of the last of three instalments,
each of £100,000 sterling, due to be paid to Scotland by England.[70]

In 1649, the story was not yet over. After the defeat of Charles II at Worcester,
loyalists moved the regalia and sword of state to Dunnottar for safe-keeping.[71]
While searching for them, Cromwell's troops were billeted in the parish of
Edzell for over three weeks, at great expense for the Laird, whose estate was
now facing ruin.[72] James Graham, Marquis of Montrose, harried the Glen in
1645, devastating the lands so thoroughly that the estate never quite recov-

[70] C. Innes, ed. *Acts of the Parliaments of Scotland*, VI (Part 1) 1643–47, London, 1850, 825. See
    also G. Donaldson. *Scotland. James V – James VII*, Mercat Press, Edinburgh, 1965, 325.
[71] Jervise, 1853, 42.
[72] ibid, 44.

ered. Because of David Lindsay's 'constant affectione and adherence to the common cause in defence of religione and Countrey', the rebel army was for long camped and quartered on the lands of Edzell and Glenesk, 'to the utter ruin and destruction of my lands and tennentis in so farre as the wholle cornes were brunt in the barn yardes and the wholle store of cattell and guides wer killed or driven away'. The whole lands of Glenesk, the yearly revenue of which was £10,000 in 1630, had ever since lain waste because the tenants had been unable to cultivate them.[73]

Lindsay submitted an estimate of 80,000 merks of loss to the Committee of Common Burdens. He complained also that he had been forced to maintain three garrisons of men to defend his tenants, 'wheroff many in ther owen defence wer most cruillie and barbarouslie killed', and had also had to keep up a constant guard of 40 men to defend his lands from the daily incursions of enemies and robbers.[74]

The Estates of Parliament agreed to exempt Lindsay from payment of maintenance, bearing in mind that national differences prevented them from giving further satisfaction for the Laird's heavy losses. He had never received any of the compensation promised, and therefore asked 'that I be somewayes releeved of my losses and my lands and tennents be able to pay the dewties as likewise that your lordships will be pleased to frie me and my tennentis from putting out of any hors or foot in this new levie and expeditione.'[75]

On the death of David Lindsay, Young Edzell, in 1648, the estate passed to his nephew, John Lindsay of Canterland, because his own son and heir had predeceased him. John Lindsay was also a staunch Covenanter. He was fined £3,000 at the Parliament of 1662 because he had raised a regiment of men in support of the Covenant.[76] Later in 1649, the Laird of Edzell complained that several times since the beginning of the late troubles 'several Companys of brokin and Barbarus hielanders' had fallen on his lands and tenants, damaging their houses and goods.[77] Several tenants had been killed in their own defence, or had been taken captive and he had been forced to give several sums of money for their release. All this meant that his tenants were reduced to great misery, so that not only did he have to do without the duties from his lands, but also had to replenish their 'rowms', i.e. their pieces of land or 'tacks'.[78]

The £20,000 granted him to supply his own and his tenant's necessities had not been forthcoming and he still had to keep a continual watch in the fields. Three houses were provided with victual, men and ammunition at his own

[73] T. Thomson, ed. *The Acts of the Parliament of Scotland, 1645–1651*, VI, London, 1819, 441.
[74] ibid, 441–2.
[75] ibid, 441–2.
[76] ibid, 8.
[77] C. Innes, ed. *Acts of the Parliaments of Scotland*, VI Part II, (1648–60), London, 1850, 484.
[78] ibid, 484.

cost to prevent rebel incursions, and 'now of lait since the doune sitting of this present sessioun of parliament the saidis hiellanders had fallin doune caried ane great spoyll with them and killed and hurt divers of his tennents'.[79] He begged for support in maintaining the three garrisons, and Parliament agreed to release him of £66.13.4 from the maintenance money he was required to pay monthly. He and his tenants were also to be free from 'all levies, quarterings and uther publict burdings whatsomevir', and the Committee recommended payment of the agreed £20,000. He was authorised 'To tak and apprehend the saidis rebells and persew them with all maner of hostilitie'. He was also to get some arms and ammunition out of the public magazine so that he could keep up his three garrisons and arm his tenants against rebels.[80]

John Lindsay, who was also Sheriff of Angus, died in 1671. Although he tried, under the most trying of circumstances, to turn around the fortunes of his estates, ruin came with the Civil Wars. He was succeeded by his son David, the penultimate Lindsay Laird of Edzell and Glenesk, who inherited the reck-lessness of previous lairds and only increased the financial burden on the es-tate. A partially discharged account made out by a merchant, James Mill in 1697, provides us with some idea of the affluent lifestyle of this Lindsay Laird. As well as giving an insight into the diet of a late-seventeenth century landed family, the bill also brings to our attention the foodstuffs that were available to the richer classes at this time. We do not know what kind of hardships his tenants were suffering, but it seems that this Lindsay laird was not going to want for much himself. The total amount owed was £196.10/-, presumably Scots, the bill being made out to the 'Rychtt honnorable Laird of Eagill's compt with James Mill 11 Desember 1697'.

Imprimis delyverit to Mr John Lambies wyff 16 lib prunes	1 16 0
Mair 2 unc off messes at 13s. 4d. a unc.	1 6 8
Mair 4 unc of gemgiber at 12d. a unc.	0 4 0
Mair 2 lib. Stifing at 3s. 4d. a lib.	0 6 8
Mair ane unc eassine	0 0 8
Mair 2 lib. currents at 10s. a lib.	1 0 0
Mair 8 lib. meatt buttor at 5s. 6d. a lib.	2 4 0
Mair 4 pynts & 3 mutchkins vinegar at 6s. 8d.	1 11 8
Mair be Mr John Lambes voman Isobel Gardyn 3 wattir potts	
Weying 7 lib. wecght al	7 0 0
Mair ane knakin of ingonis 30s.	1 10 0
Mair 16 lib. plindams at 2s. 6d. a lib.	2 0 0
Mair 16 lib. reasons for	5 6 8
Mair 4 lib. currents 13s. 4d.	2 13 4
Mair 6 drop saifrone at 5s. drop	1 10 0
Mair 4 disone trunchers at 8s.	1 12 0

---

[79] ibid, 484.
[80] ibid, 484.

Mair ane Jhone pott	2	0	0
Mair 4 unc gemgiber 4s.	0	4	0
Mair tua unc off clowis		16	0
Mair 8 unc spyce		12	0
Mar 2 unc neatt mugs at 6s. unc		12	0
Mair 4 unc cannell at 10s.	2	0	0
Mair ane punshion clarit wyne	75	0	0
Mair payit Patrick Thomsone for ane hamb	1	10	0
Mair half ane boll gryt salt & 8 peks small salt	4	0	0
Mair ane lint quhill	3	10	0
Mair 4 lib. stifen at 4s. a lib. 4 unc eassin at 8d.		18	0
Mair be John Lindsay ane stone deip plimdameis	2	0	0
Mair half ane stone blue resones at 6s. 8d.	2	13	4
Mar 4 unc spyce 5s. 6d.		5	6
Mair 4 unc gemgiber 4s. & 3 lib. ryce at 8s. lib.		19	0
Mair half ane pund currens		6	8
Mair ane pund Rochalmonds		12	0
Mar ane loaf sugar weying 2 lib. 1 unc clein sugar	2	15	0
Mair 2 buists confectiones at 12s.	1	4	0
Mair be John Lindsay 1 stone 14$\frac{1}{2}$ lib. irone at 32s.	3	1	0
Mair 5 chopins 1$\frac{1}{2}$ mutchkin vinegar at	0	19	7$\frac{1}{2}$
Mair be him ane boill gryt salt	4	0	0
Mair half ane boll small salt	1	13	4
Mair ane stone deip plimdams	2	0	0
Mair half ane st. resons	2	8	0
Mair half pund syne 10s. 1 lib. gemgiber 8s.	0	18	0
Mair 4 unc meses at 15s. unc	3	0	0
Mair half ane pund duntseids 5s.		5	0
Mar 2 lib. ryce at 5s. 1 lib. currents 12s.	1	2	0
Mair ane hambe 46s. 8d.	2	6	8
Mair be James Caithness 4 pints 1 chopin vinegar	1	10	0
Mair 2 pair wooll cards at 26s. 8d. a pair	2	13	4
Mair 8 lib resones at 6s. 8d. a lib.	2	13	4
Mair 6 lib. 5 unc clein suggar at 26s. 8d. att	8	8	4
Mair half ane gros tubacow pypes	0	12	0
Mair 4 lib. tubacow at 12s.	2	8	0
Mar 2 loufis suggar veying 6 lib. clein suggar at 26s. 8d. att	8	0	0
Mair 7 lib. 1$\frac{1}{2}$ unc pom brese at 20s. a lib.	7	2	0
Mair 2 lib. fygis at 5s.		10	0
Mair 4 lib ryce at 5s. a lib.	1	0	0
Summa extends till	196	10	0
And for the old ladie	149	9	0
Summa	345	19	0

Ressavit be me from Patrick Smairt servitor to the richt honorable the laird of Eygill the sowme off ane hundreth fourscoir sextin pounds ten shillings money and that to this abovewrittin compt and discharges him of the same be thir presents for now and ever. At Brechin the 20 off November 1698.

James Mill.

Although there are none of the luxury drinks, tea, coffee or chocolate which were the privilege of the 'big houses', nonetheless this does not read like the inventory of an impoverished laird whose estate is crippled with massive debts. The absence of the innovative hot drinks in this inventory may mean that the laird used a different supplier for these goods, rather than not being able to afford them. There were coffee and chocolate houses throughout Britain in 1697. The east coast ports of Scotland traded extensively with Holland, where much of Britain's chocolate came from, and certain merchants in the north-east would have supplied these products when available. There was also over-land and coastal trade with London, from where merchants could be supplied with these exotic goods. A thriving smuggling industry may have given some of the Laird's vassals the opportunity to sample these luxuries, but it would not be until later in the eighteenth century that they would be more widely available. In fact, it was not until the nineteenth century, when processes were developed for defatting cacao and producing it in powdered form, that the use of chocolate spread throughout all social strata.[81]

It is clear that the Laird of Edzell and Glenesk was still trying to live in the sumptuous style of his predecessors. The last Lindsay Laird succeeded to the estate in 1698 and continued the trend, even to the point of keeping 'up the parade of being attended to church by a band of armed men, who served without pay or maintenance, such duties being formerly esteemed honourable'.[82] It seems David Lindsay's extravagance knew no bounds, as he gifted his sister a very handsome dowry of 7,000 merks, burdening the estate even further.[83]

Crippled by debt, David Lindsay was forced to sell the estate on 25 August 1715 and, as a supporter of the Stuart cause, it seems only natural that he sold it to the Earl of Panmure, himself a Jacobite. The sale of the estate might have been avoided, had Lindsay accepted the aid of his kinsmen who, given time, could have helped him restore the estates' fortunes.[84] Why he refused that aid is not clear. It may be that he was too proud to accept what he may have construed as charity. On the other hand, his kinsmen may have been Presbyterian and followers of the House of Hanover, in which case he would take nothing from them. He was so anti-Presbyterian that, as an Episcopalian and patron of the parish, he would not see a Presbyterian minister elected to the charge.[85] Forbidden to preach in the parish by the Lords of Justiciary, the minister preached in the great hall of Edzell under the Laird's protection, where prayers were said for the exiled Stuart King.[86] David Lindsay, last of the Lindsay lairds

[81] A. Fenton. Coffee Drinking in Scotland in the 17th – 19th Centuries, in Daniela U. Ball ed. *Coffee in the Context of European Drinking Habits*, Johann Jacobs Museum, Zürich, 1991, 93.
[82] Lindsay, op. cit.
[83] Jervise, 1853, 44.
[84] ibid, 47.
[85] ibid, 9.
[86] ibid, 9.

of Edzell and Glenesk, sold the estate for £192,502 Scots, or £16,042 sterling. He bought a small property in Fife, then later relocated to the Orkney Islands. He died as an hostler at an inn in Kirkwall in 1744, thus ending a 360 year association with Glenesk.

FORFEITING OF THE PANMURE ESTATE

The quality of life in Glenesk during the first two thirds of the eighteenth century was partly conditioned by events of national significance, the Jacobite Risings. James, Earl of Panmure, who had bought the Panmure Estate (Edzell, Lethnot and Glenesk) from the last of the Lindsay Lairds of Glenesk in 1715, was one of those who had supported the Rising of that same year. It is thought by some observers that the Earl of Panmure bought the Lindsay estate to strengthen the Stuart cause in Angus.[87] The Earl proclaimed James VIII as King at the market cross of Brechin, and through his influence won many Angus people over to the Chevalier's cause. The Earl of Panmure was present at Sheriffmuir, where he was severely wounded. He was rescued by his brother, and the incident is recalled in a piece of Jacobite minstrelsy.[88] Under George I's Acts of Attainder (I, George I, chapters 32 and 42), the Panmure Estate fell forfeit to the Crown, as did a number of other estates. The forfeited estates were vested in Trustees to be sold for the use of the public, to give relief to lawful creditors by determining their claims, and to collect more effectively the rents and profits of the estates. Commissioners were appointed to enquire into the condition of the estates (I, George I, chapter 50).

There was much opposition to the forfeiture, as demonstrated on the Panmure Estates themselves. John Lumsden, WS, was the factor, the Earl's agent, and his most active abettor. He did all he could to make the life of the Commissioners difficult, by obstructing the planting of churches, by employing all the Earl's officers who had been most active in the rebellion, and by appointing the Countess's servants as his bailies in the Baronial courts. These courts were fenced in the name of 'the king' only, without mentioning King George I. In addition, notaries called in to subscribe for tenants who could not write, were known Jacobites. An example was John Auchterlonie, whose name is associated with the Judicial Rentals drawn up in 1716, and who, 'tho' he hath sworn the abjuration oath, frequents such church meetings where his Majesty King George is not prayed for in terms of law'.[89]

[87] Jervise, 1885, 18.
[88] ibid, 18.
[89] D. Murray. *The York Buildings Company*, Bratton Publishing Ltd, Edinburgh, 1973, 14.

Efforts were also made to obstruct the Commissioners by means of creditors setting up claims for debts, real or pretended, and presenting petitions for sequestration to the Court of Session. This would, of course, prevent the selling off of the estate until the legal problem had been cleared. When the Commissioners succeeded in ending the sequestrations, a new game was tried, by suggesting that the old proprietor had not been the owner at all. Furthermore, tenants continued to pay rents to the late proprietors in spite of the Act of Parliament, and means were sought to defeat the Commissioners' factors. For example, the Countess and her factor, Mr George Maule, persuaded the Panmure tenants to subscribe blank bills for old arrears of rent, as also a blank bond for two years from 24 June 1715. It took a little time for things to be sorted out in 1717 under a further Act,[90] (4 George I, Chapter 8), which provided means for dealing with sequestration, made the Commissioners' decisions on claims final, and vested the estates in the Commissioners for their sale by auction.[91]

In the course of all this, a Rental was compiled at the Castle of Invermark on 18 October 1716, as part of the Commissioners' enquiry into the estates 'of certain traitors'. It exists in two forms: a series of individual assessments in the Baron Court Book, each signed by John Auchterlony, Bailie, and by the tenant, if he was able to write; a list in which all the elements of the individual assessments (rent, dues, burdens etc.), which had been supplied randomly at the Baron Court in the form of marks or of pounds, shillings and pence Scots, are converted into pounds, shillings and pence sterling.[92] In other respects they agree completely.

In spite of efforts to prevent a sale, including protests by the Countess, auctioning of the estates, amongst them Panmure, the largest and most valuable, began in 1719. At the auction, Robert Hackett of London and John Wicker of Surrey acted on behalf of the York Buildings Company, a joint-stock company set up in York Buildings on the basis of what had been the Company of Undertakers for raising the Thames Water. The lot for which they were bidding consisted of the Barony of Belhelvie (Aberdeenshire), the Barony of Edzell (comprehending the lands of Edzell, Lethnot and Lochlee), the baronies of Brechin and Navar, and the lands and baronies of Panmure, Barry, Douny, Innerpeffer, Carmylie and Aberbrothock. The upset price was £54,032.11.1½. Hackett was opposed by Mr James Maule, servant of Mr Harry Maule of Kelly, WS, who brought the price up to £60,300. At this point it was found that Maule had no cautioners. He had to desist, and the estates fell

[90] *Acts of Attainder*, 4, George I, chapter 8.
[91] ibid, 13–16.
[92] NAS: *Forfeited Estate Papers*, 5, Panmure 8.

to the York Buildings Company, the most improbable of owners, for a further bid of £60,400, on 9 October 1719.

When the Earl of Panmure bought Edzell, Lethnot and Glenesk in 1715, he paid £16,042 sterling. The cost to the York Building Company of the Panmure Estate in 1719 was £11,508, and the annual rental was then £605.14.5½. The usefulness of this estate to the company can be judged by the fact that when they sold it in 1764, 45 years later, it was at a figure of £11,951.8.9, and the rental stood at £398.7.7½.[93] This is scarcely good business, and it is little wonder that it was said in a computation of April 1763 that 'upon the whole the Rents are rather lower than they were in the year 1719', and it was thought that in the case of a purchase, the farms might either bear a rise in rent or considerable grassums.[94]

Even as the Panmure estates were being sold to the York Buildings Company in 1719, Jacobite agents were active in Glenesk, inciting disaffection against the Hanoverian Government and encouraging people to be in readiness for a second rising for the House of Stuart.[95] The rebellion of 1745 brought more depredations to the Glen and surrounding areas, and the people of Glenesk suffered at the hands of Hanoverian troops and Stuart sympathisers alike.

In 1746, a company of Argyle Highlanders, billeted at Edzell Castle, allegedly harried the region while scouring the country for Jacobite rebels.[96] The Hanoverian soldiers also, allegedly, partly dismantled the castle, although it is believed that the roof and gilded vane on the tower were sold off by the York Buildings Company to pay creditors.[97] One of the most active rebels was a local man, David Ferrier, who raised more than 300 men in Glenesk and Glen Prosen alone for the Stuart cause. Another more high profile rebel sought by government troops after Culloden was the Laird of Balnamoon, who sought refuge in a cave in Glenesk near the foot of Curmaud Hill, which is still known today as Balnamoon's Cave.[98]

Charles Edward Stuart even appointed his own factors on the Panmure estates who forcibly recquisitioned the tenants' bills to the amount of £2,000.[99] It was incidents such as this which probably prevented Glenesk people from appearing on the Marquis of Rosebery's list of named rebels, it being ascertained that they were forced 'out' by intimidatory threats to their lives and

[93] Murray, op. cit. 26.
[94] NAS: GD45/16/117.
[95] Cruickshank, op. cit. 111.
[96] Jervise, 1853, 56.
[97] ibid, 57.
[98] ibid, 84.
[99] Murray, op. cit. 89.

property, and, therefore, against their will. To what extent this was true cannot now be gauged, but there is conflicting evidence regarding this claim. David Ferrier did raise a lot of men from the Glen, and Balnamoon's hiding place was never divulged in spite of the enticement of bribes and the vigilance of spies, though this may have been out of a fear of retribution.

After the '45, the Braes of Angus were a refuge for armed bands of men, some of whom probably masqueraded as rebels to give them some form of credibility. These armed bands harried and destroyed the lands and properties of Hanoverian supporters, mainly Presbyterian schoolmasters and clergy.[100] Their hiding places were never divulged, though this again may have been due to the threat of retaliation, and these 'rebels' were often given shelter by people who secretly supported them.[101]

One of the most notorious of these outlaw bands was led by one James Davidson. After the '45, he gathered up a group of Highland caterans and they, allegedly, committed a series of outrages in Glenesk and the surrounding areas. Their plundering attacks again seem to have been directed mainly against known Hanoverians. Davidson was eventually caught and was hanged on 1 July 1748.[102] How much revenue was lost from the Glen as a result of these raids is unknown, but it must have been substantial. Life could not have been very easy for the people of Glenesk during this troubled period.

The Panmure estates, which included Edzell and Glenesk, remained under the ownership of the York Buildings Company until 1764. The estates had been offered back to James, Earl of Panmure, on condition that he return to Britain and take an oath of allegiance to the House of Hanover. He refused to do so and died an exile in Paris in 1723. The Panmures had been allowed to retain one link with their forfeited estate, as the Earl's wife remained in Scotland as a tenant of Panmure on a 99-year lease agreement with the York Buildings Company.

In 1764, the York Buildings Company was declared bankrupt, and to pay off creditors the company was obliged to strip its properties of all valuable materials. At Edzell Castle the roofs and floors were ripped out, signalling the final ruin of this once magnificent structure.[103] That same year, the forfeited Panmure estates were purchased by William Maule, nephew of the exiled Earl James, at a price of £49,157.18s.4d. Other forfeited estates had been re-sold and it was considered a point of honour not to bid against the old proprietors, allowing them to re-purchase their lands at a very moderate price.[104] William Maule was created Earl of Panmure of Forth and Viscount Maule of Whitechurch

[100] Cruickshank, op. cit. 176.
[101] ibid, 175.
[102] ibid, 176.
[103] Simpson, 1930–1, 119.
[104] Murray, op. cit. 94.

in the Irish peerage in 1743. He made his fortune during the Flemish Wars, thus enabling him to re-claim what he probably regarded as his rightful inheritance.

Having no children, Viscount Maule settled his estate on his half-brother John, who predeceased him, and on his nephew, George Ramsay, later 8th Earl of Dalhousie, in life rent and on the Earl's second and other sons in fee. (William Maule's sister, Jean, had married George, Lord Ramsay, heir to the 6th Earl of Dalhousie.) This meant that when Viscount Maule died in 1782, the 8th Earl of Dalhousie's second son, William, succeeded to the Panmure estates, while his elder sibling became the 9th Earl of Dalhousie.

William Ramsay succeeded to the Panmure estates, which included Edzell and Glenesk, at age 16, assuming the name and arms of the Maule family along with the honours.[105] Like many Glenesk lairds before him, William Ramsay Maule was heavily involved in Scottish politics, being MP for Forfarshire from 1805–31. He was admitted to the peerage as Baron Panmure of Brechin and Navar. He was succeeded by his son, Fox Maule, who served at the forefront of Scottish and British politics. Fox Maule had a distinguished political career as Secretary at War July 1846 to February 1852; President of the Board of Control 1852 and Secretary of State for War from February 1855 to February 1858. In 1853 he was created a Knight of the Thistle and Keeper of the Privy Seal of Scotland.[106] As if those were not honours and privileges enough, he then succeeded his cousin James, who died without children, as the 11th Earl of Dalhousie.

Fox Maule was more radical than his father, and this is demonstrated when he joined the Seceders from the Church of Scotland in the Disruption of 1843, in direct opposition to his parent. Having previously been an elder for the established Church, Fox Maule became a faithful elder of the Free Church.

It is alleged that there was a good deal of friction between Fox Maule and his father, William, so much so that he omitted his father's name from the Rowan Tower memorial in Glenesk. The Tower was originally intended to be a memorial to his brother, Lauderdale, who died from cholera at Varna, during the Crimean War in 1854.[107] Later, knowing that he would die without male heirs, Fox Maule desired that the Tower be a memorial to the Panmure-Dalhousie family.[108] In the light of such an omission, one could be forgiven for questioning Fox Maule's motives in seceding in 1843, the implication here being that he did so partly to spite his father, who was patron of the parish and opposed to the dissenters.

---

[105] Warden, op. cit. 405.
[106] ibid, 407.
[107] Greta Michie. *The Dalhousie Family Guard Book*, 28.
[108] ibid, 27.

Fox Maule died in 1874 and the titles and honours passed to his nephew, George Ramsay, an Admiral in the Royal Navy, and now the 12th Earl of Dalhousie. George Ramsay was succeeded by his son, John. As with many of his predecessors, John Ramsay, 13th Earl of Dalhousie and Laird of Glenesk, gained high political office, being elected MP for Liverpool in 1880 and Secretary of State for Scotland in 1886. He was also an advocate of Home Rule for Ireland. The 13th Earl died the following year aged 40, the day after being informed of the tragic death of his young wife. The Dalhousie Arch in Edzell was erected in 1889 as a tribute to John, 13th Earl of Dalhousie and his wife Lady Ida Bennet. The Earl's younger brother, Charles became tutor for the young heir, Arthur, then a minor, being only nine years old. The 14th Earl, Arthur George Maule Ramsay, attained his majority on 4 September 1899. Severely wounded in World War I, he died of related injuries in 1928.[109] He was succeeded by his eldest son, John Gilbert, who became 15th Earl. John Ramsay died in 1950, unmarried, so the title passed to his younger brother Simon, the 16th, and now deceased, Earl of Dalhousie. Carrying on the tradition of previous Glenesk Lairds, the 16th Earl had a successful career in politics, firstly as MP for Angus and later as Governor-General of Rhodesia and Nyasaland. (A fuller biography of the 16th Earl of Dalhousie can be found in chapter 18.)

The Maule-Ramsay families have now been Lords of Glenesk for 283 years, ever since the Earl of Panmure bought the estates from the last Lindsay Laird of Edzell and Glenesk in 1715. However, the present Dalhousie family can claim to have an even more ancient link with the Glen, one which goes back over 640 years. In 1940, the 16th Earl married Margaret-Elizabeth Stirling, daughter of Sir Archibald Stirling of Keir, who are descended from the same Stirlings who were Lords of Glenesk in the late thirteenth century. It was Katherine Stirling, daughter of Sir John Stirling, who married Alexander Lindsay in 1357. Thus, the wheel can be looked on as having almost come full circle.

Brechin Castle is now the home of the Lairds of Edzell and Glenesk. All that remains standing of Edzell Castle is the Stirling Tower, the summer house, the garden wall with its sculptured panels and its wonderful garden, recognised as one of the most beautiful in Scotland. Nevertheless, enough of this once imposing edifice remains to impress upon the visitor the absolute power once wielded by the lairds who lived there. It is also a tribute to the spirit of the renaissance which the lairds of Edzell and Glenesk so wholeheartedly embraced and expressed. Unfortunately, this freedom of expression was also a major factor in the financial difficulties which bedevilled the estate. Admittedly, the political climate of the seventeenth and eighteenth centuries exacer-

[109] *Dundee Courier and Advertiser*, 24 December, 1928.

bated the situation. Nevertheless, the Lindsay lairds of Edzell and Glenesk must bear full responsibility for the abuse of wealth and resources which contributed so much to their final ruin. The Lindsay star rose and fell, mainly on account of their profligate lifestyle, but what hardships their tenants endured as a result of it, can only be guessed at.

4

PRE-EIGHTEENTH CENTURY
LAND USE

Prior to the eighteenth century, details of land use are scanty and must be picked up from sources dealing with other issues. Some information comes from the history of the Castle of Invermark itself.

In spite of statements that there was a castle here in the fourteenth century, there is no supporting evidence for this early date. The first official record is for 1554 in the *Register of the Great Seal* which refers to the 'tower, fortalice, and manor-place of Invermark'.[1] In 1558 there is further reference to the 'fortalice, manor-place, demesne lands, and malt kiln of Invermark', this inventory occurring in later writs down to 1715 when the lands were forfeited, Lord Panmure having joined the Jacobite risings.[2] Where there was a malt kiln, bere or barley was being grown to supply it.

The unstable political climate of the seventeenth century, and the depradations committed in the lands of Edzell and Glenesk which were, often, a direct consequence of that instability (highlighted in Chapter 3), meant that the keeping of stock and the growing and processing of crops could hardly have been comfortable procedures during those troubled times. What the situation was like in the first half of the century can be inferred, to some extent, however, from the testaments of Glen folk who had passed away. Though the evidence must be treated with normal caution, and allowances made for lapses of memory etc between the date of a death and the submission of an inventory, it is still possible to get at least a broad view of stocking levels, cropping and the value of possessions. The available examples run from 1610 to 1649; the information they contain is summarised in the following table (the total value of possession is in each case given without deduction or addition of debts, to give a truer indication of the real value):

[1] J. Maitland Thompson, ed. *Registrum Magni Sigilli Regium Scotorum*,1546–80, H.M. General Register House, Edinburgh, 1886, 206 (no. 922).
[2] J. Stuart, ed. *Registrum de Panmure*, Vol II, compiled by Harry Maule of Kelly (1733), Edinburgh, 1874, 348.

Table 4.1   *Early Seventeenth Century Testamentary Inventories*

Year	Place	Tenant	Cattle	Sheep	Horses	Crops (Bolls)		Possessions
						Oats	Bere	
1610	Corharncross	Katheringe Rawin	2	4	1	4	2	£50
1612	Bailzie	Johne Schand	21	40	5	50	20	£811
1617	Achroune	Kathrin Duncan (spouse to Alexander Mylne)	-	12	-	-	-	£28
1619	Mylntoun of Glenesk	Johne Chrystisoun	18	100	3	30	18	£765.6.8
1620	Kirktoun of Lochlee	Duncan Flagger	24	140	3	27	12	£792.13.4
1622	Hunthill of Glenesk	James Mair	14+ calves	60	1	8	2	-
1622	Migvie	Katheringe Campbell (spouse to William Nicoll)	10	30+ some hogs	2	6	2	£152.6.8
1622	Mylntoun	Bessie Ros (widow of Thomas Chrystisoun)	4	-	-	-	-	£66.13.4
1623	Glentennet	Margaret Chrystisoun (spouse to William Low)	9	36	1	10	1	£136 (in debt)
1623	Glentennet	Margaret Gold (spouse to David Low)	12	44	3	20	-	£72 (in debt)
1623	Assailrie	John Chrystisoun	10	16	2	10	-	£141.13.4
1624	Achintoull	Johne Watt	5	20	2	-	-	£84
1625	Achroune	John Mylne	7	10	-	-	-	£68.13.4
1626	Carncors	Johne Low	11	30	3	43	18	£536.13.4
1627	Achloche	Bessie Christie	5	12	1	9	4	£122.13.4
1636	Glenmark	Adame Vallace	8	30	2	2	-	£94
1636	Quhiggintoun	William Chrystie	11+ calves	130	2	15	4	£448.3.4
1638	Ardow	Andrew Lyndesay (servitor to John Gellie)	5	106	-	-	-	£426.13.4
1649	Kirktoune of Glenesk	John Watt	14	120	2	-	-	-

This sample of nineteen, covering a period of 39 years, indicates that the proportion of sheep to cattle was roughly 4.9:1 and of oats to bere 2.7:1. Though these figures would have to be subjected to other criteria – e.g. relationship of the month of death to the state of the crops-, they can at least be taken to demonstrate two basic facts, that there were considerably more sheep than cattle, and that oats was a more widespread crop than bere. The proportions might be much affected, however, if there were some way of recording the holdings of every family, for those represented in the testaments tend to be the better off (or their widows). The poorer strata, indeed the majority, do not appear as a rule. It is also evident that farmers' widows were not very well off.

There is an impression from these testaments, in the decades leading up to the Covenanting disturbances, of a reasonable degree of stability in the farming structure. Prices were fairly stable, it seems, between 1610–1630s.

CATTLE

The price of a cow or an ox rose from £8 to £10, and the price of a cow and calf from £8 to £12, though there were higher levels in the years between. The highest noted are £13.6.8 for a cow and £16.13.4 for an ox. It is, however, impossible to make acceptable generalisations, because some of the animals were old, or small, or dry, and values were affected accordingly. The most valuable were the cows and oxen. Then came 'stots', young castrated oxen or bullocks, one being valued at £8 in 1622, and a three-year-old one at £6 in 1623 and again in 1627. Dry or 'yeld' beasts, not giving milk, came next, along with 'quoys' or heifers. These were around £6.13.4, though young heifers could be £4 or £5. 'Stirks', bullocks or sometimes heifers kept for slaughter varied in value according to whether they were one or two years old, between £2 and £5. Though three-year-old stots are mentioned, presumably since they were needed for draught, no three-year-old stirks are listed, and slaughter or sale no doubt took place after two years. Calves were valued at £2, when mentioned singly, though more often a cow and calf are mentioned together and costed at £8 to £12.

The biggest number of oxen, eight, was carried on Mylntoun of Glenesk, and on Kirktoun of Lochlie, followed by Carncors with six, and Kirktoune of Glenesk with four. Other places had two oxen; like horses, therefore, they were probably worked in pairs at farm work. Kirktoun of Lochlie has eight cows; there were five each on the farms of Mylntoun of Glenesk, Achloche, Glenmark and Kirktoun of Glenesk. Glentennet had three, and other places two. Bailzie also had a good number of cows and oxen, totalling twenty-one altogether but without being separated.

Cows and 'cair', calves, are only twice mentioned together. It is likely, therefore, that the production of milk was more of an aim than the rearing of calves,

though one annual calf per cow was obviously expected since several inventories mention the same number of calves or young animals as of cows.

In only one instance, at Assailrie, was a stot kept till its third year. This may
again suggest that two years was the normal limit for keeping cattle destined
for sale or slaughter.

The five 'yeld nout', dry cattle, mentioned at Mylntoun in 1619 are a slight
puzzle. 'Nout' is simply a collective term for cattle. There is no means of
knowing if these were cows that had gone dry or as a result of being in calf. In
the case of Quiggintoun, 1636, it is assumed that the five cows and calves,
valued at £60 together, are five cows and five calves.

SHEEP

'Wedders', wethers or castrated rams, were the most expensive of the sheep,
ranging from £2 to £2.10/-. Ewes were between £1 and £2, the latter being
the commoner figure by the 1620s. 'Dulmonds', wethers of one-and-a-half to
two-and-a-half years old, i.e., between their first and second shearings, were
valued at £2. Then came 'furthcum sheep', valued at £1.10/- in 1622 and year-
old ones at £1.6.8 each in 1636. The term 'furthcum' is not to be found in *The
Scottish National Dictionary*. There is only one reference in the *Dictionary of the
Older Scottish Tongue*: an Edinburgh Testament dated 1584 mentions 'tua furtht
cummit shepe', which the editors gloss as 'Full Grown'. It is more likely, however, that 'furthcum' sheep were sheep coming originally from some other
place, and not brought up on the ground of the farm.

Roughly equivalent in value were 'hogs', yearling sheep between the time
of weaning and the cutting of the first fleece; these varied between 13/4 and
£1.13.4. Last were lambs at 16/8 or more, often £1, each. The fact that they
were worth less than 'furthcum' sheep suggests that the latter were indeed
fully grown, though this is not the main sense of the term. A 1626 inventory
mentions 'riglin' sheep at £1.11.1 and 1/3. By this is meant an undersized,
weak animal.

In three examples, 'sheep' are given as an overall number, but it is more
normal for them to be differentiated into the kinds that composed the flock.
Though sheep outnumbered cattle, nevertheless they were not kept in the
large numbers that characterised later days, nor were the south country breeds
like the Cheviot and Blackface to be found, but only the native breed.

The terminology is age related, hogs being yearlings and dulmonds in their
second year. 'Hog' goes back to 1306 in the *Acts of the Parliaments of Scotland*,
but the origin of the name is not clear. 'Dulmond' is also widespread in a
variety of forms ('dilmont', 'dinmont', etc), and goes back to 1306. It is also of
obscure origin, though lexicographers, for lack of other possibilities, think it

may be pre-Celtic. Oddly enough, the term 'gimmer', a yearling ewe, does not appear in these testaments. As far as numbers are concerned, hogs are more numerous than dulmonds, but since there is no way of checking how many of each were included under the general heading of 'sheep', the evidence is too insecure to suggest when sheep were normally killed off for consumption.

HORSES

The value of horses varied a good deal according to age. A good mare was £16 in 1610, and an old one £4. The best value for a horse was £13.6.8 in 1619, otherwise prices ranged from £4 to £10 for horses specified as old. Since horses and mares are often so described in the testaments, it looks as if their owners normally hung on to their animals once they had them. A foal was £3.6.8 in 1622. A mare and foal together were £16 in 1610, and two further examples in 1636 testaments came to £8 and £13.6.8. A horse, mare and foal came to £24.13.4 in 1620, and two entries in 1625 and 1626 for horse and mare together, each pair at £10, suggests that the concept of a pair of horses as a working unit was strong in people's minds. Horses seem to be rather few in overall numbers, which reinforces the likelihood that oxen were used for work.

CEREAL CROPS

Only two cereal crops are mentioned, oats and bere. Prices are given per boll, a measure of capacity containing four firlots, i.e. six bushels or 140 lbs. Oats ranged from £2 to £3.6.8, and bere from £4 to £6. Bere, therefore, boll for boll, was the more valuable crop. Bere-meal as well as oatmeal would have figured largely in the everyday diet.

Cereal to be valued for testamentary purposes was to be found threshed in the barn, unthreshed in the barnyard, or still uncut in the fields, according to the time of year. A standard seed yield ratio was applied for growing crops: for oats it was 3:1 and for bere 4:1. Thus, nine bolls of oats sown on the Kirktoun of Lochlie in 1620 was expected to yield 27 bolls, and three bolls of bere to yield twelve bolls. This was a standard seed-yield ratio used throughout Scotland for such legal purposes. It does not exclude the possibility that yields could be better, or worse, but it seems to have been an acceptable average.

In the testaments examined, there was a total of 179 bolls of oats against 75 bolls of bere. On this basis, over twice as much oats as bere was grown. Bere was the major infield crop in earlier days, and cultivated on the patches of good land near the houses, generally getting rather more manure than oats.

For this reason, bere was the more valuable crop. It was also the source of ale. Oats, however, was grown over a wider area, including the poorer outfield land.

There seems to have been only one variety of bere, with four or six rows of ears. There is no indication at this date of the growing of two-eared barley, which prevails at the present day. Oats, however, showed greater variety. The bulk of the entries simply mention 'oats', but there was also 'small' oats, 'black' oats, 'small black' oats, and 'brokit' oats. 'Small oats' was a name for the grey or grey-bearded oat, sown on the poorest outfield soil in higher lying districts. It is now called the Bristle-pointed oat, *Avena strigosa*. Black oats had similar qualities. 'Brokit' oats were a mixture of black and white oats growing together; the word is found in this sense as early as 1581 in Scots, and has the sense of mixed colours. A curious name, of obscure origin, for a kind of bearded black oats, *shiocks*, is recorded in Angus in the mid-nineteenth century, but does not appear in the testaments though evidently used for similar varieties.

The general impression from the seventeenth-century evidence is that the cereal crops grown, especially oats, had to be able to stand up to poor conditions. Though no great care may have been taken with the seed, the different designations of oats and the different prices nevertheless suggest an awareness of differences, even if this amounted to no more than division of types into those that were more suitable for milling into oatmeal for human consumption, and those more suitable for animal fodder.

EQUIPMENT AND FURNISHINGS.

Most of the testaments lump together the value of the 'insicht' and 'plenishing' (domestic furnishings and equipment), clothing and farm tools and utensils, and only once are we lucky enough to be given a detailed inventory. These items, when calculated as a percentage of the total value of the will, vary between two per cent and 37 per cent. This means that the stock and crops were regularly worth much more than the worldly goods. It is also noteworthy that the lower the percentage, the less well off overall is the farmer or his widow.

No details are available about the goods of the smaller tenants, but John Schande in Bailzie, one of the bigger farmers, left a substantial collection of items behind him when he died in 1612. These fall into a number of categories.

Actual agricultural implements were few. The only items mentioned were plough yokes and plough irons, and an iron 'futt' or foot. Whether this is part of a plough, is not clear. It may be that a number of iron items are simply being valued together.

Related activities are marked by 92 ells of sacks and canvasses, old and new. At £18.8/, these were valuable items, needed for jobs like the storage of grain and winnowing. Alongside this entry is one for 29 ells of Scots 'bumasie', bombazine, a kind of twilled fabric. Since it is not listed with the dresses and textiles in the house, it may also have been for agricultural purposes, though this interpretation is by no means certain.

Bere was valuable as the basis for brewing ale also, as evidenced by the brewing vat and brewing equipment, listed at £6, along with a 'brewin' zetlinge', or cast-iron pot for brewing, also at £6. Two pans, an iron crook and a pair of tongs may have been associated with brewing, though also as general kitchen equipment. There were two spits, suggesting the occasional consumption, at least, of meat in the household, most likely in the form of roast mutton. Skins and hides from slaughtered beasts were processed at home, for there was a 'bark vat' for tanning hides under preparation in the pots, and three completed 'barkit' hides, the last valued at £8 or £2.13.4 each.

The house was furnished with 'ane meitt burd with firmis' (a table with benches); three wooden beds, which seem to have been free-standing, on legs, rather than built-in, in the manner of box-beds; a 'girnell' or storage chest of fir with a capacity for holding sixteen bolls and a 'mekill kist' or large chest capable of holding six bolls; an oak chest and a new chest; and two clothes chests 'lokit and bandit', with a lock and iron bands. There were also in the house eight doors with locks and iron bands, costed at £10.13.4.

The reason for the security of the clothes chest is explained by the value of the items of clothing and textiles they contained: two 'hewd' or coloured plaids, three new plaids 'tane fra the vobster', i.e. weaver; one head plaid and two others, eight pairs of bed plaids, two pairs of blankets, four pairs of 'tuidlinge' (twilled cloth) sheets, three bolsters, six 'vairit' ('varied' with two or more colours) pillow cases, a linen tablecloth and a 'tuidlinge' table cloth. There were also two stands of clothes belonging to the dead man, one for work and one for holiday. All of these amounted to £102.0.8, i.e. nearly a fifth of the total value of the stock and crops.

The next category brings a sharp reminder of the times the Glen farmers were living in. Though in 1612 the Covenanting times had not yet arrived, nevertheless there was a need for defence against the in-roads of unruly High-landers, and the Laird had to have men ready, then, just as in later times. Johne Schand was not ill-prepared. He had a 'jack', i.e. a doublet of defence, probably of leather and lined or padded, with or without sleeves, along with a steel bonnet and a pair of 'plait slewis', iron plated or lined with mail, so that head and arms and upper body were well protected. Of weapons he had a sword, 'ane shouttin bow with ane bag of arrous', and a pair of pistols. The pursuit of farming has to be seen against the kind of society that required individuals to be ready in such a way. Weapons and coverings were valued at £29, the sword bearing the highest figure, at £10.

FINANCIAL MATTERS

Most of the wills record debts of various kind, owed by or owed to the deceased. These can comprise the normal 'mails' (rents) and duties owed to the Laird. Katheringe Rawin of Corharncross owed the sum of £12 to three servants for their year's fees in 1610; John Chrystisoun of Assailrie owed Katherine Niddrie a fee of £4.0.4 in 1623; and Johne Low of Carncors owed £10 (equally divided) for the fees of Helen Milne, John Low and Janet Low.

Individuals in the Glen had money owed to them by neighbours in the parish and by others farther afield. The same range was covered by those owing debts to the deceased. Amounts either way could range from 30/- to £69.13.4, the largest figure noted. In most cases only a small number of debts were involved, but in 1636 William Chrystie of Quhigginton had money owed to him by nine debtors, all within the Glen.

The record was held by John Watt in Kirktoune of Glenesk. Twenty seven people owed him money, some in the Glen and some well outside it. The composition of the debts is of much interest. Most were in the form of bonds for the principal sums on which an annual interest had to be paid over a fixed period. Repayment in instalments was quite usual. Watt seems to have let land for grazing, for the Laird of Balmerino owed him 40 merks (£26.13.4) for 'grasse meal' (grazing rent), and Andrew Lindesay of Old Mylne in Fearne owed £10 for the grazing of ten oxen and 50 sheep. Here we get a glimpse of the wider exploitation of the pastoral resources of the Glen. Cereals also come into the picture. Thomas Kynneir's wife in Drum owed £8 for one boll of oats and five merks (£2.6.8) for half a boll of oats, whilst John Christisone of Glenmark had a bond for 100 merks (£60.13.4), this including £8 for a boll of bere and £3 for a boll of oats. In all, he was owed £991.5/-, a very substantial sum. On the other hand, he owed ten others a total of £206.10/-.

John Christisone seems to have been something of an entrepreneur, but even if he was more so than most of his neighbours, these financial dealings over an area that stretched as far as Brechin and Montrose show a greater degree of financial sophistication amongst farmers than broader descriptions normally indicate. The point has, of course, to be stressed again that the testaments registered were those whose possessions reached a level at which 'quot' was paid, i.e. a proportion of the moveable estate payable for confirmation of the testament. It was officially set at twelve pence in the pound, though in practice less was often paid, at the discretion of the Commissioners. By the period of the testaments looked at here, the use of the income from 'quots' had been restored to the bishops through the commissariats, the jurisdictions that formed part of the bishop's courts that covered the registration of wills and inventories. This explains why the 'quot' or 'quota' of £25 was payable to the bishop of the diocese in respect of the moveable estate of Johne Shand of Bailzie in 1612.

For the second half of the seventeenth century, less information is available. The details that can be gleaned from the Testaments of 1610 to 1649 reveal a picture that goes somewhat beyond basic subsistence farming for those whose goods were substantial enough to be inventorised for the 'quot'. Towards the end of this period the Covenanting times undoubtedly disrupted an earlier degree of stability. However, recovery must have been reasonably rapid, for later in the century Ochterlony of Guynd noted that Lethnot and Lochlee paid a great rent in money and casualties, i.e. profits accruing to a feudal superior, consisting of cows, wethers, lambs, butter, cheese, wool, etc. He spoke of an abundance of venison, of moor and heath fowls, and of wood in plenty (for tools and buildings) in the forest. Nevertheless, the Laird of Edzell still had to maintain his 'great strong castle' of Invermark, and be able to raise a good number of well-armed men to keep the Highland 'Katranes' from getting away with raids.

These details confirm that the land was extensively wooded, that grazing areas were widespread, and that the products of a mainly pastoral form of economy largely paid the rents. In the lower areas crops of barley and oats were grown. We have to remember that the pattern of arable activities revealed in the Testaments was relatively small-scale within the total pattern.

All this was confirmed in 1678 in Edwards' Description of the County of Angus, which also added valuable detail:

> With regard to the valleys between the Grampians, there is some barley and oats; and the neighbouring hills are covered with grass and heath proper for pasture, where oxen, sheep and goats and thousands of unbroken horses are fed, until sold in the fairs at the foot of the mountains. After seed time when the oxen are worn out with the labour they are driven in herds to the pastures on the Grampians where they remain till they are brought back in harvest. The soil never fails to produce plenty of herbs, roots and garden fruits. Here are trees of various kinds, particularly oak and fir in the mountains; also birch, service-tree, elm, hazel, poplar and juniper. In the plantations are ash, sycamore and willows ... Here is an abundance of timber for labouring utensils, and for the houses of the common people.

The rivers too, according to Edwards, produced salmon in plenty. When the fish were running, 'the common people kindle fires on the banks of the rivers (privately in the night, because prohibited by law) and while the fish flock to the light, they are pierced with spears and carried away'.

By the end of the century, however, the stirrings of the major agricultural changes that were beginning to take place in the Lowlands of Scotland must have been finding echoes, however distant, in the Glen also. In the next chapter, evidence for an increased rate of change is examined.

Table 4.2 *Cattle*

Date	Place	Oxen	Cows	Calves/ Young Beasts	Quoys	Stirks	1yr	2yr	Stots	1y	2yr	3yr
1610	Corharncross		2									
1612	Bailzie		21									
1619	Mylntoun of Glenesk	8 5 yeld nout	5									
1620	Kirktoun of Loghlie	8	8	8 young nolt								
1622	Migvie	2	2					2				
1622	Mylntoun	2	2									
1623	Assalrie	2	3		2		2					1
1624	Achintoull	2	2			1						
1625	Achroune		2		2				3			
1626	Carncross	6	2				3					
1627	Achloche		5									
1636	Quhiggintoun	2	5	(5)				4				
1636	Glenmark	2	2	2				4				
1649	Kirktoune of Glenesk	4	5			5						

Table 4.3 *Sheep*

Date	Place	Sheep	Ewes	Wedders	Dulmonds	Hogs	Lambs	Furthcum Sheep	Riglin Sheep
1610	Corharncross		4						
1612	Bailzie	40							
1617	Achroune			12					
1619			20	80					
1620	Kirktoun of Loghlie		36	80			24		
1622	Migvie		8				4	8	
1623	Assalrie	16							
1624	Achintoull		10			10			
1627	Carncors				30 (ewes and dulmonds)				
1627	Achloche		12						
1636	Quihigginton		13	100		10	7		
1636	Glenesk		6			6	6	12	
1649	Kirktoune of Glenesk	100					20		

Table 4.4 Horses

Date	Place	Horse	Mare	Foal	Horses + Mares	Horse, Mare + Foal	Mare + Foal
1610	Corharncross		1				
1612	Bailzie	3					1
1619	Mylntoun of Glenesk	3				1	
1622	Migvie	2					
1623	Assalrie	2					
1624	Achintoull	2					
1626	Carncors				3		
1627	Achloche		1				
1636	Quhiggintoun						
1636	Glenmark						1
1649	Kirktoun of Glenesk	2					

5

EIGHTEENTH-CENTURY FARMING: THE BEGINNING OF CHANGE

Farming in a highland glen had to conform to the pressures of the environment. Options were limited, perhaps even more for arable than for grazing areas, since the uses of the latter were diversified by gamekeeping in later times. The main change as the seventeenth century moved towards and into the eighteenth was some redistribution of the older settlement pattern characterised by movement to lower lying arable areas which can be seen as a reflection of improving ideas at the time.

Nowadays, the farms lie mainly in the valley of the North Esk and some in the valleys of the Water of Tarf and the Burn of Turret. The highest are at just over 900 feet, though several ruined foundations of farms at over 1,000 feet testify to the former wider spread and greater density of population. Glenesk was once known for the large number of small tenants it supported.

Above Lochlee, for example, in a level area about one-and-a-half miles long by 300 yards broad, were three farm-village groups, named Littlebrigs, Dochty and Glenlee, the last at one time the biggest in the parish. The area contains the clusters of their foundations, and many scattered sheepfolds. Throughout the area traces of the ridges and furrows of the ploughing technique that preceded the days of systematic underground drainage can be seen. This kind of farm-village grouping was not an isolated phenomenon. It had already been noted to the north beyond the Mounth in the 1660s, when a writer described the breaking up of older grouped farms into individual units, where each farm stood on its own ground.[1]

The grouped farms were so organised that each tenant's land was in strips and patches intermingled with those of his neighbours. This was mainly true of the arable, but it also affected the use of the different kinds of grazing available. However, by the end of the century, such a community form of farming had more or less vanished, and 'every tenant received a spot of ground, of which no other was a sharer'.[2]

[1] Sir A. Mitchell, ed. McFarlane, *Geographical Collections* (SHS 1907), II, 224–306.
[2] Reverend James Roger, *General View of the Agriculture of Angus or Forfar Drawn up under the Direction of George Dempster of Dunnichen; for the Consideration of the Board of Agriculture and Internal Improvement*, John Paterson, Edinburgh, 1794, 5.

Individual use of a single unit of land was, of course, a great incentive to protecting it by enclosing it in whatever ways were most convenient; stone dykes and earthen banks surmounted by whins or, in the lower parts of Angus, thorn hedges. It was also, presumably, an incentive to clear the land 'from the dominion of the large white stones that the hand of time has thrown down from the neighbouring hills'.[3] There is no doubt that such clearance had been going on for centuries, perhaps even from prehistoric times as seen from some of the clearance heaps of stones on the hill of The Rowan.

The best arable area is the well-developed flood plain along the North Esk below the point where the Burn of Turret flows into it. Here there is a series of farms, nearly all on the north side of the River, with access to the present-day road. Earlier, however, it was the road on the south side that was the main carrier of traffic.

Higher up there is no flood-plain or haugh, and the settlement pattern is more scattered. There is some terrace development, and houses and farms are sited at the point where the edge of the upper terrace meets the hill ground. Farms with their arable on the lower slopes may lie well back from the valley and some distance from the river. It is here that the highest Glen farms are to be found. Easterton of Glentennet, for example, was at 1,075 feet; the others lay between 750–1,000 feet. It is here too, that the running together of two or more farms in recent times has been most common.

The quality of life in Glenesk during the first two-thirds of the eighteenth century was partly conditioned by events of national significance, the Jacobite Risings. As described in Chapter 3, James, Earl of Panmure, had his estates forfeited because he had supported the rebellion of 1715. The Panmure Estate was bought in 1719 by the York Buildings Company for the sum of £11,508. The Company's lack of success in managing the lands is demonstrated by the fact that they received only £450 more for the estate when they sold it in 1764, and the rental was £200 less than it had been in 1719. The implication of all this appears to be that, certainly until the 1760s, no appreciable improvement in the standards of Glenesk farmers is to be detected. On the other hand, there is no evidence of much deterioration, and it is reasonable to assume that a kind of status quo was maintained through the first sixty or so years of the eighteenth century. This does not mean that the Glen was a place flowing with milk and honey for all. The smaller tenants and cottars always had a struggle to make ends meet, and it is no surprise to learn that in 1720, the people of Lochlee, as of Lethnot, were to be seen 'travelling through neighbouring parishes with timber, heather, peat, etc., and selling the same as usual in the street', even on Fast days when the Church expected them to be more spiritually engaged.

[3] ibid, 7.

It did not take the York Buildings Company long to decide that they could not readily cultivate the estates themselves, nor manage the tenants, nor get the rents in the ordinary way, so they resorted early to the use of middlemen. In 1728, they let Panmure and other units to the brothers-in-law, Sir Archibald Grant of Monymusk who was renowned as an improver, and Alexander Garden of Troup in Banffshire. This was on a 29-year lease at £4,000 per annum.[4]

When the lease ran out in 1757, it was made over to the Hon. John Maule, one of the Barons of Exchequer, for behoof of the Earl of Panmure. By this time, the offences of the landed proprietors whose estates were forfeited had been largely condoned, and the time seemed ripe for selling the estates. The roup of the first instalment, which included Panmure, took place in the Parliament House on 20 February 1764. The Earl of Panmure was present. No one bid against him and he got the Estate back at the upset price: 'it was considered a point of honour to offer no opposition to the old proprietors, who got them at a very moderate price'.[5]

The Act enabling this sale stated in its preamble that Panmure and the three other estates in this lot 'had been long neglected and uncultivated while remaining in the hands of an insolvent company, and would, by transferring them to purchasers, be improved to the great benefit of the public'. In fact, this was an exaggeration, for Sir Archibald Grant and Alexander Garden had held the lease and Grant, at least, with his reputation, could have been expected to originate some improvements. He may have done so, for the actual rent of the Estates he and his brother-in-law held was £7,000, at least coming up to the time of the sale. Of this, the York Buildings Company was getting only £4,000 as per the lease agreement.[6]

THE LOCHLEE RENTALS

It is against this background that the Rentals for Lochlee, as part of the Panmure estates, have to be examined. A general point to be made is that the leases ran from year to year and were not on paper. Each lease was simply a 'verball sett (lease) from the ... late Earl'.

The Rentals record the holdings, the heads of households, and the payment to be made. Payments consisted of silver duty as the major element in hard cash, a grassum or amount paid by those renewing their leases, cess as the

[4] D. Murray. *The York Buildings Company*, Bratton Publishing Ltd, Edinburgh, 1973, 44, 47.
[5] ibid, 92, 94.
[6] ibid, 92–3.

king's tax or land tax, watch money to cover the cost of guarding the area, and payments of butter, poultry and wethers, commuted to money values.

Analysis of the Rentals based on the totals of all payments shows the gradation of the farm units in Lochlee. The graph table is based on the rentals of individual units, according to which Ardoch, then run with part of Nether Cairncross, comes out on top at £145.1.4. But a different pattern appears if the rentals of units bearing the same name are blocked together. In this case Gleneffock is in the lead, with its two units totalling £199.9.4. Bridge of Lee, Drousty, Auchronie, Gleneffock, Turnabraine, Keenie, Berryhill, Tarfside, Auchintoul, Betwixt the Burns and Baillie are all paired units. The rentals of each part of the pair are often equal enough to suggest deliberate halving, e.g. Bridge of Lee at £46.1.8, Auchronie at £44, Gleneffock at £98.19.8, Turnabraine at £36.14.8, Glencot at £15, etc, in each case for half the holding. In some instances the two holders are brothers, implying that splitting could take place by agreement with the Laird as families developed.

There were blocks of four units at Cairncross (including Nether Cairncross), Aucheen with its mill, and at Glentennet (including Eastertoun of Glentennet) and in the case of Arsallary, seven units were involved. These multiple units may reflect older settlement centres. It is also noteworthy that there are some short runs of rentals at the same level – e.g. three at £56, three at £39, three at £36 and three at £22, which suggests a deliberate policy at some period (not necessarily just then) of blocking out land by the estate into units of equivalent value. The reflection of estate activity in relation to its farm units and blocks of units, commonly referred to as 'rooms', is clear enough.

Where leases were being renewed, the level of grassum was normally a fifth of the silver duty; cess stood at a twentieth. Other elements were also worked out proportionally. Each individual who could write witnessed his particular Rental entry, but 57 of the 74 listed could not do so: 'depones he cannot write'.

As noted in chapter three, James Lumsden, WS, was active in obstructing the Commissioners of the Forfeited Estates. This may have a bearing on a list of rents of Panmure given by him in 1718, which tends to make Glenesk appear as a not fully desirable property on the eve of its proposed sale. In only one case, part of Gleneffock, did the same level of rental (£98.19.8) survive as in 1716. Increases of up to 100 per cent or more are frequent and there was only an occasional reduction: Buskhead, for example, was reduced from £49.2/- to £38.15/-. But many tenants were described as 'broke'. In the case of James Bowman, Betwixt the Burns, the Bailie 'took all his goods'. A total of 26 rents was said to have been unpaid in Glenesk in 1718. Again in 1719 another list showed that three out of 75 tenants had failed to pay. The majority of the tenants remained the same, however, and though changes did take place, the striking thing is the stability in the names through what was undoubtedly a troubled period.

Falling within this period is a manuscript list headed 'Lochlee Barony all Forehand Duty'. It includes 52 farm touns, names their tenants, and gives the rental payable for the for the crops 1758 and 1759. The list was compiled in the period immediately after Sir Archibald Grant and Alexander Garden relinquished their lease, and may relate to the time when the Hon. John Maule took it up on behalf of the Earl of Panmure, who was to re-purchase the Estate only five years later.

Forehand duty was the term for rent paid in advance. The Rev. Mr John Pirie, Minister of Lochlee, explained it as follows: 'The rents are paid fore-hand, that is to say, the rent for crop 1793, is paid, the first half, at Whitsunday 1792, and the last half at Martinmas 1792', i.e. payments were made after sowing and after reaping.[7]

Exact comparison between this list and the 1716 Rental is not fully possible, because a number of farms have not been included in the later Rental.

This list aligns the rentals for 1716 and for 1758–9, so that amounts paid can be compared easily. In some cases the same family names can be found in both. Women are named in only two instances, possibly because their husbands had only recently died.

Where farm units are divided into a number of parts – e.g. Arsallary, Glentennet and Migvie – it is not possible to establish which 1758–9 farmer succeeded the one in 1716. In the list, farms have been set alongside each other where the personal names coincide, since there is then a presumption of continuity, but without certainty. In some instances, there were changes between 1758 and 1759: for example, Bridge of Lee, Berryhill, Keenie Mill and Milltown, Auchlochy, one of the Arsallary units and one of the Glentennet units have different possessors between these two dates, and rent increases seem to have been applied.

Gleneffock, Baillie, Migvie and Cairncross each have two units paying separate rents. Two of the farmtouns, Arsallery and Glentennet, consisted of several units. Four of the Arsallary tenants paid just over £18 in rent, and in Glentennet two paid £14 and two exactly twice that amount. There is here again a suggestion of symmetry that implies estate planning and management.

Grading of the farms according to the level of rents paid shows a pattern broadly similar to that revealed by the 1716 Rental. If Arsallery and Glentennet

[7] *The Old (First) Statistical Account of Scotland, 1791–99*, V, 367.

Farmtoun	Tenant 1716	Tenant 1758–69	Rent 1716	Rent 1758	Rent 1759
Bridge of Lee	John Dulloch	David Kinnear	£46 1 8	£92 3 4	£92 3 4
Bridge of Lee	Alex. Duncan	John Gordon	£46 1 8		
Doughty	Thos. Annandale	David Ennerdale	£19 0 10	£19 1 0	£19 1 0
Midtown (1)	Jas. Chrystieson	Alex. Duncan	£39 8 4	£42 15 0	£42 15 0
Midtown	John Maich	–	£10		
Littlebridge	John Maich	Charles Ego	£38 8 4	£46 1 8	£46 1 8
Inchgrundle	Thos. Kinneir	David Kinnear	£86	£86	£86
Kirktoun	Robert Speed	Mr. Alex Ross	£49 6 8	£21	£21
Mains of Invermark	John Lindsay	Charles Garden		£132 13 4	£120 1 4
Glenmark	Jas. Miln	Alex. Mill	£120	£120	£120
Droustie	Donald Nicoll	Robt. Donaldson	£20 18 2	£48 5 10	£48 6 0
Droustie	John Clerk	–	£27 7 8	–	
Auchronie (2)	Alex. Chrystieson	Peter Farquharson	£80 14 8	£88	£88
Auchronie (Haugh)	Thos. Chrystieson	Jas. Thow	£44	£36 15 8	£36 15 8
Gleneffock	Wm. Archibald	David Archibald	£99 19 8	£99 19 8	£99 19 8
Gleneffock (3)	David Archibald	Thos. Jolly	£99 9 8	£98 19 8	£98 19 8
Dalbrack	Jas. Campbell	David Campbell	£94 3 0	£94 3 0	£94 3 0
Drumgreen	–	Robt. Grant		£49 6 8	£49 6 8
Tarrybuckle (5)	John Thomson	Magdalen Mill	£26 13 4	£13 6 8	£13 6 8
Whigginton	John Thomson	John Christyson		£13 6 8	£13 6 8
Buskhead	David Low	Thos. Low	£38 15 0	£37 15 0	£37 15 0
Turnabrain	John Thow	Robt. Thow	£36 14 8	£73 19 4	£73 19 4
Turnabrain	John Nicoll	–	£36 14 8	–	
Corhairncross	David Chrystieson	John Christyson	£36 14 8	£36 14 8	£36 14 8
Skelly	John Nicoll	Donald Nicoll	£36 14 8	£36 14 8	£36 14 8
Berryhill	Wm. Bowman	Jas. Thomson	£28 1 0	£56 2 0	£56 2 0
Berryhill (6)	David Bowman	Isaac Gall	£28	£56 2 0	£56 2 0
Boddom	Wm. Nicoll	Wm. Nicoll	£56 2 0	£42 8 6	£42 8 6
Skair(head)	Thos. Jollie	Thos. Edward	£41 0 8	£22	£22
Keenie	John Nicoll	Donald Gall	£22		
Keenie Mill and Miltown	Henry Lindsay	H. L's heirs	£75 12 8	£75 12 8	£75 12 8
		Alex. Mill			
Westbank	Isabell Thomson	John Crocket	£20	£52 6 0	£52 6 0
Auchlochy	David Kinneir	Robert Duncan	£33 6 8	£26 13 4	

Farmtoun	Tenant 1716	Tenant 1758–69	Rent 1716	Rent 1758	Rent 1759
Auchlochy (7)	-	John Duncan	£9 3 8	-	£26 13 4
Arsallary	John Thow	Andrew Thow	£18 7 4	£18 17 4	£18 7 6
Arsallary	Alex. Gall	Alex. Christyson and Donald Gall	£18	-	£8 4
Arsallary	Jas. Donaldson	Jas. Innes	£17 7 0	£18 7 4	£18 7 4
Arsallary	Thos. Low	Thos. Low	£26 11 0	£34 14 0	-
Arsallary	John Low	John Low	£7 17 0	£18 17 4	£18 17 6
Arsallary	John Shanks	David and John Low	£18 17 4	£30 7 6	-
Arsallary (8)	Walter Innes	Jas. Brown	£9 3 8	£18 8 0	-
Baillie	John Edward	John Low	£50 8 6	£43 15 2	£43 15 2
Baillie	David Christieson	Jas. Christyson	£50 8	£50 8 6	£50 8 6
Glencat	John Crockat	Wm. Mill	£15	£36 13 4	£36 13 4
Glencat	David Lichton	-	£15	-	-
Kedloch	Alex. Tod	Sylvester Crockat	£39 14 0	£41 1 6	£41 1 6
Shinfur	John Laurie	John Lowrie	£6 13 4	£6 13 4	£6 13 4
Eastertoun of					
Glentennet	Jas. Ewing	David Bowman	£20	£24 13 6	-
Glentennet	John Couts	Alex. Coutts	£28	£14	-
Glentennet	John Maich	Alex Coutts	£24	£28	-
Glentennet	Alex. Ross	Robt. Ross	£28	£28	-
Glentennet	-	Susanna Watt	£14	-	-
Glentennet	-	Susanna Watt	£20	-	-
Glentennet	-	David Christyson	-	-	-
Miltown of Glenesk	Jas. Gordon	Sophia Michie	£96	£96	£128 13 6
Whitehills					£96
Tarfside (9)	Wm. Smith	Robert Clark	£2 10 0	£26 13 4	£26 13 4
Tarfside	Wm. Crockat	John Webster	£20	£49 15 8	£49 15 8
Migvie	John Shaw	Robt. Kinnear	£15 14 0	£38 1	£38 1 4
Migvie	Wm. Davidson	David Crockat	£15 14 0	-	£18 7 4
Migvie					
Migvie (10)	J. Shaw, W.	-	£6 3 4	-	-

Place	Tenant(s)	£	s.	d.	Tacksman	£	s.	d.	£	s.	d.
Cairncross	Davidson, D.; Crockat	33	6	8	Thos. Christieson	33	6	8	33	6	8
Nether Cairncross	John Chrystieson	32	9	0	–	–	–	–	–	–	–
Nether Cairncross	David Nicoll	31	8	0	–	–	–	–	–	–	–
Nether Cairncross (11)	Robt. Elder; David Campbell	20	8	5½	John and David Campbell	62	9	0	62	9	9
Glack (12)	Robt. Chrystie	23	8	0	–	–	–	–	–	–	–
Burn of Coats	Jas. Webster	31	8	4	–	–	–	–	–	–	–
Ardoch	David Campbell	125	1	9	–	–	–	–	–	–	–
Auchintoul	George Wylie	61	9	4	–	–	–	–	–	–	–
Auchintoul	Andrew Malcolm	61	9	4	–	–	–	–	–	–	–
Blackcraig (13)	David and William Malcolm	45	12	0	–	–	–	–	–	–	–
Aucheen	Andrew Lindsay	46	1	8	–	–	–	–	–	–	–
Aucheen	David Low, yr.	23	0	10	–	–	–	–	–	–	–
Aucheen	David Low, sr.	23	0	10	–	–	–	–	–	–	–
Mill of Aucheen	Jas. Jollie	89	2	0	–	–	–	–	–	–	–
The Mure	Walter Lindsay	45	8	4	–	–	–	–	–	–	–
Betwixt the Burns	Walter Innes	18	7	4	–	–	–	–	–	–	–
Betwixt the Burns	James Bowman	18	7	4	–	–	–	–	–	–	–
Kirnie	Henry Crockat	30	13	4	–	–	–	–	–	–	–
Burnside	John Annandale	18	13	4	–	–	–	–	–	–	–
Middleford	Alexr. Robie	22	13	0	–	–	–	–	–	–	–
Blackhills	John Nicoll	44			–	–	–	–	–	–	–

NOTES

(1) A piece of waste ground (with a further piece in Lochend).
(2) Room and haugh.
(3) David Archibald was 'brother's son' to William.
(4) Includes a part of Burnside.
(5) In 1716, John Thomson also possessed Whigginton.
(6) William and David Bowman were brothers.
(7) Seems to have been one unit in 1716.
(8) Walter Innes also had half of Betwixt the Burns.
(9) William Smith had a quarter of the room in 1714.
(10) This was a room that had lately been waste.
(11) David Campbell also had Ardoch.
(12) Robert Chrystie paid three quarters of the rent of Glack.
(13) William Malcolm was David's father.

are kept together, as well as double units, the pecking order (in terms of fore-hand duty) is:

Glentennet	£229.7. 0	Drousty	48. 5.10
Gleneffock	197.19. 4	Littlebridge	46. 1. 8
Arsallary	192.4. 7	Midtown Glenlee	42.15. 0
Mains of Invermark	132.13. 4	Skairhead	42. 8. 6
Glenmark	120.0. 0	Kedloch	41. 1. 6
Milltown Glenesk	96.0. 0	Buskhead	37.15. 0
Cairncross	95.15. 8	Haugh	36.15. 8
Baillie	94.3. 8	Corhairncross	36.14. 8
Dalbrack	94.3. 0	Skelly	36.14. 8
Auchrony	88.0. 0	Glencat	36.13. 4
Migvie	87.17. 0	Auchlochy	26.13. 4
Inchgrundle	86.0. 0	Tarfside	26.13. 4
Keeny Mill & Miltown	75.12. 8	Keeny	22. 0. 0
Turnabrain	73.19. 4	Kirktoun	21. 0. 0
Boddom	56. 2. 0	Doughty	19. 1. 0
Berryhill	56. 2. 0	Tarrybuckle	13. 6. 8
Westbank	52. 6. 0		
Drumgreen	49. 6. 8		

If the farms are compared as individual holdings, however, Mains of Invermark is the major farm, as would be expected, closely followed by the unit of Glentennet occupied by David Christyson, and then by Glenmark. Only these three have rentals of over £100, i.e. 5.56 per cent of the total. Ten farms lie in the £70–90 bracket, so that the total of those over £70 amounts to 24.08 per cent or nearly a quarter of the whole. The number of those between £50 to £70 is low (9.27 per cent), and most lie fairly equally divided in the £10–50 band (64.79 per cent), with only one below £10. The overall impression, however, is not one of extremes with a small number of big units and a great many small ones, but of a relatively even spread. The extended community farms and one double unit outdo the mains farm when their rents are added together.

Lochlee Barony: Pattern of Farm Sizes, 1758–9

Rent	No. of Farms	Percentage of Rental
Over £100	3	5.56
80–90	8	14.81
70–80	2	3.71
60–70	1	1.86
50–60	4	7.41
40–50	8	14.8
30–40	9	16.67
20–30	8	14.8
10–20	10	18.52
0–10	1	1.86

TESTAMENTS AND ROUP ROLLS

A good deal of supplementary information can be gleaned from analysis of testaments and roup rolls covering the period. Where prices are given in Scots money, as in the 1744 and 1758 testaments, they have been converted to sterling in the notes that follow. This involves dividing by twelve; the conversions are added in brackets, to facilitate comparison with prices later in the century.

Draught animals were the most valuable stock. Thomas Christieson, tenant in Wester Achronie, had eleven horses valued at £8 each, and nine oxen at £24, in 1744. James Jollie, Mill of Aucheen, had a black mare at £15 (£1.5.0), a grey mare at £4 (£0.6.8), two foals at £9 (£0.15.0) each, and six oxen worth £26.13.4 (£2.4.5 4/12) each. The presence of oxen shows their continuing use for cultivating the soil.

Cattle Prices

Year	Name and Place	Cow	Cow+Calf	Quoy	Stirk	Stot
1744	Thomas Christieson, Wester Achronie	£16 Sc. (£1.6.8)				
1758	James Jollie, Mill of Aucheen	£18 Sc. (£1.10.0)				
1776	James Lawson, Arsallary		£2.7.0	£1.11.10	£0.8.8	
1777	Alexander Low, Keenie	£3				
1794	John Christison, Glentennet	£3.4.0		£2.8.6		£1.3.6

In some cases, individual prices were not given. James Jollie also had four cows and two calves together worth £78 (£6.10.0), two stots and a quoy at £37.16.0 (£3.3.0), two quoys and a stot at £24 (£2), and a farrow calf and a quoy at £20 (£1.13.4).

Additional description is rare, but, in 1794, John Christison's quoy or heifer was 'rigged', i.e. it had a stripe, probably white, running along its back, and his stot or bullock was black. Sheep were also differentiated as a rule. The number in brackets gives the total number mentioned.

Year	Name and Place	Sheep	Ewe	Ewe + Lamb	Ewe Lamb	Wedder	Hog	Furthcome
1744	T. Christieson, Wester Achronie	£1.10.0Sc. (£0.2.6) (112)						
1758	J. Jollie, Mill of Aucheen	£2.10.0 (£0.4.2) (45)	£2.8.0 (£0.4.2) (32)			£2.13.4 (£0.4.5) (27)	£1.6.8 (£0.2.2) (13)	£1.10.0 (£0.2.6) (15)
1762	Charles Campbell, Mid Cairncross	£3.0.0 (42)						
1776	J. Lawson, Arsallary			£0.7.3 (9)		£0.8.1 (7)	£0.6.0 (8)	
1777	A. Low, Keenie		(£0.4.0) (18)			£0.3.4	(4)	
1794	J. Christison, Glentennet		£0.4.0 (11) £0.3.11 (8)		£0.2.7 (10)	£0.3.6 (7)		
1798	D. Nicholl, Aucheen					£0.16.0 (3)		

In this list, Mill of Aucheen had the largest number of sheep, 132 in all, followed by Wester Auchronie with 112.

The number of examples of stock prices available is too small for confident statistics. Nevertheless, there is at least an indication of upward movement between the 1740s and 1790s. There is, of course, no indication of quality, but the price of a cow rose from £1.6.8 to £3.4.0. Ewes remained fairly level at 3/11 to 4/-, though wedders fluctuated from just over 4/5 to 16/-.

The details of cropping are of much interest. In 1744, bere and oats 'with the fodder' (presumably including the straw), cost seven merks or £4.13.4 (7/9 and four twelfths) per boll. The same in 1758 cost £8 (13/4) a boll, which indicates a rise in value between the two set dates, though neither period of year nor quality can be ascertained to allow exact comparison.

For the first time, however, roup rolls give us the chance to see beyond the legal figures of testaments to the appearance of the fields themselves. James Lawson, subtenant in Arsallary in 1776, had five ridges of corn and two butts (i.e. pieces of ground not forming a full ridge), and an amount of bere not specified in the same way because bought by private bargain later and not at the roup:

Purchaser	Amount	Price
Donald Gall, Arsallary	1 ridge	£0.4.3
William Crockat, Garthead	1 ridge	£0.9.4
	1 ridge	£0. 7. 0
Mr. John Pirie (minister)	2 ridges	£1.18.0
Isabell Bowman, Whitestone	2 butts	£0.7.8
David Buchan, Stylemouth	bere	£0.18.4

Two of the ridges are specified as lying adjacent to each other. The testament of Alexander Low, subtenant in Keenie, given up by his wife, Jean Robbie, on 13 August 1777, does specify four 'Riggs of Oats and Bere' at £1.10.0, an average of 7/6 per rig. But the most extensive list comes from a later roup roll for the farm of Glentennet, tenanted by John Christison. It is dated 21 August 1794. Three rigs had names: the Bog Rig, the Well Rig and the Wester Rig. There were at least 43 rigs altogether, including four butts. Of these, 24 grew oats, seven black oats, and nine bere. The crop is not specified for a small number of rigs, but clearly the proportion of oats to bere was in excess of three to one. The price of the oats averages out at 13/8 and six-twelfths per rig, that of black oats nearly 9/1, and of bere just over 16/-. Bere, therefore, was the most valuable crop, and black oats came at the bottom of the range.

Details about tools, equipment and personal possessions can also be found in such sources. They were normally of considerably lower value than the crops and stock. Percentages of the total are given in the following table:

Date	Name and Place	Crops	Stock	Equipment
1744	Thos. Christieson, Wester Achronie	11.8%	74%	6.35%
1758	Jas. Jollie, Mill of Aucheen	21.1%	40.19%	5.45%
1762	Chas. Campbell	-	66.3%	7.36%

The percentages do not total 100 per cent because the table omits debts due to the dead. The examples, though few, consistently point to the scales of values: stock came first, crops second and wordly goods well behind.

In some cases, these goods are specified. The furniture in the Mill of Aucheen in 1758 consisted of a long table, five beds and bedding, four chests, two presses, and six chairs. There were two girnels for storing meal (one of them old), and two wool wheels for spinning. Kitchen equipment included three pots and a kettle. The latter was no ordinary tea kettle, however. It was the costliest item at £18 and is likely to have been more in the nature of a cauldron, for use, for example, in brewing ale.

In testamentary inventories, it is likely that only or mainly the most valuable items were specified. Roup rolls tend to cover a somewhat wider range. The roup on 10 June 1776 of James Lawson, who was a tailor and subtenant of Arsallary, says little about domestic items, however. It mentions a heckle or flax-comb, the only thing that seems to touch on his trade. For the rest, he was disposing of farm equipment like a riddle, sieve, two weights, three hooks, three iron swivels, a calf prickle (to prevent a calf from sucking its mother), a muck hack (pronged tool for hauling out byre manure), a graip, two shovels, two sacks, and two sheep hacks, in this case meaning a 'heck' or rack, probably for fodder. Of food-related interest were the kail-gully for cutting and chopping kail, the kail-box, the use of which is not clear – perhaps for chopping the kail – and a seydish or strainer, no doubt for milk. Lawson seems also to have indulged in sports. He had a gun, which the Minister, Mr Pirie, bought for 12/2 and a fishing pirn or reel. This was a kind of preliminary clearing out, for three months later, on 10 September of the same year, he held a second roup. This included the standing corn which has beeen discussed earlier.

The testament of Alexander Low, Keenie, dated 13 August 1777, specifies as furniture three chairs, four chests, two fir beds, a 'bedding of Cloathes', two fir presses, and a plate rack and dishes. The plate rack would have been hung on the wall, above a dresser or independently. Kitchen and fireside equipment consisted of two pots, a pan, a crook from which pots could hang, a pair of tongs, a flat iron girdle and an open work brander for baking bannocks of oatmeal and beremeal. There was a spinning wheel of unspecified type, and four spades.

As for the previous century, the inventories reveal something of the money economy through the debts owed by or to the dead. Thomas Christieson, Wester Achronie, was owed £60 by several persons in 1744. Alexander Bowman, who died in Miltown of Glenesk in November 1752 (whose wife was Sophia Michie), was owed £90.10/- by Andrew Constable, flesher in Dundee; the bond was dated 1733. Robert Will, who had been servant to Robert Donaldson in Drousty, died in December 1752,when five individuals (three in Glenesk and two outside it) owed him a total of £100. The bills had been taken out in 1751 and 1752. John Innerdale at Kirn was owed £276 by ten creditors in 1753; five of these were from outside Glenesk. Debts due to his sister Jannet Innerdale, Skellie, in 1758, amounted to £200.6/-. She had eleven creditors, six of whom were from the parish.

As might be expected, the miller of Aucheen, James Jollie, had a wide range of debts due to him when he died in 1758, from 30 individuals, making a total of £866.7/-. Of these, thirteen came from Glenesk. He himself owed £185.2/- to nine servants, two of whom were women, and to two other people.

Though it is not stated, it is likely that all or most of these debts were in the form of wages to be paid. The amounts were:

John Christison	£10 (half year)
David Nicoll	£10
James Jolly	£7.10/-
Alexr. Nicoll	£6.10/-
Helen Ffergusone	£20 + £4.12/- = £24.12/-
Janet Jolly	£4.10/- + £1.10/- = £6
James Will	£6 + £6.10/- = £12.10/-
John Cattanach	£7
David Malcolm	£10

In three instances, two payments were due to be made. With the exception of Helen Ffergusone, women were consistently paid less than the men. Except for the late John Christison, whose wage was £10 for half a year, we do not know the periods covered, though half a year is likely in most cases.

The will of Charles Campbell, Mid Cairncross, throws light on the extent to which money was sometimes lent out amongst family members. At the time of his death in 1762, Sophia Michie in Miltown of Glenesk, widow of Alexander Bowman, owed him £50. But in his will, made during his lifetime, several details of financial family links are given: James Miln in Craigyshino's accepted bill for £27.6/- Scots was endorsed to Campbell's nephew, David Campbell in Dalbrack, though without obligation to make good the legacy in the event of Miln's insolvency. His niece, Elizabeth Campbell in Blackhills, daughter of his brother Alexander Campbell who had formerly been in Baillie, was to get £20 Scots out of a bill for £64.5/- Scots drawn on his nephew David Campbell in Mid-Cairncross and David Gib in Ardoch, within a year and a day of his decease.

One aspect of money lending is that the bills were frequently drawn on and accepted by more than one individual as a guarantee of security. Of the eight bills listed in the testament of James Bowman, Stylemouth, 1786, seven involved two individuals and one involved three, the amounts ranging from £1.10/- to £13.14/-, in this case all in sterling. By the end of the century, amounts stated appear to be normally in sterling, perhaps an effect of the supplanting of Scottish coinage by sterling following the Union, and actual sums of money begin to be listed in testaments. James Christison, for example, who stayed with James Cattanach at Whigginton for 18 months before he died, left bank notes and silver amounting to £8.14.6 in his chest.

THRESHING MILLS AND MEAL MILLS

Some eighteenth-century information on mills has been pinpointed. The houses and the mill of Auchmull were valued on 16 May 1709. The two stones and two wheels were apprised by John Moleson in Sclatefoord and John Innes, miller at the New Mill (later the Mill of Arnhall), and valued at £16. The houses were apprised by four individuals. They included at least eight small 'cotes', five dwelling houses, three byres, a barn, in addition to the mill house (£2), the miller's house (£2.6.8), and two kilns (one £2.16/-, the other £2). It may be significant that wooden parts – barn and byre doors, stall trees in the byre, a loose couple in a dwelling house – were specially noted, as also the lock on the barn door. Altogether, 22 units are listed for the Auchmull community. The mill and kiln elements, valued at £25.2.8, constituted approximately 28 per cent of the total valuation of £90.6.0.

THE END OF THE CENTURY

By the late eighteenth century, agricultural improvements had become well advanced in Lowland Scotland, though Lochlee remained primarily pastoral. In 1792, even hay-producing areas were limited. The Rev. Mr John Pirie wrote that there was little meadow ground, even the valleys being covered with heath.[8] The only exceptions were 'the few small stripes under tillage', along the riversides. It did not appear practicable to increase their extent.

As might have been expected, the average annual grain yield was relatively low, and not enough to support the inhabitants. One factor in this was the climate. Frost and snow could prevent the beginning of tillage till the first days of April. Only a few farms in the lower-lying east end of the parish were better off in this respect. Following a late, often cold, Spring, the crop could be checked by bad weather in the following September. If the bere survived September frosts, it filled out well enough, but oats might have to be left till mid-November and could hardly be expected to produce much when reaped.[9] For comparison, in the neighbouring parish of Lethnot, oats could be sown before mid-March and bere about mid-April, with harvesting of oats in the first fortnight of September, and of bere before 1 November.[10]

Improvements were coming, however. Potatoes and turnips had been introduced and 'if the climate would permit, these useful roots would thrive well'.[11] They sometimes played a role in the clearing of waste land (some of which is referred to in the Rentals). Cleared soil was often mossy, and had to be fed to make it produce crops. In Lochlee, as in Lethnot, and Navar, Glen Clova, Glen Prosen and Glen Isla, fallowing was little practised in the late eighteenth cen-

[8] ibid.
[9] ibid, (1792), 358.
[10] *The Old First Statistical Account*, IV, 12.
[11] *The Old First Statistical Account*, V, 358.

tury. Instead, farmers had begun to depend on turnips and potatoes for cleaning the arable, which was not extensive enough to permit very flexible use. In the lower parts, however, fallowing was a standard new element in the rotation.

Wheat was rarely or never grown in these glens, though widespread in the lowlands. Oats were common, especially Angus oats, and in some higher areas black oats were still being sown in the 1790s almost as a kind of grass seed, planted when the ground was too exhausted from alternate crops of oats and bere to grow much else. Oat crops were sown and harvested in Glenesk and other glens two or three weeks later than in the lowlands. 'Seldom is the plough drawn forth till the first week of April to prepare for the ensuing crop', said Mr Roger.[12] Barley was grown on the plains, and its hardier brother, bere, in the glens.

A major farming advance was the use of clover seed. It produced fodder that helped horses and oxen to stand up to the fatigue of cultivating the ground. Cattle that had formerly been sent to the heath to pick what they could, and horses that had been left to pasture on the roadsides or on the waste balks between tenant's possessions, and that often enough were suppered only on thistles, now began to improve in strength on winter fodder of clover-hay. This was to the great benefit of the animals and the work they had to do. The glen areas benefited as well as the lowlands, though the difference can be judged by the fact that in the lowlands a pair of horses might cost £52.10/-, but higher up, not more than £16 to £20, i.e. less than half the value. As for equipment, a lowland cart with its harness cost £9 to £13.13/-, whilst the roughness of the glens meant continuing use of currachs for the carriage of corn on the backs of horses, and creels for carrying peat, at 1/- a pair.

Another difference lay in the type of plough. Improved ploughs of the type developed by James Small, the Berwickshire ploughwright, operated in the cleared, lower-lying lands and only in Glenesk and Glenisla was the old Scotch plough, with its long sole and flat mouldboard, still in use. Its design made it ideal for shaping the high-backed plough ridges whose corrugations still mark areas of arable long since converted into permanent pasture, and often lying at surprising heights. In Glenesk, as in Glenisla, it may have been pulled by six small horses yoked abreast, with one man standing between the stilts controlling the plough, and a helper stepping backwards before the horses, keeping a sharp eye on them.[13] However, the evidence of the testaments shows that oxen were in common use in the plough.

Even the hours of work could vary in the different areas. Spring work in the lowlands demanded that servants rose at 5 a.m., saw to the horses, corned

---

[12] Roger, op. cit., 10–11.
[13] ibid, 13, 15–17, 19.

them at 6.30 a.m., had their own breakfast (by the 1790s, usually of oatmeal
and milk) and started their labour at 7a.m. They came back from the fields at
11a.m., saw to smiddy repairs, and filled the barn with sheaves, or winnowed
grain. The horses were fed at 1 p.m., the men had dinner at 2 p.m., and then
went back to work until 6 p.m. After feeding and bedding the horses, they
had supper and retired to rest.

The summer regime was to rise at 4 a.m., feed the horses with grass, work
in the fields from 5 till 9 a.m., then have an hour off for breakfast. The men
would then hand-hoe turnips and potatoes or help in hay-making, whilst the
horses fed on grass in field or stable. Dinner was from 1 till 2 p.m., and field
labour then went on till 6 p.m., after which grass was provided for the horses'
supper and breakfast.

During harvest, work began at 5 a.m. or as soon as there was light. An hour
was allowed for breakfast, which was brought to the field, about 7 a.m. A ten
minute rest was allowed at the end of every ridge of 900 to 1000 feet. Dinner
was from 1 to 2 p.m, then shearing went on till 7 p.m. or until it was too dark
to see. Work was with the sickle. Whilst it was going on, the farmer could call
away any of the hired shearers to help his own servants to carry home corn
ready for the barnyard. However, hired shearers departed as soon as reaping
was finished and the farmer and his men were left to get in the crop that was
left. Work in the hill districts was on the old, crooked, high-backed ridges,
but improvements in the lower areas had led to their levelling and straightening into parallel strips of sixteen to eight feet wide, on which three shearers
could work side by side.

In winter, servants got up at dawn, saw to the horses and stable, break-
fasted, and started work about 8.30 a.m., keeping going for five hours, till
2.30 p.m., turning dung-hills, opening and clearing water courses, bundling
straw, riddling or winnowing grain, and preparing supper for their horses.

In the hill areas, spring work meant rising between 4 and 5 a.m., feeding
the horses, breakfasting, starting labour between 6 and 7 a.m. and going on
till noon. There came a break of two hours, then an afternoon yoking from 2
till 6 p.m.

Summer rising time was between 2 and 3 a.m., with about four-and-a-half
hours' work and then a couple of hours' sleep. The men began again between
noon and 1 p.m. and did not stop till sunset.

Shearers worked from as soon and as long as weather permitted and stayed
in the farm till every stook had been gathered in. On small farms there might
be no need to take on hired hands, because there were servants enough: enough
had in any case to be available for the considerable effort of laying in adequate
supplies of peat for fuel and in winter for flail threshing and for tending the
sheep and cattle.[14]

[14] ibid, 18–20.

There were, therefore, differences in the daily hours of work and in the nature of employment between lowland and highland districts, reflecting different scales of operations. In Glenesk itself, as in other higher lying areas, even if change was not as advanced nor as marked, there is no doubt that by the end of the century there was a different atmosphere. The somewhat depressed state of affairs under the York Buildings Company had been left behind.

6

THE PARISH CHURCH

The ruined church at Lochlee is said to have been dedicated to St Drostan (*Fasti*). However, the place-names connected with Drostan – Drousty and Drousty's Well – are all a mile away at the House of Mark, which served as the parish manse from 1803 till 1931. There was also Drousty's Meadow, the exact location of which is not certain, but it is thought to have been on the lower slopes of the Rowan, near Tarfside, and not at Drousty itself. At the foot of Glenesk is St Drostan's Well, nearly a mile east of the foundations of the Church of Newdosk, in a field called Piper's Shade.

Drostan, said to have been the nephew and disciple of Columba and co-founder of the abbey of Deer in Aberdeenshire, flourished around the year AD 600.[1] Another point of view is that Deer is more likely to reflect the cult of the Pictish Drostan in the eighth century or later.[2] *The Book of Deer*, dating from the eleventh and twelfth centuries, tells that the 'Blessed Drostan, son of Cosgrach, of the royal stock of the Scot... betaking himself to this eremitical life, built the church of Glenesk. Here he gave sight to the blind priest, Symon, and resisted by compunction and maceration of the flesh the assaults of the demon'. There is a belief that Drostan died in Glenesk and that his body was carried over the hills to Old Deer, where his bones were discovered in the sixteenth century. However great the uncertainty about historicity and chronology, what remain firm are the pointers to further evidence of close links between Glenesk and Aberdeenshire, and the likelihood of considerable age for the church in Glenesk.

The kirk at Lochlee, 66 feet long by 22 feet wide, stands at the end of the Loch of the same name, surrounded by the kirkyard dyke, and with a few sheltering trees. The water laps closer to it now than in earlier days, for utilisation of the Loch in 1962 as a reservoir for a large part of Angus and the Mearns led to a rise of five feet in the water level. The ruined kirk has every

[1] 1a. Rev. H. Scott. *Fasti Ecclesiae Scoticanae*, V, Edinburgh, 1866–71, 401–3.
 1b. G. Donaldson & R.S. Morpeth. *A Dictionary of Scottish History*, Edinburgh, 1977, 60.
[2] A.M. Duncan. *Scotland. The Making of the Kingdom*, Edinburgh, 1975, 104.

sign of age. The floor is deep, and the building long and narrow. What now stands has not been the first church, since red sandstone from a previous and much superior building has been used as filling for the medieval gables, and the upper part of a carefully dressed window in the early medieval style, with a groove for glass, acts as a support in the east wall. The long walls, one of which has almost disappeared, were built after 1645 when the Church was burned by the soldiers of the Marquis of Montrose. In 1752 the belfry was added when the Session decided to replace the handbell with one now at the later Church.[3] By the end of the eighteenth century the building was in sad repair. With the deepening of the floor the congregation had actually been going downstairs to service, unless they worshipped in one of the two galleries. The leaky heather roof was replaced by a stone one, but the Kirk at the Loch had had its day.

Lochlee is mentioned in Bagimond's Roll, a valuation of the benefices of the Scottish Church made by the papal collector, Baiamund de Vicci, in 1276, and used as the basis of taxation till after 1660. In 1384, it appears as a chapel in Glenesk. Lethnot, Navar and Lochlee became a prebend of Brechin Cathedral in 1384–5, when the priest was created a canon and had to live in Brechin. He was bound in his absence to pay a curate to do his parochial work, so that for many years poorly paid, partly qualified men were all that were provided to read the scriptures and examine the people in religious matters. Lochlee,

Lochlee Church, c. 1900, designed in 1803 and redesigned in 1828. Glenesk Museum.

---

[3] Kirk Session Records.

being well out of the way, was not a favourite place, and there was seldom a resident priest. In 1517, James Foullarton is named as priest of Edzell, Dunlappie, Lethnot, Navar and Lochlee, which certainly spread his pastoral efficiency very thinly. The last Roman Catholic priest was Andrew Jolie, mentioned in 1558.

In 1803 the present Lochlee Church was built near Invermark, further down the Glen, but the old one may have continued in use for a time. The minister, the Rev. John Pirie, is said to have announced from the new pulpit: 'Next Sabbath the service will be held at the bottom of the Loch!'.

Though not in use for burials now, the kirkyard was not given up when the new church was built. Many of the gravestones have sunk below ground level or lie at various angles, while the inscriptions are becoming harder to read. Stones run in date from the early eighteenth into the nineteenth century. Built into the dyke is one for John Garden of Midstrath and his wife, whom he married on 29 October 1696. He died at Invermark, 26 April 1745, aged 73, and she on 24 November 1738, aged 62. The Latin epitaph was composed by Mr Alexander Ross, schoolmaster and poet in Lochlee. In front of this monument is a long flat stone in memory of Mr Charles Garden of Ballastreen in Aboyne, who died in 1761 at the age of 90, with an inscription: 'Entombed here lies what's mortal of this man, who filled with honour life's intended span'. These Gardens, who had Aberdeenshire links, were tacksmen and factors for the Panmure and Glenesk portions of the Forfeited Estates.

In addition to the usual emblems of mortality and immortality, crossed bones, skulls, hour-glasses and angels' heads with and without wings, there are also sexton's tools, crossed shovels and spades, and symbols of occupations. A pair of compasses and a pick-like object, on a stone for Al Broun 1732, may mark the resting place of a mason. Another eighteenth-century stone bears a plough-share and coulter, which were the valuable iron parts of the old Scotch plough, symbols of a farmer whom the earth, in which he toiled, had gathered.

From the *Fasti* (1925 edition) and other sources, the ministers associated with Lochlee can be assembled:

1558	Sir Andrew Jolie, curate.
1563	George Hay, reader. Received £13.6.8.
1567	James Fullarton MA had charge of Edzell, Dunlappie, Lethnot and Navar. Transferred to Menmuir after 1590.
	(*Fasti* has two more names not included in this list)
1607	George Donaldson, translated to Dunlappie, 1611.
1615	David Wood MA, minister of Edzell, held Lochlee in conjuction.

In 1618, Lochlee was united to Lethnot, though the two parishes were severed again on 6 February 1723.

Gravestone of Al Broun. The pair of compasses and the pick-like object may mark the resting place of a mason. G1/1/4A.

The gravestone of the Glenesk Schoolmaster and poet, Alexander Ross. Glenesk Museum.

1622	John Piggot, MA Transferred to Cortachy, 1637.
1642–83	Robert Norie, MA, master of Brechin Grammar School until 1642, and serving with the forces in 1641. He then became minister of Lethnot, Navar and Lochlee.
1685(3?)–1716	Robert Thomson. Removed 6 March 1716 for intrusion and support of the Jacobite cause.
1717–28	Robert Ker, ordained to Lethnot 18 July 1717, removed to Lochlee on erection of parish in 1723; demitted 9 October 1728, died February 1735.
1729–33	David Blair MA, ordained 10 September 1729, transferred to Brechin 6 June 1733.
1734–49	John Scott, ordained 25 April 1734; killed 23 January 1749.
1749–73	Alexander Ross MA, admitted 4 October 1749, died 20 March 1773. (The schoolmaster of the parish during Ross's incumbency was Alexander Ross 1699–1784.)
1771–1806	John Pirie, ordained 4 December 1771, died February 1806.
1806–37	David Inglis MA, ordained 1806, died 18 January 1837.
1837–41	Robert Inglis MA, son of the preceding, ordained 8 June 1837; transferred to Edzell, 20 October 1841.
1842–43	Alexander Todd, ordained 28 April 1842; transferred to Monifeith 13 December 1843.
1844–87	Walter Low, ordained 18 April 1844, died 22 March 1887.
1885–1921	John Stewart MA, ordained 22 December 1885, died 18 December 1921.
1922–32	John Rorie McKay, admitted 19 May 1922, demitted 15 May 1932, died 11 August 1960.

Some of these people have left little information about themselves, except their names on paper which can be more durable than stone. Others are documented more fully.

One name not mentioned in the list above was George Thom, described as 'somtym readder at the kirk of Lochlie!' On 17 May 1649, he begged successfully for support through Presbytery for help for his young children 'in this tyme of death', having been robbed of his goods and insight (furnishings) by Highlanders.[4] The invasion of Angus by the troops of Montrose in the course of his campaign against the Covenanters in 1645 may have created conditions which allowed Highland caterans to harry the Glen more frequently and with more ease than was hitherto possible. In 1649 John of Edzell petitioned Parliament for exemption from the levies then being raised, on the grounds that the rebel army had for a long time been encamped and quartered on the lands of

---

[4] Brechin Presbytery Records.

Edzell and Glenesk, 'to the utter ruin and destruction of my lands and tenants, the whol corns being burnt in the barnyards,and the whole store of cattle and goods killed or driven away'. The whole of Glenesk, which had been worth 9,000 merks, was left lying waste since the tenants could not cultivate the ground.[5] Times were hard for men, ministers and lairds alike.

On 28 June 1649, Robert Noray (or Norie) declared before the Moderator and other brethren that he had pressed the inhabitants of Lochlee to accept publicly the Solemn League and Covenant. This was drawn up in August 1643, when Scottish Covenanters agreed to help the English Parliament against Charles I, provided England adopted what was, in effect, a Presbyterian church system. The English agreed, with some modification, in September. The people of Lochlee, however, refused outright to do so then, but were persuaded to subscribe publicly on 29 November 1649, thus bringing to an end the state of 'malignancie', as the episcopal regime overthrown by the Covenanters in 1638 was called.[6] However, it does not appear that the minister of the time, Robert Norie, was remarkable for his activity, for the *Brechin Presbytery Records* for 5 August 1658 record that there had been 'no catechising reader at Lochlie conform to the mortification made by the last Laird of Edzell, nether has been thir many yeeres bygone'. Furthermore, the sacrament of the Lord's Supper had been administered only twice in the ten years preceding because, it was said, of 'their great ignorance and unfitness for it, quhilk he professed he was not able to help because of his great distance of way from them, and tempests often hindering him when he was both willing and in readiness to come unto them'.

Part of the 'unfitness' may have been the level of superstition that was rife at this mid-seventeenth century period. According to the Brechin Presbytery Records, 50 charmers were rebuked for casting the 'shemfur', described as 'Devil Fire', in 1649. The charmers mentioned were male. On 3 March, John Donaldson in Lochlee confessed to charming by casting the shemfur. When asked who taught him, he said 'the man was dead who learned him', and named other charmers in Glenesk: John Chrystison, Thomas Bowman, John Shanks and Alex Davidson. On 6 June 1650, John Chrystison, Thomas Kyneir and James Shanks, all of Lochlee, were further rebuked and required to make public satisfaction in sackcloth.

In 1660, the monarchy was restored, together with the machinery of government, more or less as it had been before the covenanting revolt. Under Charles II and James VII, in Scotland as in England, the constitution of the established church was of an episcopal form and continued so until the time of the Revolution of 1688–9 and the Act of 7 June 1690 which restored presbyterian govern-

[5]   Lord Lindsay. *Lives of the Lindsays*, London, 1849, II, 256.
[6]   Brechin Presbytery Records.

ment to the church on the model of 1592.[7] Despite this, many ministers remained in their charges and Episcopalians were still in a majority north of the Tay. Robert Thomson, for example, a man with strongly Jacobite sympathies and family connections, was not dismissed until 1716, and even then it was only because of keeping a 'meeting-house', contrary to law.

Thomson did not actually live in Glenesk, Lethnot and Lochlee being still united. In 1723, however, the Commissioner of Teinds again severed the two parishes and the minister of the time, Robert Ker, is said to have had his quarters in Invermark Castle. He is known to have lodged at Drousty on one occasion when he travelled from Brechin. He had been minister in Lethnot and Lochlee from the time of Thomson's departure, though his appointment was opposed in Lochlee on the grounds that nothing was known about him, and that his agent represented the Jacobite Earl of Panmure, whose estates had been forfeited. Nevertheless, he was ordained, but proved unfit to minister in the two parishes. When they were disjoined on 12 March 1723, the Minister of Lochlee was to have the usual manse, glebe, grass, fuel and other things formerly possessed by the ministers of Navar, or an equivalent in Lochlee and the former stipend of Lochlee and Lethnot, except 100 merks with the glebe and grass of Lethnot.

It is clear that Ker was not an outstanding minister. In the Presbytery records for 2 September 1728, he was asked at a meeting 'if he had been at any pains to dispose his people for the Sacrament of the Lord's Supper, by dealing particularly with them for the Effect'. He replied that he had never given the Sacrament, though he had done all he could in bygone years to prepare his people for it. At a further meeting on 20 September, he was charged with faulty conduct in having set out from Brechin too late on a Saturday to reach Lochlee the same night. He therefore lodged in the house of John Lowson in Clochy, four miles from Brechin. This was most imprudent, since Lowson was the chief supporter of the meeting-house (i.e. a nonconformist or dissenting place of worship) in Lethnot. Furthermore, he left Clochy on the Sunday morning to reach Lochlee, travelling over an unnecessarily long, rough route, 'impossible to be travelled in a short time on Horse-back, especially by a person of such a bulkish, unwieldy Body as Mr. Ker has'. He claimed he did not leave Clochy before 8 a.m. because the water was in spate, though it seems not to have been at that period. His disregard for his duties seems to have been amply demonstrated.

In due course he died. His testamentary inventory, dated 1735, was 'made and given up' by his three cousins Thomas, John and James Ker in Paisley. His clothes, some books and other small personal items were valued at £70, but

[7] G. Donaldson. *Scotland. James V to James VII*, Edinburgh and London, 1965, 358ff. Also W. Ferguson. *Scotland. 1689 to the Present*, Edinburgh and London, 1968, 1ff.

there was also a series of 'debts resting to the dead' amounting to just over £3,000. Much of this was in the form of bills or bonds, some of which were witnessed before the Sheriff of Forfarshire and registered in the Sheriff Court Books of Forfar or in the books of Council and Session, and some of which were assigned to others, for example, from father to son. Though banking goes back to 1695 in Scotland with the founding of the Bank of Scotland, no bank is mentioned in any of the entries in Ker's will, and we get here an example of how individuals could lend money widely, to fellow ministers, merchants in Brechin and Arbroath, to farmers etc, gaining interest on the principal and making modest profits. This widespread circulation of money through a personal range of loans is a phenomenon that requires closer study, but the point here is that Mr Robert Ker, whatever his failings as a pastor, was certainly not without means, even if the figures in his testament are in pounds Scots (and this is so indicated in some entries) and should therefore be divided by twelve to get the corresponding figure in pounds sterling.

Lochlee folk played a further role in his Testament. The minister, Mr John Scot, together with John Garden of Midstrath in Invermark, James Gordon in 'Inchgroundall' and David Christison in Auchrony, elders of the Church Session of Lochlee, acted as 'executors dative qua creditors' and as tutors and managers for the poor of the parish, and obtained by decreet of the Commissary of Brechin the sum of £50 Scots contained in an obligation granted by the late Robert Ker on 5 April 1721, and apparently another similar sum in another obligation dated 7 June 1722.

Ker was succeeded by David Blair, from 1729 till 1733, when he was transferred to the Second and then to the First Charge at Brechin. His monument in Brechin Cathedral relates that he was the originator of Sabbath Schools in Scotland, though it was not until the 1770s that the Sunday School 'movement' really began to spread.[8] This was sometimes done in the teeth of opposition from ministers and heritors because of 'vagrant teachers' who set up Sunday Schools without their consent, so 'committing the religious instruction of youth to ignorant persons notoriously disaffected to the civil constitution of the country'.[9]

The next minister was John Scot, who was ordained in 1734 and married Magdalen Mill, a girl from Glencat, in 1735. He was a bitter opponent of Episcopacy. By this time, no non-juring Episcopalians were allowed to officiate for more than a congregation of nine, under the Penal Act of 1719, on pain of imprisonment. The man in Glenesk, the Rev. David Rose, was referred to in

[8] O. Checkland. *Philanthropy in Victorian Scotland. Social Welfare and the Voluntary Principle*, Edinburgh, 1980, 46–50.
[9] General Assembly pastoral, 1799, quoted in H.G. Graham. *The Social Life of Scotland in the Eighteenth Century*, London, 1901, 537.

John Scot's Session records as 'the illegal meeting-house helper'. He never returned the marriage pledges of Episcopalians except to those who joined his church. Many of his parishioners thought of him as a spy, and blamed him for obtaining the order prohibiting the wearing of Highland dress, though this was in line with the law of 1746 that proscribed its use, in the aftermath of the last Jacobite rising. They also suspected that he was the cause of the visit of the Argyle Highlanders in 1746, when the Episcopal chapel on the Rowan was burned. If so, it was no more than poetic justice that in January 1749, when riding past its ruins on his way to the Presbytery of Brechin, he was thrown from his horse and killed.

The incumbent from 1749 to 1773 was Alexander Ross, not to be confused with his contemporary of the same name who was schoolmaster and poet, as well as Session clerk. The state of the church building was clearly giving him reason for anxiety, for on 20 March 1767 he wrote to John Garden, Factor for Lord Panmure, asking him for 'a Masson and a Wright to see her that they may be in case to give you proper information concerning her ... 'tis generally concluded here that heather cannot be keeped upon her but it will be in vain to attempt that anymore, and the present roof is not sufficient for bearing slats, at least a good deal of it is not so, yea not tho' she were heathered again for some of the couples have pieces of timber nailed to them as lyning to strengthen them'. He was trying to encourage the building of a new church, on a spot near the waterside a little east of the manse. In the event, the new church did not materialise for another 36 years, and it was then built farther down the Glen.

In the same letter, a postscript shows that Episcopacy was still a source of anxiety. He had learned that 'Robert Clerk in Tarfside has set a house and some lands to Mr. Davidson and his family, I mean the Nonjurant Preacher here, and that he is to settle here at Whitsunday. This is very extraordinary in Robert who is one of our Elders, therefore I have acquainted you that you may put a stop to this; I expect that my Lord will do it for I am sure I have it under the hand of Mr. Barron Maul that no such person should have a house within the lands, which I understood as denoting a house for publick worship and a house to live in'.

In the event, repairs to the church, as well as to the manse and office houses, were agreed by the Presbytery, which recommended, around 1782, that the case should be presented to the Earl of Dalhousie, so that repairs might be done without the interference of the Presbytery. The outcome was, in fact, that the new church and manse were built in the time of Alexander Ross's successor, John Pirie, who was ordained assistant and successor to Ross in 1771. The new building was ready, however, only in the fourth last year of his 35 year long incumbency.

Pirie was followed by David Inglis, MA, an evangelical high-flier, whose son Robert succeeded him in 1837. David died on 19 January 1837 and his son sent a funeral invitation to David Innes, Arsellary. Innes was also invited to the induction of son Robert on 8 June 1837. The point is of interest since Innes was an Episcopalian. Clearly, there was some degree of tolerance in the Glen. These two were popular ministers, great exponents of spiritual independence, who did much to plant Presbyterianism firmly in a parish with strong Episcopalian sympathies. Robert moved to Edzell in 1841, largely for the sake of his family's education. His replacement was a Moderate, Alexander Todd, who moved to Monifeith by 1843.

This was the year of the Disruption, when 474 ministers out of about 1,280 signed the Deed of Demission from the Established Church and formed the Free Church. In spite of Lord Panmure's objection to 'Free Kirkers', it left only a smallish congregation at Lochlee. The first post-Disruption minister was Walter ('Wattie') Low, who held the incumbency for 44 years, and produced sixteen children. He died at Carnoustie on 22 March, 1887, in his 86th year. There was a fire in the manse in 1876 and an oral memory of this survives:

> Efter the manse was burned Miss Low was feared an' couldna get
> sleepit, so she gaed an' lay doon in her ain seat in the Kirk,
> fell asleep, an' fan she waukened, she saw a coffin across the end
> fae her seat. The grave wasna ready.

Another recollection of the period is that:

> At the Manse o' Lochlee, at the Kirk o' Drousty, a coo's tail
> was bitten off by the dog. The minister took the souter's
> advice, for he thocht the coo wad be ill aff for want o' her
> tail i' the summer-time. Souter Duncan made a leather tail.
> It was a success. It was cut into guid lang strips, an' fan
> she ca'ed it roond it served its purpose.

> At the same time that was goin' on, the minister, the Rev. Walter
> Low, had a broon curly doggie. A man clippit the dog bare,
> packit up a' the hair, took it to Jess Cattanach (at Whigginton),
> an' she span't an' made a bonnet o't (Miss Lindsay, Tarfside).

Walter Low's assistant and successor was John Stewart, MA, who was ordained in 1885 and died in 1921.

In the time of the next minister, John Rorie McKay, the United Free Church, itself the result of the 1900 union of the Free Church with the United Presbyterian Church, joined the Church of Scotland in 1929. McKay continued in office till 1932, when he was replaced by the Rev. George LB McAllister, MA, the first minister of the united charge. From 1941 to 1958, the ministers were Rev. John Gordon Tosh, MA, 1942-7, then the Rev. William Ewen, MA, BD, 1947-57. The next minister was the Rev. David Stevens, MA, who came to the Glen from Kirtle, Lockerbie in 1959 and retired in 1972. His successor was the Rev. John Thomas Herbirtson Taylor, who transferred to Leslie in 1977. The parish was then linked with Logie Pert and Stracathro under Rev.

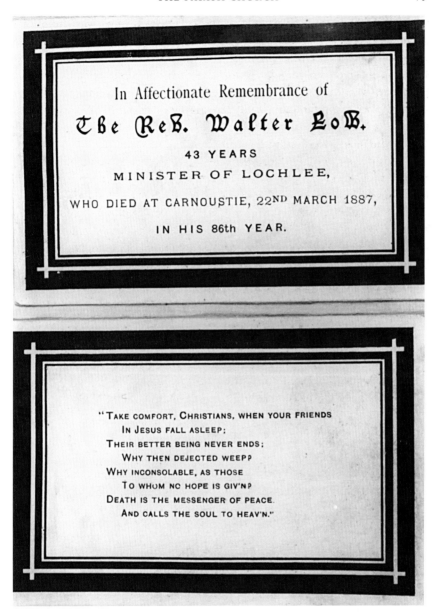

Funeral cards for the Reverend Walter Low, the first post-disruption minister at Lochlee.

William Gray until 1982 when a new linkage was formed with Edzell and
Lethnot with Rev. John William Arthur Forbes as minister. Services are held
in the Maule Memorial Church at Tarfside except once a month when the
church at Lochlee is used.

A Church outing, between the Wars. G1/16/23A.

7

THE KIRK'S CARE OF THE POOR

Care of the poor was, for long, one of the concerns of the Kirk Sessions. After 1845, it became the duty of an elected Poor Law board, but, before that, poor relief was essentially a matter for the charity of the minister and kirk session. The change was forced by the pressure of industrialisation that pulled great masses of people together into rapidly growing towns. The resulting problems of poverty and pauperism in such areas were too great for the church to handle, though it could have continued to do so for a time in rural parishes where those in need of help were not so numerous and where the old social bond between classes survived better. However, the Disruption of 1843, which split the Church of Scotland in two and led to much new and costly church building, also made the Church less able to carry out welfare (and educational) functions. It is against this background that records of poor relief in the Glen have to be seen.

As noted earlier, three elders of the Church Session of Lochlee were named in the 1720s as tutors and managers for the poor of the parish, and handled, inter alia, the sums granted by the Rev. Robert Ker in 1720 and 1721, for the benefit of the poor. The range of sources from which money could be acquired was fairly limited. It included church collections, fines from delinquents, mortifications, legacies and the like. As a rule it was used to help with matters such as food, fuel, clothes, housing and, at the end, coffins, the mortcloth and other funeral expenses. The extracts that follow give some idea of the kinds of provisions made, and of the amounts spent.

LOCHLEE. Accounts of Poors Money (Extracts)

1772 March 14	To Isabel Dunbar, younger.	5/-
	" " " elder to buy shoes.	2/-
	" Donald Gall's mother-in-law.	4/-
	Lent to John Ferrier in Woodtown by the Elders advice.	£4
	Received of Mort cloth money for Mary Smart.	1/6
	Received of Mort cloth money for John Gordon.	1/-

1772	May	17	Thomas Low paid his Penalty.	10/6
		24	Janet Crocket paid her Penalty.	8/4
		30	Susan Watt " " " .	6/8
	July	20	David Ogilvy " his " .	6/8
	Aug	18	To James Christison to help to purchase remedy for his eyes.	10/-
	Nov	27	Given back to Mrs. Scott what she gave in mistake at collecting.	11$\frac{1}{2}$d
1773	Feb	6	To Mr Shaw to buy a coat to James Ewan.	5/-
			To Donald Gall to pay out his mother-in-law's shoes.	3d
			To Katherine Edward in Mill Aucheen in great distress.	
	July	9	As there was a scarcity of meal in the Country the Session agreed that Mr. Pirie should buy some which he accordingly did, and divided as follows,	

1st. To the Poor from whom no payment was to be sought, of these were

Alex. Christison in Tarfside.	2 pecks.
Jean Brown, Auchintoul.	2 pecks.
Isabel Innerdale - do -	4 pecks.
Jean Buchan.	6 pecks.
Alaster Blair.	6 pecks.
John Sutor.	4 pecks.
James Christison.	2 pecks.
	= £1.09.10

To the following persons who were scarce of meal but were to pay as soon as they could.
viz—

To John Donaldson in Droustie	2 bolls.
" Donald Gall.	1 "
" Robert Clark in Tarfside.	1 "
" George Steven in Milltown.	2 firlots
" Jean Clark.	2 "
" James Thow in Haugh.	2 "
	= £4.07.06$\frac{1}{2}$

1773	Aug		Robert Clark paid his Bill of Meal.	
1775	June	29	Paid Isabel Innerdale's coffin.	5/6
	Oct	2	To John Donaldson, his family being in distress.	1/11
1776	April	5	To James Duncan for building Jean Robbie's house.	7/6
	June	22	William Lawson's wife paid as part of the half boll of meal given to Jean Clark. July 9, 1773.	5/-
	Nov	14	John Donaldson paid what he borrowed July 9, 1773 to buy meal.	£1.11.10
	Nov	30	To John Sutor for heather ropes	

			and prodes (thatching pins) to Jean Robbie's house. (Jean Robbie kept in meal.)	9d
1777	Sept	4	To Mary Christie for leading Jean Robbie's peats.	4d
		10	To Jean Brown in Auchintoul in great distress.	3/-
	Nov	27	Donald Gall paid part of his Bill of date July 28, 1773. The Session allowed James Gall a balance still due for bringing Jean Robbie from the Infirmary 10 May 1775.	1/6
1778	Jan	24	This day the Session agreed to give Jean Sutor five pence stg. per week for waiting upon Jean Robbie and washing her clothes.	
	June	29	George Steven paid the remainder of half boll of oatmeal got July 9, 1773.	2/10 + three quarters
1780	March	24	To Margaret Low for soap to Jean Robbie.	5$\frac{1}{2}$d
			To a peck of malt to Jean Robbie.	9d
	Nov	23	For salt to Jean Robbie.	3d
1781	May	3	This day Donald and James Gall paid bygone for £1.19.06.	
			Paid James Gall for casting, winning and leading James Christison's peats lst summer.	6/-
			Paid Donald Gall for taking care of said James Christison who has been bed-rid for some months past.	6/6
	May	20	To John Watt, Taylor, for making clothes to James Christison.	2/4
	June	16	Paid Magdalene Kinnear for attendance to Jean Robbie at her death.	3/7
			Coffin, Grave digging and funeral expenses of Jean Robbie.	6/6
1782	March	15	To Donald Gall for behoof of blind James Christison in great distress.	5/-
		21	Paid Coffin for blind James Christison.	5/-
			Earl of Panmure's legacy of £10 distributed to poor as follows—	
	Sept	7	Magdalene Blair in Drowstie.	£1.10.00
			John Sutor in Auchroney.	12/-
			Jean Gall in Arsallary.	12/-
			Margaret Dow in Turnagob.	10/-
			Margaret Low in Lochside.	12/-
			Janet Jolly in E. Auchintoul.	£1.10.00
			Jean Brown in W. Auchintoul.	14/-
			Margaret Low in Mill of Aucheen.	16/-

		Alex. Dulanach, Woodhaugh.		18/-
		Robert Clark, Woodhaugh.		18/-
		John Donaldson's daughter,		
		Tilliewell.		£ 1.08.00
				£10.00.00
1783	July	18	To Robert Thow in Bodibae by the hand of his wife, her having 7 children in straits for meal.	6/-
	Oct	13	Paid for a letter sent express from the Sheref Clerk relative to Five Bolls and a peck of meal given by Government to the poor of this parish.	1/6
		15	To expense of four horses bringing said meal from Montrose.	1/-
			To William Low and Divid Couts for bringing up said meal.	
1801	June	28	To Ann Gordon, Broomfold, to buy a bed.	3/6

In 1802, a collection was made for the children of one William Laing. This seems to have been almost a house-to-house effort. One hundred and three people are listed, and the total return was £4.03.07:

James Gall, Arsellary	6	John Watt, Baillie	1/-
Andrew Welsh, Gleneffock	3/-	James Innes, Whitestone	6
Jane Smith, do	1/-	Donald Christison Baillie	1/-
Catherine Grant, do	1/-	Margaret Will, Glencatt	6
James Campbel, do	1/-	Susan Farquharson, "	6
David Bowman, Baudy	6	John Copland, "	1/-
Alex. Stuart, Dalbrack	1/-	Wm. Crockat, Burnfoot	1
Mr. Ramsey, Drumgreen	1/-	Donald Innes Wife, Kedloch	6
Agnes Ramsey, do	1/-	John Dun, Shinfur	6
Charles Moir, Kirn	00	Jane Dun, "	3
James Innerdale wife, do	6	William Dun's wife Shinfur	6
John Donaldson Tilleybuckle	1/-	John Middleton Middleford	8
Charles Catenach Whiginton	2/-	James Bowman's wife Midtown	6
James Catenach	2/6	David Christison East Town	6
Robert Thow East Turnabrain	2/6	John Christison, Cove	1/-
David Kinear, Boddam	6	David Christison, Townhead	1/-
Thomas Kinear, W. Migvie	1/-	Alex. Will, Mid Cairncross	2/-
Thomas Christison Migvie	6	Alex. Webster, "	6
John Innes, Twixt-the-Burns	6	Margaret Watt, Cairncross	6
John Henry, Buskhead	1/-	John Christison, Townhead	6

John Mitchell, W. Turnabrain	1/-	Charles Brown,	"	6
John Mitchell, Buskhead	6	Janet Christison,	"	6
Robert Middleton, Berryhill	1/-	Janet Crockat,	"	6
Alex. Watt, do	6	Janet Bowman, Ardoch		1/-
David Toash, Drum	1/-	Robert Kinear,	"	1/-
James Beise, do	6	David Low,	"	1/-
John Gordon, do	6	John Findlay,	"	1/-
David Toash, Jr, do	6	James Crockat,	"	6
David Dunbar, Garthead	1/-	David Lowrie,		6
Margaret Gall, Arsellary	2	John Dildarg,		6
Joseph Gall, do	6	Margaret Crockat		6
James Christison, Bodiebae	6	Sarah Webster		6
Jean Malcolm,		Anne Finlay		
Betwixt-the-Burns	3	(Beside Stylemouth)		3
William Low, "	6	David Gib		2/-
Alex. Bowman, Boghead	6	John Gib, Keenie		2/-
John Bush, Whitehill	6	Thomas Innerdale, Keenie		8
Thomas Gordon, do	6	William Mill, Smith		1/-
James Towns, do	6	John Dun's wife, Shank		1/-
Helen Malcolm, do	6	George Caithness,		
		Blackhills		1/-
Agnes Henrie, do	6	James Bowman		6
William Mitchell,		Jane Caithness		6
W. Turnabrain	6	Elizabeth Lamont		6
Margaret Middleton	3	John Edward, Blackcraig		1/-
Jean Mitchel	3	David Edward, "		1/5
Jean High	1/-	David Edward, E. Aucheen		1/-
Peter Grant, W. Migvie	6	John Watt, do		6
James Henrie, do	6	David Christison,		
Jane Lindsay, do	6	West Aucheen		2/-
Hellen Thow, do	6	John Daldarg, W. Aucheen		6
David Christison, E. Migvie	6	David Christison, Westbank	1/-	
Margaret Crockat, do	6	Jean Christison, do		2
Jean Malcolm, E. Auchintoul	1/-	Mr. Pirie, Minister		5/-
Alex Malcolm, do	1/-			

£4.03.07

There were, of course, always problems under the old system in covering the difference between the real need and the amount of money that could be found. In 1792, the Rev. John Pirie's account of Lochlee Parish noted that the number of poor on the roll did not often amount to twelve. The interest of a small fund, plus the weekly collections, amounted to about £6 sterling per annum, and this was divided amongst them. If any were bedridden, it was the custom to hang up a bag in the mill for them, and tenants put a handful of meal in when their corn had been ground.

There were then no travelling beggars in the parish, and very few passed through it except in June and July, at which time 120 or more might appear begging wool. Many of these appeared to be real objects of charity, and others not. They were not natives of the parish, but came from the towns, Dundee, Arbroath, Montrose, Brechin, Stonehaven and Aberdeen.[1] By way of comparison it may be noted that the average sum spent each year on the twelve poor of the much richer parish of Edzell was £18 – i.e. three times greater.[2]

Consideration of how to treat the poor was a solemn matter, especially at times of death when the ability to cope became extremely difficult and required special measures. Some of the problems and procedures can be seen in sample extracts from the Records. Whether Episcopalian or Church of Scotland, the same needs were felt.

MANSE OF LOCHLEE

8 January 1813. The Session being met and constituted Sederunt the Revd. David Inglis, Moderator, Andrew Welsh, David Gib and John Jolly, Elders, Mr. Inglis Clark p.t., the Session being convened to consider the state of the poors' funds and the high price of meal. After examining the state of their funds they found that the expenditure last year far exceeded the Income and that owing to the high price of meal this year and the number of poor upon the roll as well as others who stand in need of occasional supply they, with the advice of other intelligent people of the Parish, unanimously resolved to call a meeting of the tenants and others within the Parish to convene at the Chapel on the 21st of January in order to adopt such measures as to them may seem proper for affording relief to the poor during the continuance of the present dearth for this year, and the Moderator was requested to make public intimation from the pulpit next Lord's day immediately after Divine Service in the forenoon.

21 Jan. 1813. Contributed for the Poor and other householders in this Parish on account of the high price of Meal by the Tenants and others. A donation from the Hon. WM Maule of Panmure of 10 Bolls Oatmeal to the Poor valued at £1.14.- per Boll.

BRIDGE OF TARF

21 Jan. 1813. The Which day, in the Chapel, a meeting of the Tenants, Householders and others in the Parish of Lochlee convened to consider the state of the Poor, and to adopt such measures as to them may seem proper for alleviating in some measure the distressed condition of the Poor owing to the unprecedented stagnation of Trade and the high price of the first necessaries of life by voluntary contribution to reduce the price of Meal so much per peck. The Rev. Peter Jolly

---

[1] *Old (First) Statistical Account of Scotland 1791–99*, Angus XIII, EP Publishing, 1976.
[2] ibid, Parish of Edzell.

in the Chair. The following resolutions were moved by the Rev. David Inglis, Minister of the Parish, and unanimously adopted. Resolved:

1. That a Committee be appointed consisting of 7, three to be a Quorum, Mr. Robert Pirie Clerk and collector of contributions in aid of the Poor.
2. The whole money contributed to be laid out to reduce the price of meal so much per peck. In the first instance Oatmeal to be reduced 6d and barley meal 4d per peck.
3. That relief shall be afforded in proportion to the number of Persons in each Family, to those who are in straitened circumstances as well as to those who are on the Poors Roll.
4. That all those who are able and willing tenants, as well as others though absent from this Meeting, shall be invited to contribute to this fund. Two men were appointed to collect in each district of the Parish.
5. A list of the Poor and those in straitened circumstances being made up and approved of by the meeting, a copy of such list with instructions was ordered to be sent to James Jolly, Mill of Aucheen, and another copy to John Gib Junr. Mill of Keeny, to supply those contained in said list with meal at the reduced price as stated in this Minute.

The following persons were appointed for managing the Contributions and auditing the accounts viz.

> The Rev. David Inglis
> The Rev. Peter Jolly
> Andrew Welsh, Gleneffock
> David Gib, Ardoch
> James Bowman, Glentenet
> James Jolly, Mill of Aucheen
> and Mr. Robert Pirie Clerk

24 Jan. 1817. This day the Session met and being constituted the Minister laid the state of the Poors' fund before them and the Expenditure for the last year, and the Session, taking into their consideration the unprecedented stagnation of trade and the high price of the first necessaries of life and that many families and individuals are requiring assistance who are not on the Poors Roll and finding that the Collections in the Church, the Interest arising from £50, the whole stock that belongs to the Poor of this Parish, and other casualties are inadequate for affording relief to those in distress. They unanimously resolved to call a meeting of the Tenants and Householders of this Parish to meet in the Chapel on the 8th of Feby. next in order to commence a voluntary contribution for the above purpose. They resolved also that intimation of this should be given to the Hon. William Maule of Panmure the sole Heritor of this Parish.

8 Feb. 1817. The which day a meeting of the Tenants, Householders etc. in the Parish of Lochlee convened to consider the state of the poor, and to adopt such measures as to them may seem proper for alleviating in some measure the distressed condition of the poor owing to the unprecedented stagnation of trade and the high price of the first necessaries of life, by voluntary contribution to reduce the price of meal so much per peck.

Amount paid by the Tenants and others: £19. 01/-
Owing to failure of a number of tenants and the poverty of other subscribers the

fore-going subscription amounting to £23.17/- fell short by £4.16/- The real
amount came to £19.10/-.

Poors Money altogether came to £54.05/- in 1817.

1833. The Session have further to state that there is no fund here to the Poor,
and they depend solely on the ordinary collections and a few casualties, the
average amount of which for these 27 years past has been £33.06.- per annum of
which £2 is paid for Presentor and Session Clerk's fee, leaving £21.06.- to divide among 16 paupers, or £1.06.7$^{1}/_{2}$ for each pauper allowing all to receive an
equal share, and we have still greater objects here than Samson is reported to be.
This is the utmost Samson can receive, if he be forced upon us, unless an assess-
ment take place – and before the Session here will have recourse to that measure, every individual will give up all charge of the Collections and poor, because
such a measure would be decidedly opposed by the Sole Heritor of the Parish.
Had this case been reversed, and Samson a native of Lochlee, the Session have no
hesitation in saying that no other parish would have been troubled by him.

1837. Inter alia – the Kirk Session being satisfied that the School at Tarf under
the Patronage and superintendence of the Society for Propagating Christian
Knowledge has been by the blessing of God the means of great benefit to the
young and willing generation of an extensive district of this Parish – that the
said School has always been numerously attended and taught with the full ap-
probation of the Presbytery of Brechin -that the present Teacher Mr. Peter Duncan
having a wife and three young children has now taught the same school for
nearly fourteen years to the complete satisfaction of all concerned in the institution – and that with one of the least salaries allowed by the Society as also that
the fees are small and not very regularly paid in many cases – the Kirk Session,
being satisfied that Mr. Duncan's means of providing for the necessary comfort
of himself and his family are very inadequate and that some increase of salary
might be very beneficial for promoting his usefulness in his present situation,
did and hereby do resolve to transmit extract of their proceedings in the case to
the Revd. the Presbytery of Brechin with a view to solicit their concurrence and
co-operation in such measures as may be thought necessary to bring Mr. Duncan's
case under the consideration of the Society, and they instruct their Clerk to
furnish the Moderator of Kirk Session with a copy of this extract to lay before
the Presbytery of Brechin for the above purpose – Sederunt closed with prayer

Robt. Inglis, Sess. Clk.

The records show that there was seldom enough money in the Poors' Fund
to provide a level of relief for the poor that was sustainable. One can sense the
frustration and concern of the committee, who were naturally distressed at the
scale of poverty within the parish. Voluntary contributions from other tenants
fell as they suffered from the combined effects of a trade slump and high prices.
The resources of the Church were drained by the new church building programme following the Disruption, which made it very difficult for the church
to carry out its welfare functions. Nevertheless, as an early form of community
aid, it could rightly be seen as a precursor of the welfare state.

8

THE EPISCOPAL CHURCH

The story of Episcopacy in Glenesk has already been touched on. In spite of strong feelings that manifested themselves at times, Episcopacy and Presbyterianism have made a strongly complementary existence in the Glen. The list of Episcopal ministers is as follows:

Rev. Robert Thomson	1684–1716	
Vacancy		
Rev. David Rose	1723–58	
Vacancy		
Rev. James Brown	1763–66	
" Alex. Davidson	1766–82	
" Peter Jolly	1782–1839 (first resident Episcopal minister in Glenesk since the time of the Revolution).	
" Alex. Simpson	– 1871	
" Wm. Presslie	1871–1914	
" Wm. Aldous		
" Wm. Beveridge	(last resident minister)	
" Wm. Wimberley		
" Canon Miller		
" J.D. Bisset		
" G.L.A. Hick		
" Ian Hay		

In 1717, Rev. Robert Thomson was ejected from Lochlee and Lethnot by the Presbyterians. He moved to Stonehaven, where he ministered until his death in 1737. A blank period of six years followed. From 1723 to 1759, Rev. David Rose acted as Episcopalian Clergyman. A chapel was built, 75 feet by 14 feet, with a floor of earth and gravel, a heather-thatched roof, and an aisle on the north side. This was at the time of the strongly anti-Episcopal Mr Scot, the parish minister, who may have hardened Episcopal feelings because of his efforts against them.

On 16 August, 1745, Bishop Raitt confirmed 70 candidates at the chapel on the Rowan, and on the preceding day, 25 in Mr Rose's house at Woodside of Dunlappie (see Mr Lunan's Diary, Queen's College, Dundee). When the 1745 Rebellion broke out, Scot persuaded the Episcopalians that if they would burn down their chapel, they would be spared a visitation from the red coats, but the Hanoverians came all the same. It was Scot, too, who was responsible for Rose's imprisonment on board the sloop 'Hazard' off Montrose. On 23 January, 1749, Scot was thrown from his horse and killed as he passed the ruins of the chapel.

As related in a letter from the Rev. John Moir to Bishop Alexander Penrose Forbes, of Brechin, dated 9 December 1863, Mr Rose's habit was to stand in the door while officiating, with the people gathered about on the green.

> From this they were after a time driven out by the tenant of the farm, some influence having been used to prejudice him against them. They then used to assemble for Public Worship behind a portion of the wall of the old Church on the Rowan. Some of the flock inserted their walking sticks in the wall, stretching over them one of their plaids, which formed the only protection their Pastor had during the service. Mr Rose did not reside in Glenesk. At one time he held the farm of Tillyburnie in the Parish of Menmuir. Afterwards, he resided at Woodside, part of the farm of Western Dunlappie, about 4 miles from Brechin, where he died. Mr Rose had a wide district under his charge, and he officiated alternately in many parts of it, at Glenesk, Lethnot, Brechin, and at Arbuthnott, Careston, Balnamoon, and other families attached to the Church: a laborious charge it must have been.
>
> His son was the Honourable George Rose, connected with Pitt's Govt., and I think Treasurer of the Navy. There had been another brother, for Bishop Low mentioned to me that he had either himself seen, or had been told of, the two boys being seen coming into Brechin, without shoes or stockings, like country lads staring at all the novelties the toon, though nothing to boast of, presented to them.
>
> I was also told by someone, I cannot recollect who, that Mr Rose collected a sum of money with which two bridges were built in Glenesk, one at Pons-Kiny, the other at Tarfside. After finishing these, a few pounds remained, which, by deed under his own hand, he committed to the management of the congregation for the benefit of the poor, I think. The fund has been lost sight of. But the deed was preserved and sent about 1811 to Mr George Rose. There is still in the possession of the congregation of Glenesk a small bell which Mr Rose had presented to them. His name is upon it.
>
> Mr Rose died about the year 1759. Among my grandfather's papers I found a curious document in Mr Rose's hand-writing. I sent the original some years ago to the descendants of Mr George Rose, thro' Mr C. Innes, Edinburgh, who applied to me for some information about the family. Before sending it off I took an exact copy. It ran as follows:
>
> A brief account how I have been supported in the exercise of my priestly office since its commencement Barnabas Day, one thousand seven hundred and twenty-three. I passed my Tryals in the Old Town of Aberdeen; the Very Revd.

Dr. George Garden, Doctor James Gadderer, Doctor George Middleton, the R. Revd. Mr William Murray, all living in the New Town of Aberdeen, June ninth and tenth, 1723. Upon St Barnabas Day said year, Present the above mentioned Clergie and several Laiety, I was ordained a Deacon by the Right Reverend Dr James Gadderer, Bishop of Aberdeen, in the House of Dr George Garden in New Aberdeen. I was consecrated a Priest in the same year upon St Bartholomew's Day by the above mentioned Bishop in the House of the Revd. Mr William Murray in the Old Town of Aberdeen.

In the said year Bishop Gadderer in his visitation course of his Diocese, during which time (ten weeks) I officiated for him in the Honble. The Viscount of Arbuthnot's Family, settled me optionally in Skeen Elder and Younger their Families, for which cure I was to have twenty lib. st. yearly. At which juncture of time I had an unanimous call given by the Lochlee and Lethnott Parishes, which I preferred to the above mentioned settlement. Lochlee parishioners bound themselves to pay me yearly fourteen lib. st. which they paid me punctually for some years. Lethnott promised me five lib. ten sh. st. yearly, qch they never paid me. The collections of both Houses were applyed by proper Managers and me to pay all publique things and satisfy the demands of the Poor, the superplus was given to me.

Since my entry to my present charge to 1745 I was privately supported by the Interest and addresses of Lord Panmure and his family, but nothing from their own Pocket. Some years before 1745 to 1747 I was greatly supported by the Right Honble. Lady Sinclair, and from 1747 my wife and I have an annuity during Life five lib. ster. From 1750 to his death Sir Alexander Ramsay was my benefactor, and from 1747 I was much obliged by the good offices of John Erskine of Dun, Esquire and James Carnegy Arbuthnot of Balnamoon Esquire for several years. And for the space of thirty years George Skene of that Ilk was my true friend.

My present sallary arisable from the goodwill of the after-mentioned Families and places: From Balnamoon's Family four Bolls of Meal, one Boll of Oats and one of Bear. From Keithock a Boll of Malt, from Lady Smiddyhill half a guinea, from Lady Findowry two Bolls of meal besides Altar Collections. From Lady Balbegno and Miss Ogilvie three Bolls of Meal besides Altar Collections. From Lochlee House at Milltown yearly nine pounds stg. From all the Retainers to Woodside from Caraldstone, Brechin, Lethnott and Navar parishes three pounds sterling. From Woodside collections Altar and daily deducing publick charges three lib. sterling. From Lochlee Collectors deducing publick charges three lib. sterling. By prudent management and timeous application these funds and my share of the Charity Fund maybe continued with my successor in office. The truth of their Presents is attested at Milltown in Glenesk, January the eleventh one thousand seven hundred and fifty-eight by the subscription of (signed) David Rose, Priest of the Scots Church.

On Mr Rose's death in 1759 there seems to have been a vacancy for $3^1/_2$ years, and during that time many of his congregation attended service at Dalladies where Mr Simon officiated. Mr Rose was succeeded in Glenesk by a Mr Brown. I never heard many particulars about him; indeed none except that in his Incumbency and at his suggestion the church was rebuilt. The work of rebuilding, I have been told, was very expeditiously gone through. On a set day the congregation all arranged to meet, and each bear a part in the work – and in this

way the walls were raised in one week. A very short period after saw the rest of
the work completed. The Roof was of Heather. A few years ago I met at Old
Montrose a son of this Mr Brown's. He lived in London and was rather an eminent Botanist.

Mr Brown continued about 3 years in Glenesk, when he went to Montrose.

Details of Mr Brown are available from other sources. He was ordained on
29 June 1763, and on 28 October he wrote to Bishop Alexander at Alloa:

> When I wrote you last we had met with no opposition, but before I received
> your answer, we were obliged to remove out of the House (which my Predecessor
> used since the burning of the Lochlee Chapel in 1748 till his Death) by the
> malicious Waspishness of the P...b.tn Teacher there who had wrote Lord
> Panmure, and his Factors wrote a threatening letter to the Ground Officer of
> Lochlee to warn any person that from that Time should give encouragement to
> any such Practices to leave the Parish Whitsunday first. This menace was disre-
> garded as an empty Blast. But the House I had officiated in for some Sundays
> had been let us by a P...b...tn woman, whom the P...b...tn teacher upon receipt
> of Lord Panmure's Answer went and threatened to such a degree that we thought
> proper to give her no more Trouble by staying any longer in her House at that
> Time ... till the Blast was over. I officiated two Sundays to a very numerous
> audience at the Ruins of the old Chapel ... and we removed again to the House
> we were in before the Persecution and have continued in it about five Sundays,
> without Molestation. Ross has not above 20 left him ...
>
> And our honest Folks in Glenesk are not at all intimidated but as it has
> pleased God to send us favourable weather, they have been employed in build-
> ing a large house at the Ruins of the one that was destroyed in the 1746 since
> Monday last, and D.J. (Deo Juvante), as there is such a number of hands at
> Work, we shall have it finished and covered within three weeks.

According to Miss Lindsay, Tarfside, 98 able-bodied men came to help. The
walls were built in a week and the roof in a fortnight. The next incumbent, Mr
Alexander Davidson, lived at Balzeordie. An anecdote is told of a precentor
named Crockett. On the occasions when Mr Davidson announced a psalm
with a tune unknown to the precentor, he would look over the church and say,
'I doot ye'll need tae try that ane yersel', Mr Davidson'.

After a year's vacancy, Rev. Peter Jolly was appointed, from 1783, and his
incumbency lasted for 57 years. His daughter married D. Moir, Bishop of
Brechin and Incumbent of Brechin, 1812 to 1847.

Balzeordie was on the Estate of Balnamoon, not far from Woodside where
Mr Rose lived, and he officiated at Tiggerton, Brechin and Glenesk. He died
in 1782. It is perhaps a commentary on the difficulties such clergymen had to
face that the distance from Balzeordie to Lochlee is fourteen miles, over
Caterthun and through Lethnot across the shoulder of the Wirren. For a Sunday
service in Lochlee, Mr Davidson had to go there on Saturday afternoon. There
was apparently a small room on the hillside near the Rowan where he had
more or less to look after himself on these occasions, for there was no house
near. It is said that on these long walks, he carried an onion in his pocket, in

case he should become faint and weary. The story may be taken up again by the Rev. John Moir:

> After a vacancy of one year he was succeeded by my Grandfather, the Revd. Peter Jolly. He held the Incumbency for 57 years. Grandfather was one of the young men trained by Bishop Petrie at Meikle Folla, Aberdeenshire: as you know, he passed a quiet, uneventful life in his retired little charge. About 1811 the present Church and Parsonage were built; and considering the time, and the little interest that was then felt in the extension of the Church, the obtaining of the necessary funds must have cost him no little effort. I think he was much assisted in his gatherings by that strange man, Mr Gray of Carse. Mr Jolly officiated only at Tarfside, and he was the first resident clergyman in the glen, as they call it, after the Revolution. A large body of the farmers on the West Water, in the upper part of Lethnott Parish, adhered to that charge. Tiggerton and Brechin were detached.
>
> You ask about his knife. He used to mention the circumstances, as an instance of the primitive state of things in the glen that there was at that time, it was early in his Incumbency, hardly such a thing as a knife and fork among the people. This knife and fork he had in a small case, which he carried in his pocket, when going to a christening or any occasion where there was likely to be an entertainment. He used to act as carver, sending round the portions in large dishes among the guests, who made the best of it with their fingers. I do not remember anything about a kettle. But he mentioned one other trifling incident which shows the simplicity of their manners. Towards the end of the last century, before umbrellas came into general use, one of the good folks of the Glen had been on Deeside visiting his friend. Heavy rain came on, and on starting homewards he was offered and urged to take an umbrella, which was put up and placed in his hand. The worthy man reached home safely; but all the art of his own household and the neighbourhood could not get the strange machine closed. It was too large to be got in at the door of the cottage, and after consultation, it was secured by a rope to the carthouse, apparently with a feeling that perhaps it was just as well there, and that somehow it might turn out not altogether quite canny.
>
> You have heard of the sad night he once spent in the middle of the winter in the hills. He and a lady, Miss Douglas of Brechin, who boarded with them, had gone to a wedding at Millden. They left for home early in the afternoon. But before they had reached the top of the Mudloch a severe snowstorm came on. Though so familiar with the country, he lost his way in the drift, and they wandered in the hill all night. About 4 in the morning, as he supposed, his companion overcome by the cold and fatigue, sunk and died beside him. He remained by the body, moving about, and at break of day knew where he was and soon reached a cottage. A party of several men went out in search of them. He had observed several times flashes of light, which proceeded no doubt from the lanterns they carried. But in the wildness of the night he thought it was lightning. Mr Jolly suffered much from the exposure, but he was able notwithstanding to go to church next day and return thanks for his deliverance and take a good part of the service; it was Sunday morning.' (Rev. J. Moir, letter, Dec. 1863).

According to Miss E. Davidson, Migvie, the church of St Drostan was built by the congregation largely assisted by friends, using stones gathered in the neighbourhood, on a perpetual feu granted by a predecessor of the Earl of Dalhousie. It was 40 feet long by 24 feet wide, with a belfry on the west end and a Latin cross of Aberdeen granite on the east. Part of the east end was railed off for a chancel and also contained the pulpit. There was a small gallery at the west end. The pews were brought down from the church on the Rowan. Miss Davidson's grandmother, Ann Grant, attended the first service on 11 August 1811, and noted the text. It was from Isaiah 56, verse 7: 'mine house shall be an house of prayer for all people'. This church was pulled down in 1879. The Latin cross was kept and placed over the porch of the one that replaced it.[1]

About this time, Bishop Gleig of Brechin held a Confirmation in the Old Chapel in the Upper Wynd in Brechin. He seems to have thought Glenesk absolutely out of this world, for he directed all the Glenesk candidates to meet him there. They had had no opportunity of being confirmed for a long time. Between 80 and 100 folk came down, riding in carts which the farmers had lent, the event making quite a commotion in the Glen. When they finally reached Brechin, the upper room was so small that they had to be dealt with in groups. The Bishop was possibly the one who saw most light, for after this episode he never refused to go to Lochlee, and is said to have greatly enjoyed his confirmations there.

A great deal of the upkeep of the new church in the Glen was carried out by the congregation itself. A stable was built to accommodate those who drove from a distance. It was recommended on 18 July 1842 that Elizabeth Smart should get something 'for sweeping the chapel and keeping her clean'. It is perhaps noteworthy that the ministers of both denominations thought of their church or chapel in the feminine gender. In bad weather, the service was conducted in the parson's own house, and, at least in the time of the Rev. Alex Simpson, hospitality was not unusual. According to the Lochlee Episcopal Chapel Records, on 7 August 1843:

> The business of the meeting being over, the managers present partook of their worthy Pastor's accustomed liberality in meat and drink.

The term 'managers' is worthy of note, since it is normally understood as referring to members of the board of management of the temporal affairs of certain Presbyterian churches. Here, however, it clearly relates to the Episcopal church.

The Records throw further light on church activities at this period. In 1844:

> As James Innes at Whitehouse being many years a Manager and now unable to gain anything for a livelihood, it was agreed on at the last January Meeting to give him a small supply for necessaries from the Funds, as he is very unwilling to be cast on the Parish Funds, some giving meal and others potatoes. It being reported that the Parish Funds were nearly exhausted and that the Poors Rates

---

[1] Letter in *Dundee Courier*, also quoting a letter in the *Dundee Advertiser*, 27 August 1879.

were to be laid on, it was agreed among the Managers to collect a small sum to keep him off our Funds until it would be seen what was done. The sum collected amounted to 16/4.

He did not long survive. On 20 January 1845 his will was read. He left to the church all his possessions, valued at £20.03.07, but after deducting the cost of his keep and funeral expenses, only £10.17.09$^1/_2$ remained. This figure, however, may be compared with the clergyman's half-yearly salary of £12.10/-.

In 1851, the members of the Vestry were:

> Rev. Alex Simpson, Incumbent.
> David Mitchell, Farmer, Turnabrain.
> Jas. Will, Farmer, Milton.
> Alex. Christison, Farmer, Woodhaugh.
> Jas. Watt, Shoemaker, Tarfside.
> Wm. Duke, Farmer, Migvie.
> David Low, Farm Servant.
> A.B. Donald, Teacher.

Alex Simpson died on 22 February 1871, at the age of 56. He farmed part of the ground now on Tarfside farm, so was not entirely dependent on his salary as a clergyman. A cart-plate with his name on it, found by Mr Ramsay Guthrie in the parsonage grounds, under an uprooted tree, is now preserved in the Glenesk Museum. Alex. Donald may have been the teacher for the school that was proposed in 1850 in connection with St Drostan's. He was dismissed in 1856, and succeeded by Mr David Lord, who was still keeping a Log Book in 1863. The school and schoolhouse were let to Dr Mackie of Brechin in 1872.

The number of Episcopalians continued to decline. In 1857–60, there were 115 on the roll. Seat rents numbered 37 in 1858, 33 in 1872, 30 in 1880. Yet in 1778, there had been 600 Episcopal Communicants.

Peter Jolly was succeeded by the Rev. Alex Simpson. In the Rev. John Moir's words:

> You know well that, during his Incumbency, the Church, Parsonage and small farm has been considerably improved – a school and a master's house have been built, and the ground on which all the buildings stand secured on a 99 years lease.
>
> My Grandfather, I should have mentioned, told me he had often heard that when the Episcopal Incumbent was forced out of the Parish Church in 1717, from 400 to 500 of the Parishioners kept steadfast to the Church, out of a pop. of 600 or so.
>
> As you know, the Surplice has never been used in the Glen. I remember my grandfather often substituting the 'Short Law' for the 10 Comts. I do not recollect any other peculiarity in the way of conducting the Service. They have always used the Scottish Office for the Holy Communion.[2]

---

[2] Moir, letter, 9 December 1863.

In 1880, the present St Drostan's Church was consecrated. For some time before that, the services had been conducted in the schoolroom, or in the dilapidated structure of the old church. The new building was erected by Lord Forbes, as a memorial to his kinsman Alexander Penrose Forbes, Bishop of Brechin from 1847 to 1875, and an outstanding personality in the history of the Episcopal Church in Scotland.

The new church stands close to the roadside, not far from the earlier structure. The design, by Messrs Mathews and Mackenzie, architects, Aberdeen, is in the first pointed Gothic style. There is a nave and chancel, a porch on the south side, and a vestry on the north side of the chancel. The west gable has a three-light lancet window, with a canopy above for the bell. On the south side there are three double-lancet windows. The north side has no windows. Five crosses, three of them in granite, decorate the exterior. The three windows in the chancel contain stained glass representing the Good Shepherd, St Andrew and St Peter. The principal dressings of the church are of Aberdeen granite, brought by rail to Laurencekirk and carted from there. The rest was found locally.

Inside, the passages and chancel are laid with encaustic tiles. Those in the nave and porch are plain black and red; the others in the chancel and within the altar rails are more ornamental. The pulpit, like the pews and chancel stalls, is of pitch pine varnished. The roof of the nave, open to the ridge, is of stained and varnished wood. The chancel has a waggon-head arched ceiling of timber. The baptismal font, of Binny stone, is supported on four Peterhead granite columns, the capitals of which were carved by Mr Goodwillie, sculptor, Elgin. The altar was purchased by Lord Forbes in London. It is of Derbyshire marble, with marble columns relieved with alabaster. Seating is for about a hundred worshippers.

The ceremony was in accordance with the form laid down 'with Episcopal sanction'.[3] The clergy who were to take part arrived shortly before noon, and proceeded to vest in the schoolhouse. The procession left there precisely at noon and walked slowly towards the church: first came the choir of St Salvador, Dundee, followed by Deacons Radcliffe and Allan, then the clergy of other dioceses, the Brechin clergy, Lord Forbes, the Dean of Brechin, Mr Cowper, representing the Bishop of Aberdeen's Chaplain, Bishop Suther, Staff-bearer Rev. Jas. Crabbie, Brechin, Bishop Jermyn, Bishop of Brechin, and Chaplain Rev. J.W. Hunter, St Mary Magdalene's, Dundee. At the church the procession walked slowly around reciting the usual service of the Church of England for the consecration of a church, the consecration ceremony being performed by the Bishop of Brechin.

---

[3] A Form of a Consecration of a Church, used at the Consecration of St Drostane's Church, Lochlee, Thursday, 9th of September, 1880, Edinburgh, 1880.

At the close of the ceremony of consecration, a sermon was preached from Luke 14, verse 22, by the Bishop of Aberdeen. Before beginning the discourse, he said:

It is seldom that members of the Church meet under more interesting circumstances than those which bring us together this day. In general, when churches are erected, they are the result of the wants of those who build them. For their own benefit they give their means and in gratitude to God for what they themselves have received at His hands, they build houses to His glory, in which they hope to enjoy spiritual blessing, to share in all the holy ordinances of the sanctuary, and to receive instructions in that wisdom which maketh wise unto salvation. But in the present case this house, in the solemn dedication of which we have just taken part, owes its origin not so much to those now around it who will enjoy its precious privileges, as to the love and piety of one individual whose name is dear to Scottish Churchmen, the head of a family, distinguished in Scottish history, from which have sprung names which are household words in the annals of Scottish Episcopacy. It is a venture of faith on his part to rebuild the waste places. It is the pious offering of a loving heart to the Almighty Father of all. It is an act of pure Christian charity to give his fellow-Churchmen what he so dearly values himself. It is a memorial of a friend and a kinsman to one who, though dead, speaketh to us, who knew him on earth, by example of his unspotted and laborious life in the Divine Master's cause, and by his learned writings on the mysteries of redemption and the great verities of the Catholic Church. He was taken from us in the Providence of God just when we seemed most to require him here; but in his name and his work and his virtues will be held in everlasting remembrance. On all those accounts, therefore, the work this day finished and solemnly consecrated has a special interest to all Scottish Churchmen; and we hail it with joy because of the generous and pious motives which have prompted it, of the ends which it is intended to serve, and of the invaluable advantages which it will confer on the present and future dwellers in this sequestered glen, where the lamp of the sanctuary, notwithstanding persecution and difficulties, has always been kept alive, though sometimes with a feeble and glimmering light.

After the service, luncheon was served in a marquee in a field not far from the church. Lord Forbes occupied the chair, and was supported on the right by the Bishop of Brechin, and on the left by Bishop Suther. There was a large company, including many ladies. Among many others, there were present Lord Clinton, Lady Kinnaird, The Knapp, the Hon Waldegrave Leslie, Mr Irvine of Drum, Chancellor of the Diocese, Colonel Ogilvie, yr of Baldovan, Colonel Drummond Hay, Dr Grub, Aberdeen, etc.

On covers being removed, Lord Forbes gave 'The Health of the Queen, the Prince and Princess of Wales, and the other members of the Royal Family', a toast that was loyally pledged. Lord Forbes then proposed 'The Episcopal Church of Scotland', coupled with the name of the Bishop of Brechin, whom it was a pleasure to see amongst them that day. He hoped his Lordship would now think that a stain had been taken away from his diocese by the old church being pulled down and a new one substituted. There had been some rather remarkable churches built there – one of them, he thought, was built in a week. This one had taken a rather longer time than that, and he hoped it would be more substantial than the one that was built in a week. The Bishop of Brechin returned thanks, proposing in conclusion 'The Health of Lord Forbes'.

Lord Forbes, in acknowledging, said he did not consider the new church perfect, but he thought it was a very good model. He thought, however, the chancel might have been larger. Lord Forbes proceeded to say that that day was rather remarkable in the history of the Episcopal Church in Scotland, for, had it not been for another consecration elsewhere, he might have secured more bishops of the Church of Scotland to be present; but both the Primus and Bishop of Argyle and the Isles were engaged in the consecration of a church elsewhere. It was a great thing to find two new churches consecrated in one day.[4] At this time, the incumbent was the Rev. William Presslie, who ministered from 1871 to 1914.

By 1970, however, the church was in use only on every second Sunday in summer, services being conducted by the Rev. G.L.A. Hick, St Andrew's, Brechin. On 10 August 1980, the church's centenary was celebrated by the Bishop of Brechin, with singing by the choir of St Salvador's Episcopal Church, Dundee, a walk in Glenesk before the service and a barbecue afterwards. This, the fourth Episcopal Church in sequence, remains a symbol of the long story of Episcopacy in Glenesk, as do the Episcopal Communion vessels of pewter, stamped 'Adam Anderson, Edinburgh 1734', now on loan to Glenesk Museum from the Bishop of Brechin, and a mort bell rung at funerals, inscribed 'From Rev. David Rose, Glenesk, 1728', also in the Museum.

[4] Newspaper cutting, 1880.

9

THE FREE CHURCH

The Disruption of 1843, one of the major events of the nineteenth century, saw 470 ministers, over one-third of the clergy, secede from the Church of Scotland. The repercussions were felt throughout Scotland, with Glenesk no less affected than other areas of the country. In the Glen, it was reported that nearly all of the Rev. Todd's congregation left him, apart from one elder and a couple of others who, the Rev. Paul rather scurrilously remarks, had received or expected to receive favours either from the Laird or his Factor.[1]

Lord Panmure was of the opinion that not many of his tenants would join the Free Church, perhaps thinking that they would be influenced by his own opposition to the new institution. Therefore, it was a great shock to him when he discovered that nearly all of them had done so, despite alleged threats, which included removal from the Glen by Whitsunday 1844, made by the Laird to his tenants.[2] Lord Panmure was obviously just posturing here, as it was not in his interests to get rid of one of his main sources of income. Nevertheless, he did his utmost to persuade his tenants to return to the Church of Scotland, as witnessed by a letter that he sent to three former elders of the established Church. Dated 3 August 1843, the letter reads as follows:

TO MESSRS DAVID AND JAMES LOW, AND JOHN ARCHIBALD, FORMERLY ELDERS, PARISH OF EDZELL

YOU FOOLISH MEN,

RETURN to your good Old Kirk where there is plenty of room and when more is necessary you will be provided with it. –

RETURN to that Moderate, Useful and Harmonious Church for the establishment of which your Forefathers Fought and Bled. –

PAY due and proper respect to that Minister placed in the Parish of Edzell by Her Most Gracious Majesty. –

LET PEACE, AND COMFORT, AND HARMONY surround your Firesides, and you will always find me, (as Principal Heritor,) a Friend ready to promote your Welfare and Happiness. –

Yours faithfully,

PANMURE.

[1] Rev. James Paul. *Up Glenesk*, D.H. Edwards, Brechin, 1894, 25.
[2] ibid, 26.

The letter is carefully worded and is, on first reading, paternalistic and conciliatory in tone. The first point addressed by the Laird refers to the fact that the Free Church congregation were obliged to use the Masonic Hall as a place of worship, mainly because Lord Panmure would not permit the erection of a church for that purpose.[3]

In the second point the Laird resorts to a form of emotional blackmail by reminding the former parishioners of the various bloody conflicts in which their forefathers fought in defence of the established Church. Therefore his tenants owe it to the memories of their ancestors to return to the Church that they fought so valiantly to establish and preserve.

The third point addressed by Lord Panmure concerns one of the main grievances of the Evangelicals within the Church of Scotland, and that was the contentious issue of patronage. Previously, the Laird, in his position as patron of the parish, could present his own preferred candidate for the post of minister, with no obligation to consult the congregation in the matter. This rather undemocratic process led to the passing of the Veto Act at Westminster in 1834, for which the Evangelical party within the Church were primarily responsible. This Act meant that presbyteries were obliged to accept any objections made by the majority of male heads of families within a congregation to a presentee.[4] Finally, the last sentence contains a veiled threat, in which Lord Panmure reminds his tenants that he, as Principal Heritor, while willing to promote their 'welfare and happiness', could equally make things very difficult for them.

The Secession of 1843 not only disrupted the Church, it also brought discord into the home and broke up life-long friendships. The Rev. Low, minister of Lochlee was verbally abused, if not actually threatened, in the street by a Free Church minister.[5]

There was still the problem of finding a place to worship for the Free Church congregation. Although the Laird would not permit the building of a church, David Inglis of Baillies knew that the Earl would not refuse him permission to build a shepherd's house. David Inglis duped the Laird by erecting a building large enough to afford room for the shepherd and his family in one end, while using the other end as a place of worship for the Free Church congregation, which even included a rough hewn pulpit and pews.[6] Later, on hearing of this, Lord Panmure acknowledged that 'Baillies had out-generalled him'.[7] So it was that the Free Church Congregation at first worshipped in the Masonic Hall, with Rev. Robert Inglis in charge. Thereafter, for twelve years, services were held at Burnfoot, in a barn next to the house, in an atmosphere so domestic that it was said, 'at the time o' the service, ye could hear the rock o' the cradle'.

[3] ibid, 30.
[4] Ian Donnachie and George Hewitt. *A Companion to Scottish History*, B.T. Batsford Ltd, London, 1989, 58.
[5] Cruickshank, op. cit. 310.
[6] Paul, op. cit. 31.
[7] ibid, 31.

Through the General Assembly of 1845, application was made for the congregation to become a sanctioned charge. People were weary of trudging over the moors in all kinds of inclement weather to their place of worship, only to find that no preacher had turned up, which meant that they just had to turn around and go home again. The request was acceded to, but it was two years before the congregation received a minister of their own. Rev. A. McIlwraith became its first minister in 1847, when the congregation was still worshipping at Burnfoot.

It was not thought expedient to ask for a site for a new church from Lord Panmure. Fortunately, however, for the congregation, his son and heir, the Hon. Fox Maule, later Lord Dalhousie, was a strong Free Churchman. In 1852 he granted a site, and contributed £500 to the building fund. Lochlee Free Church, built by Robert and Donald Dinnie, was completed in 1857. Later it became Lochlee United Free Church, and, in 1931, the Maule Memorial Church. Midtown of Cairncross was used for a short time as the Manse and School. Lord Dalhousie, when he died, left £20,000 to be divided among four Free Churches, one of which was Lochlee. Mr McIlwraith was followed by Mr Dickson, MA, James Paul, MA, R.H. Glendinning, MA (who died in 1970 at the age of 83) and Cameron Dinwoodie, MA, PhD.

It used to be the custom to christen Glen children with Lochlee water, perhaps honouring an old tradition. Mr McIlwraith liked to christen children outdoors, seemingly in imitation of Thomas Guthrie (1803–73), the Brechin man who became a recognised authority in Britain on the care of criminal and destitute young people.

The Rev. Thomas Guthrie preaching in Glenmark.

The new church was formally opened on 12 May 1857 by the Rev. Mr Nixon Montrose, who preached to a full audience and achieved a collection of £15.13.2.[8] Apart from Lord Dalhousie's contribution of £500, more money was still required. By the date of opening, about £100 had been gathered within the bounds of the Presbytery to help clear the debt, which applied to the cost of the manse as well as of the church. A subscription list was circulated in January 1858, with the aim of getting 100 subscribers at £1 each for three years, to clear the debt in that period. This was easier said than done. The amount collected in January 1858 was £12.8/-, which was paid into the hands of Duncan Michie, consisting of sums ranging from 1/- up to £1. In the spring of 1881, two stained glass windows were placed in the church. One was gifted by the family of Dr Guthrie and the other by Lady Christian Maule, in memory of her brother, the Hon Fox Maule Ramsay, Earl of Dalhousie. Dr Guthrie preached his last sermon in the Maule Memorial Church on 25 August 1873, and his text was 'The just shall live by faith'. Included in the congregation was HRH the Duke of Edinburgh (Prince Alfred), then Lord Chancellor of England.[9] The church has a massive square tower, and internally it has an open roof.

In 1930, the basis of union for the united congregation of Lochlee Church and the Maule Memorial Church was approved by the Brechin and Fordoun Presbytery, and the deed was consummated on 22 May in that year. The Rev. T.C. Sturrock, Edzell, was made interim moderator for the united congregation. The terms of the union were that:

> The congregations shall be united in the name of Glenesk, and the property and funds belonging to each church and congregation shall be transferred in accordance with the title deeds. Both churches shall be used as places of worship as shall be arranged by the minister and kirk-session of the united congregation. The elders of both congregations shall be elders of the united congregation, and form with the minister the kirk-session. The manse of the Maule Memorial Church shall be recognised as the manse.
>
> As soon as the union of both churches is effected the united congregation shall proceed with the election of a minister. The present minister of Lochlee, Rev. J.M. Kay, on retiring for the sake of union, shall receive £300 per annum from the endowments of the parish until he reaches the age of 75, when he shall revert to the allowance made to ministers, retiring in ordinary course from age and infirmity.
>
> Mr Kay shall also have the free income of the let or sale of the manse and adjacent glebe for life. He shall be allowed a reasonable time from the date of union to occupy the manse and glebe, and arrange for the disposal of its crop, &c.

---

[8] *Brechin Advertiser*, 19 May 1857.
[9] Paul, op. cit. 48. For a life of Guthrie, see C.J. Guthrie. *Life of Thomas Guthrie, D.D.*, Edinburgh, 1897.

These arrangements shall begin as from the date on which the union is effected, and shall terminate in the event of Mr Kay being inducted to another charge or receiving salaried appointment.

In that case, however, sufficient of his retiring allowance shall be retained by him to bring his stipend up to his present stipend.

The manse and glebe of Lochlee Church shall be sold or let or otherwise disposed of subject to the approval of the Presbytery, and subject to the title on which the properties are held. The stipend of the minister shall be at least £330, with manse, &c.

Mr Kay sent a letter indicating that in the interests of local union, he wished to intimate to the Presbytery demission of his charge as minister of the parish of Lochlee.[10] The first minister of the united Charge was Rev. George LB McAlister. The recent history of the United Church can be found in Chapter 6, 'The Parish Church'.

[10] Newspaper cutting 1930, probably *Dundee Courier*.

10

TEACHING THE BAIRNS

From early times the Church had been responsible for education, and in the early days of the parish school, the minister conducted it unless there was a schoolmaster or reader who was usually one and the same person. The general standard of literacy, however, was not high.

In the first Book of Discipline it is clearly stated clearly that the Reformed Church will continue its predecessor's responsibility for education. Before the Reformation it is known that apprenticeships played a large part in the training of youth in trades and crafts. In the towns, these apprentices were trained under the auspices of the craft guilds.[1] The Act of 1496 compelled all barons and freeholders to send their eldest sons to grammar schools at the age of eight or nine, until they were well grounded, thereafter to the schools of the arts and law. The aim of the Reformed Church was education for all, but through lack of money and possibly unwillingness on the part of the parents who may have feared a loss of valuable workers, this was not achieved until education was in secular hands and compulsory, but even then this was not without difficulty.[2] Only ten parishes in Angus had a school in the seventeenth century.

In 1616, the Privy Council issued an Act for establishing schools in every parish.[3] This Act was ratified, altered and added to by the Acts of Parliament of 1633, 1646 and 1696. There was to be a commodious school with a schoolmaster in every parish, maintained and supervised by the Church of Scotland. Heritors contributed to the support of these parish schools by providing a school building and living quarters for the schoolmaster, and also paying the teacher a salary.[4] Parents augmented the schoolmaster's salary by the payment

---

[1] J. Scotland. *The History of Scottish Education*, I, University of London Press, London, 1969, 8.
[2] People were unwilling, on the whole, to send their children to school as they were employed from an early age in the keeping of cattle and sheep, there being few or no dykes or hedges to stop the animals from straying.
[3] H. Paton, ed. *Register of the Privy Council of Scotland*, X (1684–85), Edinburgh, 1927, 671–2.
[4] Scotland, op. cit. 63. See also D. Myers. Scottish Schoolmasters in the Nineteenth Century:Professionalism and Politics, in Walter M. Humes, & Hamish Paterson, eds. *Scottish Culture and Education 1800–1900*, John Donald, Edinburgh,1983, 76.

of fees. Often heritors did not fulfil their responsibilities, taking advantage instead of the schools planted by the Society for the Propagation of Christian Knowledge, a practice which led to the Society withdrawing their charity schools in some areas.[5] In many cases the buildings provided by heritors were inadequate for the purpose.[6] Unrest in the country prevented satisfactory results, but David Lindsay of Edzell had been considering the matter. In a Deed of Mortification dated 1639, he binds and obliges himself, his heirs and successors:

> yearly to content and pay to ane Catechising Reader at the said Chapel of Lochlee, whom I and my foresaids shall present and the ministers of the Presbytery of Brechin shall think qualified, the soume of ane hundred merks money usual of Scotland at two terms in the year, Whitsunday and Martinmass, in winter equal proportions, six bolls of meal yearly betwixt Yuill and Candlemass, ane good and sufficient house of stone and faill (turf) to dwell in with ane yaird; and the Croft at the back of the chapel within the stone dyck, and another Croft before the said chapel and nearest the Loch mouth, with ane cow's grass, and pasturage to twenty sheep with faill, fewell and divvots sufficient. Quilk duty above mentioned I do by thir presents mortifie to the Reader at the said Chapel allenarly (only), and for observing thereof I am content and consents that thir presents be insert and registrat in the books of Counsil and Session, or Comisars books of Brechin 'ad futuram rei memoriam'.[7]

In 1631, the presbytery found that the Parish of Lochlee had 'sufficient Salary for a Schoolmaster by Donation'. David Lindsay of Edzell had obliged himself in 1639 to pay yearly the sum of a hundred merks and six bolls of oatmeal 'with other benefittes and priviledges to be employed allenarly for the Maintenance of Ane Catechising Reader' at the Kirk of Lochlee. His nephew John Lindsay did in 1659 draw up a Deed of Mortification, and did:

> in corroboration of his said Uncle, find and oblige himself, his heirs and successors, to make good and thankful payment, in all time coming, of Ane hundreth marks Scotts money, yearlie, at two terms in the yeare, Whitsunday and Mertimes, with six Bolls good and sufficient Oatmeal, betwixt Yule and Candlemas, yearlie, for the use and maintenance of ane catechising Reader, to be established at the Kirk of Lochly ... farther binds himself and his foresaids to give peaceable possession to the said Reader and his Successors of that Manse, and two Crofts of Land, with the privilege of the pasturage of twentie sheep, ane Cow and horse grasses, which my deceast Uncle dedicat for that use, together with the liberty of casting fewell, feall and divott on the Landiss.[8]

---

[5] ibid, 61.

[6] S. Leslie Hunter. *The Scottish Educational System*, Pergamon Press, Oxford, 1971 (2nd edn), 4.

[7] *Deed of Mortification*, dated 1639, in G. Michie. Guard Book Number 5, *Church and School*, 163.

[8] *Deed of Mortification*, dated at Edzell, 22 August 1659.

In 1658, there was no catechising reader 'conform to the mortification made by the last Laird of Edzell'. Lochlee was 'in a desolat and deplorable condition', which explains the need for the Deed of 1659.[9] It has been suggested that the people of Lochlee had at that time been Gaelic-speaking, and had been unable to understand their minister. At least some of them may have been, for in 1618, John Taylor, 'The Water Poet', did go through a country called 'Glaneske … At night I came to a lodging in the laird of Eggels land, where I lay at an Irish house, the folkes not being able to speake scarce any English'.[10]

From 1723 until the late 1790s, the parochial schoolmaster enjoyed the benefits of the Laird of Edzell and Glenesk's Mortification, as he received no other salary.[11] For much of this time the schoolmaster at Lochlee was, from 1732, the well-published poet Alexander Ross (1699–1784), whose *Helenore* or *Fortunate Shepherdess* was popular reading in Angus and the Mearns for several generations, and some of whose songs have endured. Ross was born in Kincardine O'Neil, the son of a farmer, and graduated in 1718 from Marischal College. Although he acquired several well-known friends including Dr James Beattie, he was content to raise a numerous family on the small stipend (worth about £20 a year) that Lochlee afforded. His accommodation for himself, family and school was a small house containing two twelve-foot-square apartments beside the loch. Some of the epitaphs he composed can still be found on the tombstones in Lochlee kirkyard.[12] In the schoolhouse, the room to the west was occupied by the schoolmaster and his family. It had two windows, one facing south and another facing west to the Loch. The east end of the house was the school. In 1805 the school was moved to Invermark.

In the Lochlee Session Records of 1829 there is a note of an increase in the Salary of the Schoolmaster, Mr Masson. The value of two chalders of oatmeal (sixteen bushels) at £17.2.2d. per chalder is to be collected from the preceding Martinmas 1828. The fees are to be as follows:

For reading English	2/-
Reading and Writing	2/6
Reading, Writing & Arithmetic	3/6
Latin & Mathematics	5/-

All per Quarter.

A condition was attached. The Schoolmaster shall teach such poor children as are recommended by the Heritor and the Minister *gratis*. In the Glenesk Museum are two Angus Club prizes awarded for Latin and Arithmetic respectively, to Alexander and Harry Michie, in 1849 and 1852.

---

[9] W. Fraser. *History of the Carnegies, Earls of Southesk and Their Kindred*, Edinburgh, 1867.

[10] J.C. Jessop. *Education in Angus*, University of London Press, 1931, 60.

[11] *The Old (First) Statistical Account of Scotland*. XIII. Angus, Parish of Lochlee, EP Publishing, Wakefield, England, 1976 (Re-issue), 435.

[12] R. Chambers. *A Biographical Dictionary of Eminent Scotsmen*, Glasgow, 1835.

The parish school was moved again in 1863 on the retiral of Mr Masson, when the Earl of Dalhousie suggested that it be transferred from Invermark to Tarfside along with the population. This took place, although Invermark is known to have been closed in 1865 and open in December 1870 under Mr Alexander Bowman. At one time it was described as a 'side school'. Side schools came about through the 1803 Education Act. Where parishes covered an extensive area, as in the case of Lochlee, and one school was not sufficient to serve the whole population, then the heritors were authorised to provide a salary of six hundred merks (approximately £36.6.6) for two positions, dividing the money as they saw fit.[13] The heritors did not have to provide a house and a garden for the second school, and these institutions then came to be known as side schools.[14] The side school at Invermark closed in 1920 for two years, re-opening again in November 1922. The school finally closed in 1930 with a roll of three who were transferred to Tarfside.

St Drostan's Episcopal School and Schoolhouse, Tarfside, with Mr Lord and his pupils. About 1860. Glenesk Museum.

The relocation of the Parish School to Tarfside presented a problem. There were already three schools there. The Episcopal School, built in 1850, lasted until 1865. Greek was taught there and there were evening classes. The Free Church School was temporarily at Midtown of Cairncross and later at Burnfoot.

---

[13] J. Scotland, op. cit., 176.
[14] ibid, 176.

There was also the 'Society School' below the post office, probably on the site of the building once tenanted by Miss Lindsay, last of the name in Glenesk. However, the Education (Scotland) Act of 1872 brought them all together. There had been small schools run by groups of parents in outlying places at Skelly, Arsallary, East Auchintoul and Corhidlin (in the Aucheen area). The Society School is recalled in the diary of George Webster Donald, later custodian at Arbroath Abbey, who applied for the post of teacher there in 1847:

> On the recommendation of the Rev. Robert Stephenson, parish minister of Forfar, I now set out for the Normal School, Edinburgh. I remained in the capital for four months, visiting every place of interest that I could think of. I returned home when I found that all my cash had evaporated but two shs. and sixpence to pay the boat.
>
> Next Spring I observed an advertisement in the Montrose Review for a teacher to take the management of the Society School at Tarfside, Lochlee, applications to be lodged with the Rev. Walter Low, minister. I lost not a moment in applying, but received no word back from the mountains for four months. At the end of that time I had a kind letter from the minister, stating that the situation had been conferred on a young man, a Mr J. Lee, from Montrose, but that my certificates and recommendations stood high in the esteem of Lord Panmure. He also added that they, the inhabitants of Lochlee, had been shut off from all communication with the outer world by a severe snowstorm, or I should have heard from him much sooner – date of this letter was 26th March, 1847.
>
> Sultry day – month of July – little man dressed in black enters my school at Kingsmuir – desires me to drill my pupils before him – nothing forbidding about him – act according to his wish – quite satisfied – Walter Low, minister of Lochlee – sent by Lord Panmure – Mr Lee had broken down – Tarfside School still vacant – Mr Low strongly advises me to go to Edinburgh to stand an examination before the commissioners – agreed – lights his pipe with one of the eyes of his spectacles – shakes hands – departs – I now employed a person to take charge of my school, and set out for Edinburgh immediately – could find none of the commissioners at home – only the secretary, James Tawse, WS, – wait three weeks and returned unexamined – borrowed the skeleton of an old grey mare, which might have passed for a lineal descendant of Rosinante, from a neighbour – rode up to the mountains with all speed – much struck with the surrounding scenery – stop at 'White Horse Inn' – Auld Nelly Smith – regular Nancy Tumock – offered a dram – refused – chose milk – remark – last Dominie who came up looking after school drank deep, and slept all night in swine crue – I passed over the shoulder of Rowinhill – arrived at Manse – Highland welcome from minister, Mrs, and all his 'eighteen children' – ushered into Panmure Hall – merry-making with elders and neighbours – almost torn from the wrists by shaking hands as hard as leather – plenty of toddy – minister sings 'Willie brewed a Peck o' Maut' – all shake hands again and disperse – half-past one – remain all night at the manse – get up in the morning – visit grave of Alexander Ross, author of 'The Fortunate Shepherdess' and 'The Rock an' the wee Pickle Tow' – old Castle of Invermark – stronghold of the Lindsays – visit the school – lone barn-like place – strong smell of peat-reek – parted – promised to return and open school by the end of September, whether examined or not – another letter from the minister – date 1st September, 1847 – to meet him in

Brechin with gig – sorrowful reflections on leaving my father's house – arrive in Brechin – meet the parson – some 'wauchts' of punch – turn to the mountains – long road – arrive at manse – school opened in a few days – stupid set of children – taught till 1st November – received a letter from James Tawse to attend a diet of examination – travel thirty miles down the country on foot – arrive at Usan, small fishing village on the coast – to await the Aberdeen steamer – take quarters in an inn – get on the steamer next day – tremendous storm – small sloop lost with all hands – quit the steamer, and betake ourselves to a small boat – landed at Arbroath, and take the train to Edinburgh – attended examination next day – full meeting – came off well – returned to Lochlee not so poor as when I set out from it – taught the school during the winter months – examined again by the Presbytery of Brechin – strange scene – visit Lord Panmure at the castle – adds £6 more to my salary – returned to meet Mr Low at Dr. Gardener's manse – half-seas over – treated with great kindness and loaded with presents – start for home – three-quarters past 11 p.m. – excessive cold – frost and snow – lost the way above Auchmull (sic) – reconnoitre – perilous position – met the old shepherd of Mill of Aucheen – got home during the morning by his aid – settle down in school – feel something like a glow of sunshine flooding round my heart while pronouncing my name: my own land, my own cow, my own house, but not yet my own *wife*, that was to come soon – too happy to last – making rhyme, love, and friendship at every turn – got married on the 30th May, 1849.

Applied for another situation, the Society School of Luthermuir, am successful – entered on my duty about midsummer, 1852 – school a preaching station – officiated for clergymen frequently – quite happy for four years.

George Webster Donald's 'examination before the commissioners' was standard practice for Society teachers. All teachers employed by the SSPCK had to undergo an examination by an Edinburgh based committee in reading, writing, arithmetic and religion.[15]

Lord Panmure concerned himself not only with the Church but also with the school. In 1843 he persuaded Brechin Presbytery to libel the Schoolmaster for joining the Free Church, and the latter agreed to resign at Martinmas. This must have been rescinded, as Mr Masson appears to have continued as schoolmaster at Lochlee until 1863.

The imminent removal of the Parish School had hastened the withdrawal of the SSPCK from Tarfside, since that organisation supplied a teacher only in the parts of parishes without schools. This left vacant the Society building and land, which may have been the perquisites which the Earl of Dalhousie made available for the new Schoolmaster, Mr John Sutherland. The house may have been renewed as its style is mid-nineteenth century. This, however, amounted to far less in value than that which the latter had enjoyed at Invermark. Mr Sutherland, although disappointed, was unwilling to complain, and it was Rev. Walter Low, parish minister, in conjunction with Brechin Presbytery,

---

[15] ibid, 100.

who lodged a protest and delivered it to Brechin Castle. It was made clear that the Reader at Lochlee and subsequently at Invermark, had been entitled to the Mortification previously described dating back to the seventeenth century, initiated by the Lindsays and acknowledged by the Panmure family on their purchase of the Barony of Glenesk. This had been paid until 1852, when the Earl of Dalhousie had succeeded his father. As it ensured that there was a proper school and schoolmaster for the parish, the Rev. Walter Low and the Presbytery demanded a full equivalent in land at Tarfside for the same at Invermark.

At the time of the protest Mr Sutherland had instead been put in possession of:

> a School and Schoolhouse, an insufficient Cowhouse or Byre, a portion of ground for a Garden which had been imperfectly redeemed from a state of nature ... with about three acres of very inferior land instead of the large, excellent and productive Garden, and eight acres of good land which his predecessors had ... occupied and enjoyed at Invermark, along with ample accommodation for four cows, a stable, cartshed and convenient barns – the stipend of 100 merks in money and six bolls of meal, having been converted into a money payment of £15, but which your Lordship declared and intimated you did not consider yourself bound to make, for any period of time beyond your own pleasure.

Lord Dalhousie was therefore sued as heritable proprietor:

> ... in the right and possession of the Barony of Glenesk including the lands and Estate of Edzell, for withholding the perquisites due to the Parochial Schoolmaster and his successors in office, and it was clear that he was bound by law to honour this old Mortification. Indeed, the Presbytery described his behaviour as illegal and incompetent, that he was liable in all loss and damage that the schoolmaster had already suffered and might yet suffer. The date was 5th October, 1865.

Following this powerful protest and threat of litigation, Lord Dalhousie provided an excellent school and schoolhouse which is still in use. It was opened in 1873.

Mr Masson, the schoolmaster at Lochlee, was in receipt of the Mortification in 1854, as his and other schoolmasters' salaries for that year are known. As the entries show, the salaries differ from parish to parish, but Mr Masson at Lochlee does quite well compared to his colleagues in other districts:

1854 April 25	By cash paid William Masson value of six Bols of Meal Mortified by the late John Lindsay, Laird of Edzell to the Schoolmaster or Reader in the *Parish of Lochlee* for		
	1853 @ 20/3:–	£6.1.6	
	Under deduction of Income Tax:–	3.6 = £5.8.0	
May 27	By cash paid William Masson half a year's Salary as Schoolmaster of Lochlee to Whitsunday:–	£11.6.8	
	Under deduction of Income Tax:	6.7 = £11.0.1	

1854 Dec 13 By cash paid William Masson *Lochlee* half a year's
school Salary to Martinmas:– £11.6.8
Under deduction of Income Tax 13.2 = £10.13.6

One can only assume that the salaries shown here do not include school fees as they are considerably lower than the salaries being paid twenty years earlier to parochial schoolmasters. Rev. Robert Inglis records in the *New Statistical Account* that '... the parochial schoolmaster has the maximum salary of £34.4.4d besides what was mortified by a catechist ...'.[16] Assuming that Mr Masson's half-yearly salary paid to him in December 1853 had also been in the region of £11.6.8, then his net annual salary would have amounted to around £22. On top of this he received the cash equivalent of six bolls of meal amounting to £5.18s net. Mr Masson received relatively more than his fellow teachers in the surrounding areas. By comparison, James Mitchell, Schoolmaster of Lethnot Parish, received an annual salary of £13.6.4 net. William Ayre, Schoolmaster of Edzell Parish received £15.11.11 net annual salary. In contrast, Alex Jaffray in the Parish of Kinnell received a half year's salary of £2.14.0 net, payable from the lands of West Brakie in that Parish.

Westside, 26 May 1865
Received from Mr David Innes Arsellary
the Sum of Eleven shillings and four pence
Sterling, being the amount of Schoolmaster's Salary, due
at Whitsunday Eighteen hundred and Sixty five
£ : 11/4 · Robert Stock

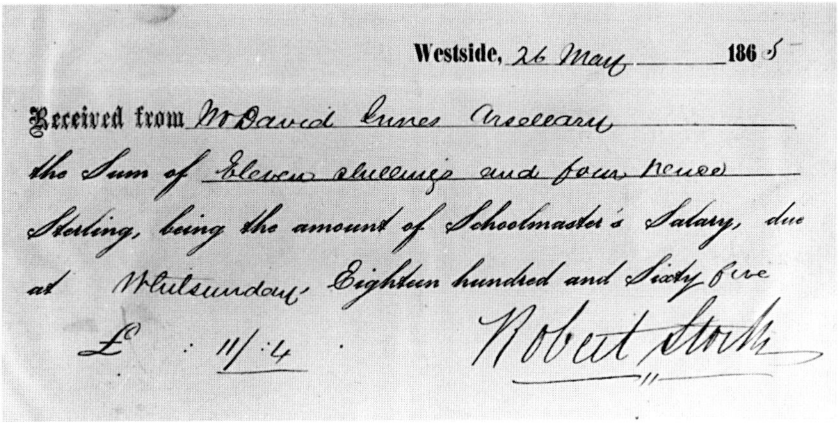

A receipt acknowledging payment towards the schoolmaster's salary by David Innes, Arsellary, and witnessed by the factor, Robert Stock. 1865. Glenesk Museum.

From the time of its opening, the attendance at Lochlee Public School, Tarfside, appears to have been poor until 1884 when there were sixteen pupils, rising soon after to nineteen. On Mr Sutherland's resignation, the school was closed for a short time until the appointment of Mr Lyall on 10 December 1888, and on 4 January 1889 there were 36 pupils, rising in December of the same year to 42. Owing to a bad water supply, Mr Lyall and his housekeeper

[16] *The New Statistical Account of Scotland:* Forfar and Kincardine, XI, Edinburgh, 1845.

died tragically in August 1890. He was followed by Mr Samuel Cruickshank
who stayed until 1921, and whose successors have been fairly numerous. Gradually, the school and its water supply have been modernised.

Tarfside School with the headmaster, Mr Samuel Cruickshank. About 1905. C.12635.

Subsequent to the Education Act of 1872, there was considerable difficulty in enforcing attendance from the age of five. There were reasons and
plausible excuses; delicacy of the child, bad moral atmosphere of the school
and the inefficiency of the teacher. But the chief difficulty was the determined opposition of certain parents who had children able to work for them.
Entries in the log book of Lochlee Public School are of great interest in this
connection.

By all accounts the quality of the available schoolmaster was frequently
poor. About 1865 a Master was at Tarfside, and the pupils each carried the
usual daily peat for the fire, an old style open one, level with the floor. The
Dominie was feckless and the boys were often wild. One frosty day a number
of them brought a sackful of icicles from outside, two kept the door open
while one 'curled' icicles along the floor into the fireplace. The Dominie was
helpless, and sat down among the girls. A boy of sixteen named James Dunbar
from Garthhead in Arsallary, was perched on the Teacher's desk, frowning at
the performance. Another boy called out, 'Look at Garthy. Hey, Israel'. James
Dunbar removed himself from the desk, collected his books, and returned
home. He informed his people that he would never enter that school again,
that he would find a way or make one. He went to the University of Aberdeen

and eventually became Lecturer in Greek in the University of Otago, Dunedin. Oddly enough, many years afterwards he met the Dominie in New Zealand, almost destitute.

The strict discipline to which teachers were trained in the years that followed had its effect on school punishment, and in some cases an element of cruelty seems to have entered school life. Children used to be sent outside to bring in their own weapon of punishment. In another part of Angus, an uncle of Greta Michie braved the Dominie and brought in a paling post. A Glenesk Dominie of the period used to send the children out for birch twigs to cut them over the ears with. Greta Michie knew two witnesses of this performance. A Dominie at another Glen school, allegedly, nearly killed Greta's father, who said nothing at home consciously, but told it all in his sleep. The youngest Christison from York Redoubt fell through the ice, either on Cairncross Dam or Mrs. Lowden's Lochy. The schoolmaster made the boy sit until his teeth chattered. After school his companions raced him home to get some warmth into his body. They were also wet to the skin. Mrs. Davidson at Dykeneuk found them on the road, dried them out and fed them. These stories were told to Greta Michie by people now long dead.

A change came around 1890, with a new generation. Mr Lyall, he who died because of the bad water supply, was, according to one of his former pupils 'an artist, an athlete and a boy's man'. His successor, Samuel Cruickshank, whom posterity recognised as a teacher of outstanding qualities, had great difficulty with school attendance during busy times on the farms and during the grouse shooting. He took education beyond the four walls of the classroom.

Although there is really no space to mention all of the assistants, one exception must be made. Miss Minnie Lindsay taught needlework at all three Glen schools. The last Lindsay in Glenesk, she had wonderful creative gifts from which all those whom she taught have benefited. One of the greatest contributors to the Glenesk Museum, she had a complete understanding of what was required.

The poorly paid Dominies had hard lives, and were answerable to Church, School Boards and the Inspectorate. They were expected to rule with a rod of iron. Some of the conditions under which they lived would not be tolerated today. In the 1880s, when Invermark was still open, the schoolmaster was Alexander Bowman. In spite of an extension leg-boot, he walked, part of the time at least, daily from Tarfside and back, probably over the Rowan. He lived with his mother in the first house to the west of the present school. The Dominies had to suffer from the performance of their duties quite often. When one Dominie died there was no grief. The children merely said, 'The Dominie's deid'.

The Education (Scotland) Act of 1872 came not before time, and presented many problems to all concerned. Schools had not been related to the size of the population in the vicinity and frequently were inaccessible to many in the parish.

In 1864, Rev. Dr Guthrie of Ragged School fame, gave evidence before the Education Commission:

> I know country parishes where the parochial school is so situated that it cannot teach the whole children of the parish ... In Lochlee, a parish of 15 to 16 miles long, there is a place called Tarfside, which is situated about five miles from what was the parish school; in that small village you had a school for the SPCK, a Free Church school, and an Episcopalian School, while between that small hamlet and Edzell there are twelve miles without a school at all, though it is a well-peopled glen.

In fact, there were vast differences in opportunity in general, including suitability and quality of school buildings, equipment, teaching and government. As Dr Guthrie pointed out, schools maintained by different organisations were often in close proximity. Compulsory school attendance was desirable, but everyone knew it would be ill-received, involving as it did the loss of cheap labour for the parents. Not even after 1872 could it actually be enforced if the child was receiving instruction elsewhere.

After administration by the Church for centuries, an organised State system of schools was created, administered by School Boards and responsible to the Board of Education. More or less compulsory education from the ages of five to thirteen years was introduced, with limited authority on the part of the Education Department. Teachers were to be appointed and paid by the School Boards. It was indeed a leap in the dark, a situation bristling with difficulties, but the disorganisation preceding 1872 could no longer be ignored. The number of schools belonging to various denominations throughout Scotland in 1864 shows the scale of the problem:

Society for the Propagation of Christian Knowledge	202
Church of Scotland	519
Free Church	617
Roman Catholic Church	61
Episcopal Church	74

The Church came very creditably out of the situation. The Church of Scotland and the Free Church gave over their schools unconditionally, and various Church Training Colleges continued until 1906 to undertake the responsibility of preparing teachers for their profession, as they had increasingly done throughout the nineteenth century. In the early part of the century many teachers had been ill-qualified for their task.

The preceding account of the national situation explains what happened in Glenesk. Two parishes were involved, Lochlee and Edzell, the two meeting at Millden. In Lochlee, at the new school and schoolhouse at Tarfside, the accommodation was adequate. So also was the side school at Invermark, re-opened in

1870. Edzell, however, was in a different situation. Although the village of Edzell is outwith this study, it is worth recording that its parish school was only 30 by 23 feet, and required considerable enlargement. In the Glen portion of the parish was a Subscription School, at Bentyfauld, not far from the boundary, now a ruin. It was situated about 150 yards north-east of the later site of the school at Bridgend of Dalscampie (Greenburn Croft), described in Edzell School Board Minutes, 1873, and mentioned on one occasion as Millden.

A Subscription School provided superior education, although in this case, the housing was inadequate. The 1865 Report by the Commissioners describes it as a 'rented hovel', and recommends that a new school be built for a population of about 250. The grandmother of Mrs Main of Dalhestnie told her what the old school looked like. There was a form right along the back wall, so that the children sat with their backs to the road. In front of them was a long table, there was one window with several small panes of glass and shutters. The floor was of clay.

In that area there was no parochial school whatever. The only suitable existing quarters in the Parish of Edzell were at Balfour, maintained by Lady Gladstone, and which were eventually abandoned through lack of numbers.

On 4 April, 1873, the examiners from Edzell School Board were highly satisfied with the state of the Glen school, so far as education was concerned. The Board, taking this into consideration, unanimously agreed to fix the Salary of Mr Aikenhead, the Teacher, at 18/- per week including fees, instead of 16/- as previously decided. The building was, however, ruinous.

Apparently, in the past a teacher had been engaged for five months each year by parents who wished their children to receive an education. Schools of the kind, run by groups of parents, are said to have been Arsallary, Skelly, Cornhidlin, Broomfauld and East Auchintoul. Unlike Bentyfauld-Dalscampie, these did not survive so long. The only known written record is one dated 1819. It gives a list of pupils and their attainments, and was discovered in a book in the possession of Miss D.M. Skene.

Like members of other school boards, the Edzell representatives were taking their duties seriously. To enlarge one school and build another from the foundation was likely to be no small financial burden. They counted the children in the Edzell village area and those in the Glen area, who would attend the schools, and included those from the parish of Lochlee who were over three miles from their own parish school. For the new Glen School, to be named Waterside Public School, that made a probable total of 46 pupils.

Therefore, with a view to the future, the School Board looked for a site to accommodate a school for 60 scholars and a schoolhouse of four apartments. Finally, they chose a place a little below Bridgend of Dalscampie, where the building stands to this day, although no longer a school. The Clerk to the Board remarked that they had examined the district, ascertained the wishes of the inhabitants, and believed they would meet every want and give general satisfaction. The school was opened in 1876, and in the 1880s it was attended by 40 to 50 pupils.

Grants had been available, but not sufficient for Edzell's commitments. Apart from their expenses in the village, £750 had to be found for Waterside. Borrowing was inevitable. The local farmers, no doubt realising the dilemma, offered to help with the carting of stones from Craigoshina, Dalforth and Greenburn, on condition that Lord Dalhousie donated £100. His Lordship was agreeable. The architect was Ross of Inverness, and the building was occupied by 1876, although there was a good deal of trouble later on with smoke coming down the chimney, a leaky roof and rainwater coming under the door.

The Master, Mr Munro, had been temporarily accommodated since 1873 in a house on Mill of Aucheen, tenanted at the time by John Jolly. Mrs Jolly taught needlework. There was not, unfortunately, a good understanding between Mr Munro and the parents, even though the teacher was an intelligent, fully qualified man of whom the Board of Education spoke highly.

The problem of school attendance was always a subject of controversy during seasonal work on the farms and at the time of ghillying. Prior to the Education Act, the problem had been solved by boys working when required, and attending school in winter until the age of roughly eighteen to compensate for absences.

Mr Munro left in 1876, but an interesting case arose during his schoolmastership at Waterside. John Bruce of Waggles refused to send his daughter, Anne, to school, as he intimated his intention to superintend the education of his children personally. The Board considered he should be prosecuted, but the Sheriff found the charge 'not proven', as John Bruce was not bound to send his child to any school, but was bound to provide elementary education for his family. The Education Department upheld the verdict. At the end of 1876 Mr Munro resigned.

He was followed by schoolmistresses, who were not so difficult to pay. The reasons for this had their origins in the 1872 (Scotland) Act. The rule that all children over the age of five should attend school meant that there was increase in demand for teachers, especially in the infant age group.[17] Women were cheaper to employ and more eager to work and the school boards urgently required a large supply of teaching staff.[18] Some women resented not receiving equal wages despite having the same qualifications as their male colleagues. Others saw it as a chance to be independent in terms of career and salary, and accepted the wage difference either as simply the way things were,

[17] H. Corr. An Exploration into Scottish Education, in W. Hamish Fraser & R.J. Morris, eds. *People and Society in Scotland*, II 1830–1914, John Donald, Edinburgh, 1990, 304.
[18] ibid, 304.

or that a man was the breadwinner 'and so required higher pay to keep his family'.[19]

Two of the schoolmistresses stayed for short periods, and were followed in 1880 by Miss Black who stayed so long that she became an institution. She was much appreciated, and seems to have spent her whole life teaching at Waterside. On her resignation in 1925, she was followed by Mr Crowe, who had previously taught at Invermark. According to James Caithness, who was born in the parish of Lochlee in 1917, Mr Crowe was quite strict, '... using a strap or cane, to rap the pupil over the hand for not holding pen or pencil properly'. The teachers who followed Mr Crowe were all female, namely, Miss Meldrum, Mrs McDowal, Miss Dallachie and Mrs Batchelor. A second teacher also came to teach during the war years, as there was quite an influx of evacuees from Dundee, although James Caithness recalls that '... some of them only stayed a short time due to no Picture Houses or shops'.

Mr Crowe, the Dominie. Back row: James Lowden, Charles Duncan, James Stewart. Middle row: Greta Michie, Davina Skene, Lily Leighton, Ella Jolly, Duncan Michie. Front row: Ruby Lowden, unknown, Mary Crowe.

[19] Willis. B. Marker, Scottish Teachers. In H. Holmes, ed. *Institutions of Scotland:Education*, (Scottish Life and Society. A Compendium of Scottish Ethnology, XI, forthcoming).

With general depopulation the numbers began slowly to decrease until at Waterside only three pupils were left. In 1965 the school was closed. Mrs Batchelor was the last teacher. Children from this area now attend Edzell Primary and Brechin High School.

Until the Local Government (Scotland) Act of 1889, which brought free schooling, fees were payable in the schools in the parish of Edzell. The fees were to be paid monthly in advance.

For English or English and Writing	3d. per week
For English, Writing & Arithmetic	3$\frac{1}{2}$d. " "
For English, Writing & Arithmetic with Grammar & Geography	4d. " "
All other Subjects	5d.

Also in Edzell was a Dame School. A dame school was really a type of 'adventure school' run by impoverished people trying to eke out a living in their rooms, garrets or barns, using what knowledge they happened to have. There survives from Inchbare an example of an alphabet taught about 1825 in such a school by a Miss Jean Smart.

Muckle Ah
Little Ah
Bey
Say
Day
Fat's in yer heed? E
Fat's like yer Mither's glasses? G
H
I
J
Fat's in the byre? K
Fat has ae leg? L
Fat has 3 legs? M
Fat has 2 legs? N
Fat's like the Mune? O
Pey
Q
Err
Fat's like the crook? S
Fat's on yer feet? Tae
U
Vey
W
Fat does yer Mither brak sticks wi'? X
Y
Izzit

The Cooper Bequest preceded the Education Act. It was frequently referred to in the Minutes of the Edzell School Board. The Bequest was intended to help poor children, and for the provision of ground for a school and a garden upon the Mill of Dalbog, and also on the east side of the river on the west extremity of the farm of Bonhary, or as near to these places as circumstances permitted. Those concerned had to build the schools and schoolhouses at their own expense, the interest to be applied towards paying school fees and books for children in poor circumstances. Sir Thomas Gladstone provided both ground and a school at the Kirkton of Balfour, and it was proposed that the Kirk Session should build a 'Bridge of Communication for children on the West side of the River North Esk with convenient pathways to and from school'. They would then pay over to Sir Thomas not less than £200 from the Legacy. The plan was turned down. This is here fully described, as a fictitious tale persists that there was once a school at Dalbog. The building at Balfour is still in existence.

At the time of the 1872 Compulsory Education Act, it was calculated that the total number of children in Edzell Village and nearby was 144. A few more would be attending from that part of Stracathro which was a fair distance from their own parish school.

The Parochial School in the village, although substantial, was inadequate in size, as were so many schools of its kind before compulsory education. The Free Church School had poor quarters, vividly described by Inglis in *Oor Ain Folk*. The Dame School was in a rented room. The School Board decided that there should be one school with a Master, Mistress and one or two pupil teachers, and in order that future needs should be supplied, accommodation for 200 children was planned. Such a programme necessitated an entirely new school, but want of money limited the building of an extension. It was not until 1902 that the substantial new school that now exists was built.

In Lethnot, as in Glenesk, there was one parish and one Society school. There was also Westwater School, the description of which in 1805 speaks for itself:

> Westwater School is taught only in Winter and sometimes in alternate winters only, and there is no other school in the district which the children can attend, the parish school, which is the nearest, being five miles distant. The district in question is intersected by hills and rivulets, its extent being four miles long by one broad; population 40.

In 1901 a number of educational reforms started with the raising of the school leaving age to fourteen, and, eventually, to fifteen after World War II. In 1908, Scottish School Boards were given the further duties of providing school meals, and the provision of free books and stationery. Until the stock went done, every child at that time received a schoolbag presented by Coats of Paisley. The boys' type was slung over the shoulders, and the girls' had a handle. Two are preserved in the Glenesk Museum. The schoolbags bring to mind the daily routine of the school itself. Listed below are some of the mid-nineteenth century schoolbooks that were used, formerly the possessions of John Jolly of Mill of Aucheen who died c.1875, and whose collection of exercise books and text books came to light in 1945:[20] Ingram's *Principles of Arithmetic*, price 1/-, was described as 'the cheapest and most complete elementary treatise on arithmetic that has ever appeared'. It contained 28 tables of weights and measures. Even the Scots money table was included, since 'valuation of lands, some few duties, ministers' stipends, schoolmasters' salaries and other public and parochial burdens are still reckoned in Scotch money'.

In Glenesk it was only the more able pupils who progressed from the elementary rules to Proportion, Practice and Interest. Exceptional scholars reached the heights of Vulgar and Decimal Fractions, Evolution, Discount, Barter, Loss and Gain. At the back of Ingram's Text-Book were the answers, doing no harm to the child, and a tremendous help to a harassed schoolmaster dealing with all stages at one time. Also available in this subject was Dr McCulloch's *Arithmetic*.

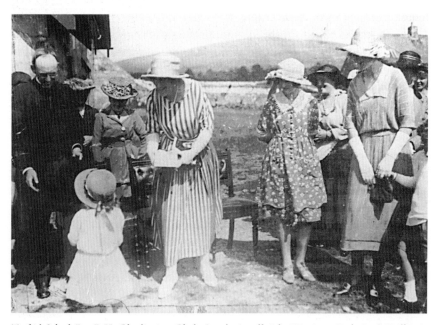

Tarfside School. Rev. R.H. Glendinning, Gladys Lowden (small girl), Miss Agnes Duke, Lady Dalhousie, Lady Jean Ramsay, Lady Ida Ramsay, Hon. Simon Ramsay. 1926 or 1927. Glenesk Museum.

In many diaries and exercise books are included maps, usually drawn by the pupil. The World and Angus seemed to be the most popular. White's *Geography*, price 1/3d, is undated, but the material is so short and so antiquated as to

[20] *The Scottish Educational Journal*, 21 December, 1945, 640.

indicate that the book is of great age. Another popular course book was Dr McCulloch's *Lessons in Prose and Verse*. There was also time for the art of penmanship and it was said that in the Glen 'they were braw writers'. And all of this was achieved in an old style school, which we can try to imagine, with its glowing fire and lamplight on dark winter days, and the children, who had perhaps walked a long distance from outlying places, and had carried their 'pieces'. Ham in two bannocks was popular, with a cup of cocoa. At the turn of the century, Glen schools began to have soup kitchens, with white enamel bowls. At Tarfside, the kitchen was called 'The Soupie'. The temperatures in the schoolrooms were often low in the winter, and the heat of the fires of the time often went up the chimney.

Tarfside School. Greta Michie, schoolteacher, and pupils. 1952. G1/27/17A.

Although there have been as many as three schools in Glenesk at one time, only Tarfside School in Upper Glenesk has a sufficient number of pupils to continue. After Greta Michie retired in 1965, she was succeeded by Mrs Omand, who was followed by Mrs Skene. The current teacher at Tarfside is Ms Sandra Guthrie, who has taught at the school since she succeeded Mrs Skene in 1976. The school currently has ten pupils, which is a far cry from the days when there were as many as 42 children in attendance. The Secondary pupils all attend Brechin. In isolated districts the problem today is not the want of schools but the want of scholars.

Tarfside School. Mrs Skene with pupils. Moyra Duncan, Colin Osler, Gordon Bain, Glenda Hale, Christine Bain. 1970. G1/27/34A.

11

LAND USE AND LABOUR:
THE NINETEENTH CENTURY

Farming in Glenesk in the nineteenth century is dominated by changes in land use, which brought about a reduction in the number of holdings in the Glen. As with many other highland estates, Glenesk was moving into a different economic pattern, with more emphasis being placed on sporting interests. Much grazing land and many small farms, such as those at Glenlee and Inchgrundle, were given over to deer forests and grouse moors. The Smarts had Inchgrundle for many years. They left to go to Dalbog in 1853–4 when Fox Maule received permission from the Crown to create the Forest of Mark. Consolidation of farms saw many small holdings disappear, as they were either combined to form larger, single units or added to bigger farms. These factors created a redundant population. Combined with agricultural depression in the last quarter of the nineteenth century, this resulted in a movement of people away from the Glen, mainly in search of regular employment.

Evidence for the reduction in holdings can be seen clearly by comparing the Lochlee rentals of 1759 (see Chapter 5) and those of 1875. In the 1759 rentals 52 holdings are listed but by 1875 the number has dropped to 39.[1]

The Barony of Lochlee Money Rents for Martinmas 1875 lists 39 farm touns, names their tenants, gives the rents payable and includes the terms of the leases.[2] The rents were probably paid 'forehand', that is the first half paid at Whitsunday and the second half at Martinmas. It must be pointed out that the place-names are reproduced according to the spelling in the sources.

Many of the farms changed hands in the period between 1759 and 1875, but there is evidence of continuity in a few cases, though it is harder to trace in some instances as the names of the tenants in the 1759 rentals have not been included. At Arsallary in 1875, David Innes was the tenant, while Walter Innes was tenant of part of the same farm in 1716, and James Innes tenant of part of Arsallary in 1758–9. David Christison is listed as tenant of Auchronie in 1875, while Alex and Thomas Chrystieson held the tenancy in 1716, but

---

[1] Barony of Lochlee Money Rents, Martinmass 1875, NAS GD45/18/1790.
[2] Dalhousie Muniments, NAS GD45/18/1790.

Tenants	Possessions	Marts 1875	Entry	Endurance	Expiry	Tenant in 1759
Charles Mair	Drumgreen	£18.10		At Will		Robt. Grant
John Cattanach	Whigginton	£ 2.10		"		John Chrystison
David Mitchell	Turnabrain	£20.00		"		Robt. Thow
Burnett Gibb	Glentenant	£31.15		"		Bowman, Coutts, Ross, Watt, Chrystison
David Innes	Arsellary	£13.00		"		Innes, Low, Brown
John Paterson	Tarfside	£10.00		"		Robert Clark
James Heigh	West Migvies	£ 2.00		"		Webster, Kinnear
David Gibb	Ardoch	£32.10		"		-
D & A Christison	Auchintoul Hill	£ 4.00		"		-
" "	Hall of Aucheen	£ 9.00		"		-
David Jolly	Mill of Aucheen	£29.00		"		-
Duncan Michie	Mid Upper Cairncross	£23.10	Whit 1875	19 years	Whit 1894	John and David Campbell
Archibald Stewart	Buskhead	£ 7.10	" "	At Will	" "	Thos. Low
John Pirie	Auchintoul	£26.00		"		
Alexander Christison	Cohairncross	£ 7.00		"		Innes, Low, Brown
John Dunbar	Arsellary	£11.00		"		Henry Lindsay's heirs and
David Christison	Milton	£ 5.00		"		Alex. Mill
Archibald Campbell	Haugh	£ 5.00		"		Jas. Thow
William Duke	West Migvies	£ 9.00		"		Webster, Kinnear
John Edwards	Blackcraig	£30.00		"		-
George Campbell	Keenie	£45.00	Marts 1864	19 years	Marts 1883	Donald Gall
	Common Hills of Berryhill	£17.10	To run out with Keenie			Jas. Thomson, Isaac Gall
Thomas Christison	East Hall East Migvies	£ 5.00		"		Webster, Kinnear
W. Paterson	West Hall "	£ 6.00		"		" "
William Lindsay	Dalbrack	£72.10	Whit 1872	19 years	Whit 1891	David Campbell
" "	Westbank	£35.15	Marts 1874	"	Marts 1893	John Crocket
Alex Eggo	Kidderich	£ 4.10		At Will		-
James Caithness	Blackhills	£15.00		"		-
		£ 6.00		"		-
David Christison	Auchronie	£11.00		"		Peter Farquharson, Jas. Thow
Andrew Campbell	Baillies	£35.00	Whit 1871	19 years	Whit 1890	John Low, Jas. Christyson
Archibald Campbell	Gleneffock	£85.00	" "	"	" "	David Archibald, Thos. Jolly
Alexander Eggo	Common Hill	£ 2.10		At Will		-
David Stewart	Haugh Pendicle	£ 3.10	Marts 1859	19 years	Marts 1878	-
Col Guthrie	Fernybank? Land			At Will		-
David Moir	Tarfside Smithy	£ 3.10		"		-
W. Watt	House Tarfside	£ 2.00		"		-
Wm Davidson	West Migvies	£ 1.00		"		Webster, Kinnear
John Pirie	Auchintoul Pendicle	£ 2.10		"		-
John Sutherland	Tarfside	2s.9d		"		-
David Lowden	House Tarfside	15s		"		-

had changed by 1758–9. David Jolly was tenant at Mill of Aucheen in 1875, while James Jolly is recorded as being the tenant in 1716. Finally, William Davidson was tenant at West Migvie in 1875, while another William Davidson was recorded as tenant of two parts of Migvie in 1716, although it is not clear if it is the same individual who had both holdings.

Whereas the Rentals of 1716 and 1758–9 point to a period of relative stability in Glenesk, the Rental of 1875 reflects a time of instability for the tenants of the Glen, though not for the Heritor and his estate. Many of the names from the 1759 Rental have gone by 1875, to be replaced by newcomers to the Glen, marking a tendency for in and out movement. This period witnessed an increase in the mobility of farmworkers, and as some people left the Glen to seek better opportunities elsewhere, their places were taken by others from Aberdeenshire and the surrounding areas.

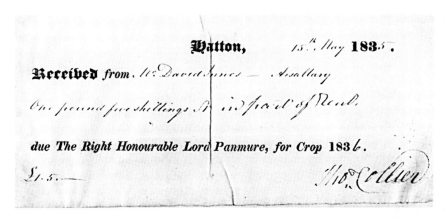

Arsallary rent paid by David Innes to the Panmure estate, paid in advance in May 1835 for the crop 1836. 1835. Glenesk Museum.

The grading of the farms according to the level of rents paid shows a vastly different pattern to that revealed by the 1759 Rental. Assuming that the rents from Whitsunday to Martinmas 1875 were approximately the same, and all the double units are kept together, then the order in terms of annual rent paid is:

	1875 Rental	*1759 Rental*	*Increase/Decrease*
Gleneffock	£170.00	£197.19.4	13% decrease
Dalbrack	145.00	94.30/-	55% increase
Keenie	90.00	22.00/-	300% increase
Westbank	71.10	52.06/-	36% increase
Baillies	70.00	94. 3.8	25% decrease

Ardoch	65.00	-	
Glentennet	63.10	229.07/-	72.5% decrease
Blackcraig	60.00	-	
Mill of Aucheen	58.00	-	
Auchintoul	56.10	-	
Arsallary	48.00	192. 4.7	75% decrease
Mid Upper Cairncross	47.00	95.15.8	50% decrease
West & East Migvies	46.00	87.17	47% decrease
Blackhills	42.00	44.00	5% decrease
Turnabrain	40.00	73.19.4	45% decrease
Drumgreen	37.00	49.06.8	23% decrease
Berryhill	35.00	-	
Auchronie	22.00	88.00	75% decrease
Tarfside	20.00	26.00	23% decrease
Hall of Aucheen	18.00	-	
Buskhead	15.00	37.15/-	49% decrease
Haugh	10.00	36.15.8	28% decrease
Milton	10.00	75.12.8 (with Keeny Mill)	86% decrease
Fernybank	10.00	-	

If the farms are compared as individual units, then only two farms, Gleneffock and Dalbrack, have rentals of over £100, i.e. 5.2 per cent of the total, which is fairly close to the 1759 figure of 5.56 per cent. Three farms lie in the £70–90 bracket, or 7.7 per cent of the whole, which is low compared with 1759 when there were ten farms in this bracket. There are five farms between £50–70, which makes up 12.83 per cent. Seventeen farms lie between £10–50 (43.6 per cent), leaving twelve farms (30.79 per cent) with rents of under £10. The picture here is slightly different from that of 1759 when there was a more even spread in the size of units.

The most notable aspect of the above table is that the majority of units have far lower rents than in 1759. Only three show an increase in rental, while thirteen of the twenty-four show a decrease of 20 per cent or more, with three of those over 70 per cent.

Consolidation of farms and a dramatic reduction in the number of multiple tenancies would account for the decrease in the rents of many holdings. Both Glentennet and Arsallary are listed as having seven units each in 1759 and rents of £229 and £192 respectively. By 1875, Glentennet has been reduced to one unit with a rent of £63.10, and Arsallary to two units whose rents of £13 and £11 suggests that they are of roughly similar size. The fact that the farms of Glentennet and Arsallary are still going by the same names is evidence that they were not split into smaller, different units. The one exception is Migvie, which was divided into four parts in 1759, but is listed as East and West Migvie by 1875, consisting of two and three units respectively paying separate rents. The area no longer supports a 'Mains' farm. Mains of Invermark, once the major farm, is not included on the 1875 Rental, presumably having been broken up when the Forest of Mark was created.

Payment of Arsallery rents to Dalhousie estate paid in advance for 1863. 1862. Glenesk Museum.

Two units are described as 'pendicles', at Haugh and Auchintoul. 'Pendicle' is the term given to a small piece of ground which forms part of a larger farm and is frequently let to a sub-tenant. In the case of David Stewart, he would have been granted a nineteen-year lease for his Haugh pendicle directly from the estate. Of the 39 holdings in the 1875 Rental, nine are held on nineteen-year leases. These nine are mainly the larger farms with half-yearly rents of over £35, as one would expect, although Mid Upper Cairncross at £28.10/- and Buskhead at £7.10/- are also included. The nineteen-year leases start either on Whitsunday or Martinmas and run out on the same festival day in the appropriate year. The remaining tenancies are held 'at will', which simply means that the tenants were liable to be dispossessed without notice, thereby making it easier for the estate to implement change.

Concern among Glenesk residents regarding the suppression of small farms was brought into the public domain by a letter published in the *People's Journal* on 13 July 1867. The letter is a reply to statements made by the Earl of Dalhousie in the House of Lords, in which he castigated the larger class of farmers in Scotland for wishing to dispose of their smaller tenants. The Earl is accused of hypocrisy as '… no one in this county, and for a good distance out of it, has put down more small industrious tenants than he (Earl of Dalhousie) has done himself'. The author of the letter, who signed it C.F., then supplies a list of farms suppressed or added to others by the Earl on his Edzell and Glenesk estate, viz:

1. Farm of Glenlee, now deer forest.
2. Inchgrundel, Kirkton and Glenmark, also deer forest.

3. Muirton and Crosstile – houses thrown down.
4. Broomknowe, houses thrown down and families removed.
5. Stylemouth and Westbank added to Glack.
5. Badabae, a small farm, now to Garthead.
6. Middleford and Easterton to Glentennet.
7. Townhead to Midtown.
8. Dalhestnie and Dalscamphie to Haughead.
9. Burnside to Dalforth.
10. Latch and Rannach to Holmhead.
11. Blackhills to Shank.
12. Shanna and Cornescorn added to Dalbog.
13. Easter Auchintoul to Wester Auchintoul.
14. Bothybrae to Arsillery.
15. Stoneyhill added to Garthead.
16. Gleneffock added to Baillies.
17. Craigshinie to Haughead.
18. Woolmill to Inveriscandy.

The letter also states that nine pendicles have been suppressed in Edzell parish, and a great number of houses have been thrown down in Lochlee parish and the families removed from the Glen. Further, 'the parish school has been removed three miles lower down the Glen, as the whole population above the old site had been removed, except gamekeepers and their families'.

Despite the author appearing to have the advantage of local knowledge, the above list may, however, contain some discrepancies. It is cited that Gleneffock was added to Baillies, yet in the Lochlee Rentals of 1875, both of these farms are listed as separate holdings, paying rents of £170 and £70 respectively. Similarly, Westbank, along with Stylemouth, is reported as having been added to Glack, yet the former also appears as a separate holding in 1875. One can only surmise that Westbank was the larger farm and so it was decided to keep that name for the new amalgamated units. The removal of the parish school refers to that building being moved to Tarfside in 1863. The estate would have had no option but to move the school further down the Glen. After the creation of the Forest of Mark, resulting in the loss of farms, there would have been no children in that upper part of Lochlee parish as families would have been removed to relocate either elsewhere in the Glen or furth of it. Moving the school further down the Glen meant that it was closer to those pupils who previously had to walk a few miles to Lochlee.

The Earl of Dalhousie vehemently denied the accusations made against him. The fact remains, however, that farms and land did make way for deer forests.

TESTAMENTS AND ROUP ROLLS

As with the previous century, testaments and roup rolls provide a good deal of supplementary information. Glenesk has always had an emphasis on stock grazing. Since the second part of the eighteenth century, sheep farming has come to dominate. Hardy breeds, especially the Blackface, are pastured on the mountain grazings. Ewe lambs wintered in the lower grounds or lowlands, return to the higher areas in April and May. This emphasis on stock grazing can be seen by examining roup rolls and inventories.

In a roup roll of a Displenish sale at Garthead, Lochlee, 10 May 1876, there were 119 ewes and 110 lambs; 76 two-year old wedders; 84 wedder hoggs, 52 ewe hoggs and three tups. In most cases the individual prices are given, though they varied according to kind and quality:

10 Ewes & 10 Lambs	@ £1.17. 6	20 2yr old Wedders	@ £1.10
26 " & 30 "	@ £1.10. 6	36 " " "	@ £1.11
10 " & 10 "	@ £1.10.	20 " " "	@ £1. 1. 6
10 " & 10 "	@ £1. 9. 6	20 Wedder Hoggs	@ £1. 2. 6
20 " & 20 "	@ £1. 8. 0	20 " "	@ £1. 2. 0
10 " & 10 "	@ £1. 7. 6	20 " "	@ £1. 1. 0
10 " & 10 "	@ £1. 7. 0	4 " "	@ 8/6
10 " & 10 "	@ £1. 6. 6	20 Ewe Hoggs	@ £1. 9. 6
13 Ewes	@ £1. 6. 6	20 " "	@ £1. 6. 6
1 Tup	@ £1.14. 6	12 " "	@ £1. 0. 0
1 Tup	@ £1. 6. 0		
1 Tup	@ £1. 4. 0		

As with the sheep, cattle were also differentiated. Three cows were sold at £16.5/-, £14.5/- and £15.5/- respectively. Two stirks were sold for a combined price of £21.10/-, while another went for £8.2.6. Two calves were purchased for £10.10/-, while two others were sold at £2.12.6 and £1 respectively. The bull was sold for £12.12.6, while the most valuable of the livestock was the horse, purchased for £35, and which provided the draught power.

The majority of these prices compare favourably with those listed in an Inventory and Appraisement of Farm Stock Crop which belonged to David Innes of Burnside and was made up in 1865. Roup rolls do not give an accurate indication of market prices because the stock was purchased at the lowest price possible, or the lowest price that people thought they could get away with. Nevertheless, they do show some form of stability in prices.

The agricultural depression in the last quarter of the nineteenth century saw a drastic fall in the price of both cereals and wool, which would have undermined the economy of the Glen to a certain extent, dependent as it was on both these products. Although the effects of recession were felt in Glenesk, evidence from roup rolls and inventories indicates that it does not seem to have had a disastrous effect on everyone in the Glen. The market prices recorded in the Buskhead farm cash book, kept by Archibald Stewart from October 1885 until November 1898, support this evidence.[3] By studying the 1865 Inventory of David Innes, the roup roll at Garthhead 1876 and the Buskhead Farm cash book, it can be seen that although there were serious fluctuations in livestock prices, they steadily picked up again. Analysis of these sources show that sheep provided most money. The table below charts the price of sheep in the second half of the nineteenth century, with the assumption that the highest price represents the best quality stock:

Year	Wedder Lambs	Ewes	Wedder Hoggs	Ewe Hoggs	Tups
1865		16/- each		£1.0.0 each	
1876		£1.6.6 each	£1.02.06 each	£1.09.06 each	£1.14.6each
1886	13/3 each				
1887	10/3 each				
1888	11/9 each	£1.03/- each			
1890	14/6 each	£1.06/- each			
1893	9/9 each	18/9 each	£1.06/- each		
1895	15/6 each	19/6 each			
1897		£1.04.3 each		£1.0.0 each	
1898		£1.05/- each			

The recession would have presented a dilemma for many farmers in that they could not plan too far ahead, such was its unpredictability, though planning may not have been part of their mental make-up then. The sample of figures above reflects the turbulent nature of the depression and its effect on prices in the last fifteen years of the nineteenth century. 1893 was a particularly bad year for wedder lambs, and ewes were at their lowest price since 1865. However, by 1895, the selling price of wedder lambs had risen to 15/6, the highest for almost a decade. Crisis periods for ewes were 1893 and 1895, but they were picking up again within two years.

In contrast, wool and corn, by which is meant oats, showed a sharper fall in price. Archibald Stewart sold wool at $5^{1}/_{2}$d per pound in 1888, and by 1891 this peaked at 6d per pound. It then declined steadily to $5^{1}/_{4}$d in 1895 and a low of five and one-eighth pence per pound by 1897. Oats were sold at 18/- per quarter in 1888, dropping to 17/6 the following year. The price of corn reached a high point of £1.2/- per quarter in 1891 but fell to 19/- in 1893 and 16/6 by 1895. Clearly, cereal prices fell at a more alarming rate than wool and sheep prices, dropping by approximately 25 per cent between 1891 and 1895. However, the relative stability of sheep prices may have helped to off-set the worst effects of recession, although 1893 does seem to have been a very poor year all-round.

[3] A. Fenton, ed. *At Brechin With Stirks*, Canongate Academic, Edinburgh, 1994.

Oats were the most widely grown crop, valued at £5 per acre in 1865, followed by barley, potatoes and turnips. By the latter half of the nineteenth century, the average amount of arable land on a Glenesk farm amounted to about 45 acres, about three times what it had been in the early part of the century according to the inventories. The 'Seven Year Shift' was adhered to in Glenesk as a rule, following the introduction of root crops, ley, oats, awal (second crop of oats), potatoes and/or turnips, clean ground (oats and grass seed grown), hay and grass. The flocks of sheep averaged 220 to 250, although Burnside in 1865 had 311 sheep, while Garthhead in 1876 had 434. Very few places in the Glen now kept sizable cattle herds, there being seventeen beasts at Burnside in 1865 and only eight at Garthhead in 1876.

The main difference between Inventories and Roup Rolls is that the former list the value of the goods as they were appraised, while the latter list the purchase price which appears to be invariably lower than the appraisal value. As mentioned in chapter five, roup rolls also tend to cover a wider range, while inventories concentrate on the more valuable items. These sources also contain details about tools, equipment and personal possessions.

The importance of stock is reflected in the lay-out of inventories. In the 1865 Inventory and Appraisement of Farm Stock Crop and other effects, which belonged to the late David Innes, Burnside, Lochlee, livestock is listed first, followed by crops, implements and, lastly, domestic items and other worldly goods. The farm equipment consisted of such items as barn fanners (winnowing machines), three riddles, three graips, a drill harrow and an iron plough.

Furniture included three fir tables, seven chairs, a plate rack which housed the dinner ware, three bound (built-in) beds and presses, a tea kettle, and five pots and boiler. The 'South Room' had a 'clouty carpet', which was made out of old clothes or rags stitched together on a base. The bedding included four chaff mattresses, which were filled with chaff from the mill. The chaff bolsters were placed under the head with feather pillows on top. Fireside equipment is specified as a grate and fire irons. The most expensive piece of furniture was an eight-day clock valued at £2. Personal possessions, i.e. the deceased's body clothes (worn) and an old silver watch, are the last items on the inventory, perhaps suggesting how little value was placed on such material goods.

The roup roll of William Findlay of Whitestone in 1861 and the inventory of David Innes, Burnside in 1865 are evenly divided between farm equipment and domestic items. In contrast, the roup roll at Garthead in 1876 deals mainly with livestock and farm implements, while the roup roll of the late John Bowman's effects in 1863 contains chiefly domestic goods. The mention of a trout creel and a gun suggests that John Bowman indulged in fishing and hunting.

No. 333—1.

INLAND REVENUE.

— LICENCE.—FOR ONE HORSE OR MULE £0 10s. 6d.
32 & 33 Vict., cap. 14.

No. *608* *Dundee* Collection.

Brechin Div. or Ride.

Mr David Innes

of *Arsallan* in the Parish

of *Lochlee* in the County of *Forfar*
is hereby authorized to keep ONE HORSE or MULE from the day
of the date hereof until the 31st day of December next following;
he having paid the sum of TEN SHILLINGS and SIXPENCE for
this Licence.

Dated at *Brechin* this *Thirtyfirst*
day of *January* 1879.

Granted by

NOTICE.

If the HORSE or MULE be kept after the 31st December in any year, a fresh Declaration must be
filled up and delivered, and a new Licence obtained before the expiration of the month of January
following.

Licence allowing David Innes to keep one mule or horse for one year. 1879. Glenesk Museum.

Apart from the 1876 roup roll, the nineteenth-century roup rolls differ
from those of the eighteenth century in that many more domestic items are
contained in them. This may be telling us something about the affluence of
nineteenth-century farmers/tenants compared with their eighteenth-century
counterparts. The nineteenth-century inventories do not give any information
on the finances of the deceased, mainly because people were dealing through
banks by this time. One can also recognise change in agricultural methods
and land use as the eighteenth-century roup rolls see many 'rigs' of land and
crops being sold off, whereas the 1865 inventory of David Innes mentions
land and crops being sold off by the acre rather than by the rig.

It is still possible to find traces of the medieval to early modern system of agriculture, including 'run rigs'. They can be clearly seen on the Drum, parts of Gleneffock, the Baillies, on the hills above Buskhead and Turnabrane after a slight fall of snow, on the Skairs, in Berryhill, Bulg, Craig of Dalhestnie and on Lady Jane above Cornescorn. Where there has been recent cultivation, only the consumption dykes remain, as on Craig Cane, Craig Soales, Hillock and the Rowan. The older rigs are more irregular than the later. Those on the Craig of Dalhestnie are 'rowed rigs', the ground having been levelled up along the contours by rolling stones into position, the whole resembling an enormous staircase.

Generally, there were several tenants on a farm, and in early feudal times the land was held in rotation, each tenant thus having his chance of the good and bad land, the sunny and the backset. Later, each tenant's share became fixed. This stage took different forms. The various tenants who supplied the full team of oxen may have had their land lying along a waterside, with houses a distance apart, as in the Whigginton area, or they might have been living in a community in the centre of their field system, as in Berryhill at the back of Keenie. They could also have been clustered at the foot of the arable ground as at Fauldhead, now on Gleneffock.

The infield was beside the township and was well manured. The last place to 'ca' oot muck fail' (peat manure) in the parish of Lochlee was Stylemouth. The infield was cultivated year in, year out, apart from the ley which had a chance of

A late nineteenth-century scene which may be the Hillock. The haystacks are interesting because they either have a tuft on the crown, known as a 'peerie', or a straw cross. A sign of change is the wooden fencing replacing the stone dyke in the lower left of the photograph. C4266.

resting. The outfield, a larger and less cultivated area, was beyond it. There is a tradition that on the Rowan, high fields were burned and the ashes brought to the lower ground. Although there was little cultivation on the outfield compared with the infield, there was probably a crop every four years or thereabout on part of it. It was convenient for grazing cattle. Beyond the outfield was the hill dyke, still often visible in snow, and beyond that was the extensive common hill, where many fat wethers were reared, a valuable source of living. Groups of tenants had shared a common hill, and this custom continued well into the nineteenth century. Before the mid-nineteenth century, Craig Soales was common to five tenants, and similarly Buskhead, Whigginton and Kirn had a common grazing, as did Keenie, Skelly, Corhairncross and Turnabrane.

Other manifestations of change include the technologies used in the eighteenth and nineteenth centuries. From medieval times until 1800 the hook (heuk) was chiefly used for shearing grain crops, and sometimes also for mowing grass. It was always used by the threavers, the name given to travelling harvesters from the north. The scythe, on the other hand, was from the sixteenth century and earlier used for mowing grass. It became popular in the nineteenth century as a harvesting tool, its speed counteracting a shortage of manpower. Women cut the corn with the heuk, while men tied it in sheaves and stooked it. On the other hand, men scythed while women tied and gathered.

David Lowden using a scythe and cradle. Cradles were not commonly used. His daughter, Nellie, is 'tying the stooks'. Pre-1914. C9349.

The first experiments with reaping machinery go back to 1805, but it was long before a good one was on the market.[4] Only by the end of the nineteenth century did reapers become popular on small family farms. At that time, sitting alongside each other were the three holdings of Whigginton, Buskhead and Turnabrane. At Whigginton the Cattanachs used the heuk. At Buskhead, the Stewarts used the scythe, because it made a better job than the reaper, while at Turnabrane the Skenes had a reaper. When Charles Skene brought it home, one of his elderly aunts, living in a nearby house, said, 'Fat are ye daein' wi' a nesty new-fangled thing like that?'.

Charles Skene's wife, Mary Agnes Birse who was born in 1851, remembered the threavers, twenty or thirty of them, coming across the hill, singing. This may have been the song:

Bonnie lassie, will ye gang
Tae shair wi' me the haill day lang?
Love will cheer us as we gang
Tae jine the band o' shairers.

In the foreground are stooks of oats, each of eight sheaves. In the background is Invermark Castle before the ivy was removed in 1898. Note the use of wire fencing just in front of the old Invermark school. 1890s. Glenesk Museum.

[4] A. Fenton. *Scottish Country Life*, Tuckwell Press, East Linton, revised edn, 1977, 66ff (1976).

Another sign that times were changing was the exodus of tradesmen from the Glen. The countryside still had tradesmen, and there were still small and large holdings from three acres upwards. Even as late as the 1850s there were townships, huddles of tradesmen and tenants of land partly worked in common. There is a good example at Dalforth, between Waggles and Colmeallie in the parish of Edzell. According to the 1851 Census, 33 people lived there. John Christison was a farmer of twenty-four acres arable, employing three labourers, with hill pasture for 130 sheep. He, his wife, two sons, a heather besom maker and his wife, comprised the household. Isabella Middleton, farmer, had twenty acres arable and hill pasture for 130 sheep. Two of her three sons were employed elsewhere as agricultural workers. David Louden, master shoemaker, employed three men and one apprentice. He, his wife and growing family, along with his employees, lived in the same house.

Two other houses were occupied by the Christisons. One was occupied by three elderly sisters, retired house servants, and, across the burn, another John Christison, a stone dyker, lived in the other with his wife and three young children. From a collection in the Museum archives there is evidence of a smiddy having been at Dalforth. There is also evidence that in 1846/7 a threshing mill was installed by Peter Brown of the Forest of Birse (Finzean).

Joint tenancy of this kind must have involved work in common, but of course it has never entirely disappeared from the Glen. The best evidence we have of the working lives of nineteenth-century agricultural workers in Glenesk is to be found in two day labourers' day books which have survived from that time.

TWO DAY LABOURERS DAY BOOKS

These two sources are remarkable because both were written by day labourers in the same relatively isolated part of Scotland. Diaries and account books kept by day labourers are in any case rare; but to find two from one place, for the periods 1826–56, and 1866–73, is quite exceptional. It must say something about the educational level in the country districts of Scotland at this mid-nineteenth century period.

Although there is no through road, Glenesk is no backwater. Before the building of turnpike roads that took people up the coast to the East, the valley was an important shortcut to the north-east shoulder of Scotland. In addition, there was from time to time an influx of outside visitors, especially after the sport of grouse shooting developed, which helped to keep the local folk aware of the wider world. Service on the estate might also have had an effect on educational levels. At any rate, both day labourers could wield pens and put the details of their daily work on paper.

THE WRITERS

The writers were James Stewart and Robert Middleton. James Stewart lived at Burnfoot on the farm of the Baillies. He was born in 1800 at Alyth in Perthshire to the South, and his wife, Mary Calder, at Birse in Aberdeenshire to the north. Neither was a native of Glenesk, and James presumably had his school education before he moved there. His wife was eight years younger. Her widowed mother, Isobel Stewart, born in Kincardine O'Neil, had been a midwife, and now lived with them. James and Mary had a son, John, born in Burnfoot, through whose descendants the day book eventually returned to Glenesk Museum.

James Stewart was 26 years old when his day book began. He lived in one of a group of four houses at Burnfoot, having it rent free from the farmer, David Inglis, in exchange for a certain number of days of bondage work each year. These days regularly covered the entire harvest period. They also included four days' digging potatoes in October 1846, the hoeing of potatoes and turnips for single days in July 1850 and 1851, and '1 Day Spreading dung to David Inglis' in April 1851.

Robert Middleton was the son of John Middleton, farmer at Middleford. For a time he worked as a shepherd, living at his father's holding (1851 Census), and shepherding at the Mill of Aucheen in 1855. By 1866 he, like his elder brother John, had become a day labourer, living at Burnfoot, as James Stewart had done. He described himself as being in bondage to the Baillies: in June 1869, he spent 20 days working in the peat moss, of which eight days were described as 'Pet Moss Bondage Baillies', and in July, he spent '3 days turnip howing, Boundge'.

These nineteenth-century day labourers were reflecting in this practice of bondage the last remnants of a feudal system of dues to a superior. However, it was no longer the medieval range of services – including cutting and carrying peats, shearing cereal crops, carrying manure – due from a tenant to a proprietor but had simply become services due from a farm worker to a farmer in lieu of rent. The system fitted easily into a day labourer's varied world; but for farmers who had to set their own needs aside whilst tending to those of the proprietor, it was more difficult, and therefore more likely to be commuted for money payments.

JAMES STEWART'S DAY BOOK

In 1826, James Stewart listed hours worked for named individuals, along with the payment received. From 1827, he named the tasks undertaken. After 1832, he gave specific timings also and continued this system till the day book ended in 1856. The changes perhaps suggest a growing skill in book-keeping and the fuller part, 1832–56, permits an examination of Stewart's annual personal rhythm as well as of the rhythm of his work for others. There are, however, some puzzles. It is not clear, for example, why the entries often do not start in January, but in February or even May or June, and sometimes run up to November only. Was he simply neglecting his book-keeping?

Clearance and Improvement

The account of the kind of work undertaken, and for whom, tells a good deal about what was happening in the second quarter of the nineteenth century and about the year's rhythm of activities. Fresh ground was still being broken in for farming by the laborious process of deep digging with spades, or trenching. Stewart did a good deal of trenching for a small number of farmers; in addition he carried out drainage and fencing work, and the blasting of earth-fast stones. These activities all point to ongoing clearance and improvement. Added to this was the breaking of limestone to be burned in the local stone-built limekilns, for fertilising the ground. Such work was all part of the dynamics of continuing nineteenth-century farming improvement.

Clients and Community Service

Some of his other major tasks, however, were not carried out on behalf of the bigger farmers, but rather of a whole range of individuals amongst whom women's names are not infrequent. They also included tradesmen like James Esplin the blacksmith. A five year sample gives the following figures:

Tasks, Time and Numbers Worked for

Mossing (Peat cutting)	1827	1828	1829	1830	1831
Days worked	17	21	$15^1/_2$	$17^1/_2$	$17^1/_2$
No. of people served	11	7	5	10	7

Grass Cutting					
Days worked	21	$20^1/_4$	15	$22^1/_2$	$11^1/_2$
No. of people served	10	12	7	10	8

The grass or hay was, of course, being cut as fodder for cattle, presumably milk cows, in the byres.

Some other tasks were also in part of a 'community service' nature and in part undertaken for the bigger farmers. The former were short term, 1–4 days, for a number of people; the latter long term, 6 month blocks, for a small number of individuals. They included the cutting of turf and divots, and threshing with the flail. In such ways the work of a day labourer touched on all levels of the rural population. It also touched on the gentry levels, for James Stewart regularly acted as gillie for General Balfour and Sir David Moncrieff, when they came to the Glenesk hills to indulge in the developing sport of grouse-shooting.

Levels of Payment

The tasks undertaken had their own status levels, as indicated by the rates of payment. In the 1820s, spring, autumn and winter tasks such as mossing, cutting turf, thatching buildings, threshing, cutting sticks, breaking lime-stone, pulling heather, turning dung, etc, fetched one shilling to one shilling and three pence a day. The cutting of grass was consistently higher at one shilling and sixpence to two shillings and sixpence. Best paid of all was acting as gillie for wealthy visitors at from three shillings to five shillings a day.

It is hard to assess Stewart's annual income, because not every year is com-plete. A base-line of £10 per annum can be set up for 1837, when he seems to have engaged as a farm servant with Thomas Jolly (possibly at Mill of Aucheen), at the May and November terms at £5 a term. But apart from this, sample years give the following figures:

Samples of Annual Income

Year	Income	Days Worked	Percentage of Year
1832	£16. 6. 0$^1/_2$	105$^1/_4$	28.8%
1842	£10. 8. 6	279 2/3	76.6%
1852	£12. 3. 7$^1/_2$	306$^1/_4$	83.9%

He therefore appears to have been marginally, and at best a good deal, bet-ter off as a day labourer than as a full-time farm servant.

These figures remained remarkably stable for the period of the Day Book, though by the 1850s, slight increases begin to be identifiable, i.e. the one shilling and three pence of the 1820s was now as often as not one shilling and sixpence to two shillings. This may be taken to indicate a modest rise in living standards by the mid-nineteenth century.

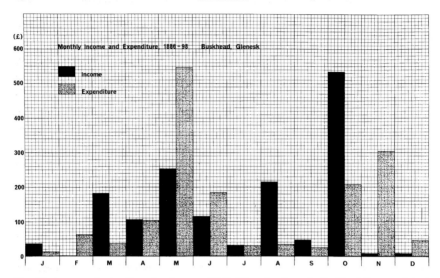

Monthly income and expenditure for the years 1886–98, taken from the Buskhead Farm cash book.
C19182.

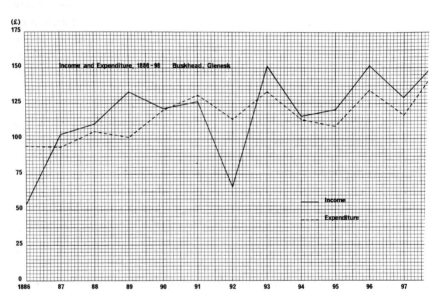

Annual income and expenditure for the years 1886–98, taken from the Buskhead Farm cash book.
C19183.

The annual round of work for James Stewart did not vary greatly. To some extent it reflected the farming year, and to some extent also the ad hoc needs of individuals for house repairs and the like. The major regular annual fixture was the bondage work that took up the whole of the harvest period, i.e. about six weeks' work that could range in date from the third week of August to the beginning of November, depending on the weather conditions.

Analysis of what Stewart did for himself rather than for others is revealing. Many days were spent at home because of high winds, rain, frost and snow. He repaired his own house and outhouses, thatching the roofs with straw or with heather, which had to be pulled, and making straw ropes to tie down the thatch using a system of vertical and horizontal roping that made a pattern of rectangles on the roof. Fuel had to be got for the fire; the cutting of peat (mossing), setting the peats up to dry, taking them home, stacking and thatching them, took seven to nine full days, from June onwards, each year.

He had a garden that he dug in February, and he grew potatoes to help to feed the family. These were not only grown at home, but also in parts of fields on the nearby farms of Buskhead and Dalhastnie. It is not known if he paid for the use of such potato ground, but he may have provided services in exchange. The planting, hoeing and lifting of potatoes, followed by pitting near his house, took about four to six days a year. He killed a swine for family use on 20 December 1843.

Another source of food and certainly of income was honey. He spent up to eight days a year making straw bee-skeps, and up to three days a year draining honey. He also seems to have had wooden hives. This argues for a reasonable scale of production and may have been a substantial element in the diversification of sources of income that is the mark of a day labourer in such rural areas.

The dressing of lint took up three days in 1842, no doubt to provide household linen. On one occasion (1844) he went to Mains of Fasque near Kirriemuir for wool, presumably to be spun and knitted into garments by his wife. Two or three days each year were spent on mending shoes.

Personal Life

Very little is said of himself and of his family directly. He attended local farm sales (which often followed funerals), fairs, funerals and marriages. He had occasional days outside the Glen, at the towns of Brechin, Aberdeen and Kirriemuir, and on one occasion he sought and got work on the railway in the Kirriemuir area, between 12 May and 5 June 1847. Such extended trips to a maximum distance of less than 100 miles were rare, however, and James Stewart remained very much the creature of a localised environment.

He suffered sometimes from illness, mostly resulting from the heavy work to which he was habituated. Between 1843 and 1856, he was off for 98 days through illness. The reasons were 'unwell', 'sore back', 'sore ribs', 'under medicine', 'broken ribs' (not literally, but possibly some kind of skin eruption over his ribs), 'strained hand', 'bealing (festering) knee', 'sore side', 'bruised foot', 'sore breast'. Though this averages seven days off a year, the actual numbers ranged from one to sixteen days, with a decidedly regular increase as the Day Book moved towards 1856 and James Stewart approached his 56th year.

For entertainment, he had his rare outings to local towns and days at local events. Sunday was never a day of work, and there is no reference to this day in the Day Book. The major annual Church event was in July. In 1842, for example, Fast Day fell on Thursday 14 July, Preparation on Saturday 16 July, Communion next day, then Thanksgiving on Monday 18 July. Communion took place once a year. There were other Fast Days, e.g. on 1 December 1842. On these days no work was undertaken. It is not known, however, if he was a regular churchgoer.

The only other regular festivals to which attention was paid were Christmas and the New Year, but this was still Old Style:

1843,   5 Jan   2 Days unimployed being Christenmas
        12 Jan   1 Day unimployed New years day

Education and Work Ethic

James Stewart's handwriting is accomplished. He was taught well. Inside the front cover of his Day Book is 'A Map of the Tropical Regions of the Globe for illustrating the Account of the General Trade Winds and Monsoons', engraved for the journal, *The Bee*. In it, Australia is still described as New Holland. Also at the beginning is a page of multiplication tables in the style of Pythagoras, in his own hand. These are pointers to his educational background.

His life was one of hard work, though he had some freedom to choose to work or not, even if the weather sometimes chose for him, except for the bondage work of harvest. Work was his ethic; to be unemployed or unable to work through illness was more than loss of income. It was also against his creed. And perhaps as part of his character, as it was of most men of his time, he has little or nothing to say of his wife Mary, nor of his four children, Elizabeth, William, Mary and John, nor of Jean Brown, the fifteen-year-old farm servant girl who boarded with the family in 1841.

In spite of the signs of increasing physical troubles, he passed 71, for at that age the Census Returns show him to be still living in one of the houses at Burnfoot, though now alone. A source of 1870 shows that he was by then requiring help to get his peats home.

Robert Middleton's Day Book

Robert Middleton's Day Book moves into the second half of the nineteenth century. There are many parallels to that of James Stewart. The entries are still one-liners, though the pages of the Day Book are divided up the middle to allow comments on the weather on the right hand side. Such deliberate and regular comment on the weather appears to reflect more of the viewpoint of a farmer than of a day labourer. Payment for the rent of Burnfoot was still covered by bondage work. Improvement of the surrounding farms proceeded as before, with trenching, the blasting of stones, breaking of limestone, surface draining, the building of stone dykes and the erecting of wire fences to enclose the fields. The length of the working day was ten hours, reducing to nine hours or less in the dark days of winter.

The pattern of work for others was very similar to that done by James Stewart, though it was much more oriented towards the bigger farms than towards other members of the community. Middleton never seems to have acted as gillie to the gentry, though he enjoyed his own kind of sport – an occasional day's fishing (1 October 1868), and hare hunting on the hill of Craig Soales (1 and 3 February 1869).

Personal Life

He took part in the Church routine in August of Sacramental Fast on the Thursday before Communion Sunday. Sundays are regularly mentioned, but very often he was 'At Home Keeping house', no doubt whilst his wife was at Church. He has few comments on his own health except for a headache once (1 July 1868) and in May–June 1869 he had a 'Sor(e) hand not able to work', which took over a week to heal. He mentions family illness when it occurred. He made trips to Luthermuir, where his wife's grandmother lived, to the market at Edzell, and to the towns of Forfar, Brechin and Kirriemuir, but nothing further.

Outside Harvest Work

He did not do bondage harvest work to David Inglis at the Baillies, but from 1866 to 1869 he regularly went down the Glen to the Lowlands near the town of Laurencekirk, where he took a harvest at Waulk Mill of Halkerton. The harvest dates reflect the variability of the Scottish weather:

1866	1–28 Sept	1868	5 Aug–3 Sept
1867	16 Sept–19 Oct	1869	24 Aug–25 Sept

It was on one of these expeditions (1868) that he let his thoughts be seen in a way not entirely common in such sources:

Saturday 29 (August) fine calm lead all the corn in all 36 good stack. We had very Ackward hands for thaching the stacks – James Anges and self did therrty of them some of them not very well don Strong brezies of wind annowed us very much. The forman William Matches a strong not so strong either as a blustring blockhead a bad stackyard man the Thaching went fa(i)rly up his back as the saying is when they cant do the work in fack (fact) he was no hand at any thing I saw hime begin to …

Such bursts of feeling, which again seem to reflect a farmer's rather than a day labourer's attitudes, appear in the Day Book only for the harvest period, however.

Education and Work Ethic

Another difference is that scattered through Robert Middleton's Day Book, normally on the right side of his divided pages, there are extracts evidently taken from books and papers he had been reading. These include an Acrostic on Garibaldi, recipes for removing grease spots and oil paint, wise saws and precepts, cooking instructions for fresh vegetables, poems, a reference to a paper on the Game Laws read before the Gaelic Society of London, and a Latin poem. As a rule an attempt is made to write these entries in a more careful hand, almost, it would seem, as a writing exercise. Taken together, a good educational level is indicated.

This does not mean that Robert Middleton did not share James Stewart's attitudes to work. The work ethic was just as strong in both men. To be at home doing little or nothing was clearly anathema to Middleton also: 7 January 1869, 'At hom A little indisposed'; 21 January 1869, 'At Home Still dont know what to do'. There may have been a scarcity of work, allied with poor weather, in December 1868 and January 1869, because he was at home a great deal during these two months. That is perhaps a main reason why, on 1 February 1870, he went into the Earl of Dalhousie's service to run the sheep farm of West Bank, to which he moved from Burnfoot on 11 March. The physical style of the Day Book entries changed from this time. Instead of a central page division, entries now ran right across the page and there are no more asides. The Day Book became, in effect, the diary of a sheep farmer.

SOCIAL STRATIFICATION

A comparison of the two Day Books (excluding Robert Middleton's diary entries from 1870–3) and of the two individuals involved, even with the selection of material presented, shows that the two represent different strata within a fairly limited social spread. The Day Books, in fact, emphasise the need for deeper research into such clear, but not always readily observable, social variations. It is the interpretation of such stratifications, which are not fixed but can flow into and out of each other according to age and circumstances, that constitutes the main importance of such study.

END OF THE CENTURY

An account book kept by Peter Brown, of the Finzean Bucket Mill near Banchory, includes entries for threshing mills erected by him in Glenesk. They were put in for various farmers in Lochlee: Mr Lindsay, Dalbrack, in July 1876; Joseph Dunbar, Kirn, in 1883; James Innes, Burnside, in 1877; Burnett Gibb, Glentennet, in 1878.

In 1891, he erected the mill for Archibald Stewart at Buskhead. He is said to have been the only millwright who worked in Glenesk. He preferred water power where he could get it, and horsepower where there was none. Peter Brown's grandson said of him in 1965 that he went to the Glen every summer for a number of years, putting in mills. He left his foreman joiner in charge at the Bucket Mill, where he employed two joiners and two apprentices. He is known to have stayed at Glentennet during the three summers of 1883–5.

In spite of Jim Stewart's idea that Peter Brown was the only millwright in Glenesk, Peter was nevertheless only one in a series. Though no threshing mills were to be seen in the 1770s, by 1792 there were three in the parish of Lethnot, each with a set of fanners. There were few farms that did not have a mill in the barn.

Meal mills in and around Glenesk were surprisingly numerous, which no doubt indicates their relatively small size and also the need for reasonably limited areas to be properly served, in the days before motors made it easy to move loads for long distances. Mill sites for the parishes of Lochlee and Edzell, are:

1. Mill of Inchgrundle
2. Mill of Auchronie
3. Mill of Milton
4. Mill of Cairncross (site unknown: marked in Roy's map, possibly in wrong position)
5. Mill of Aucheen
6. Mill of Keenie
7. Mill of Auchmull
8. Mill of Dalbog
9. Waulkmill of Dalbog
10. Mill of Inveriscandye

These mills ground mainly oatmeal, with barley also being mentioned for the mill of Aucheen. Two accounts exist for the Mill of Aucheen. They were from the miller, David Caithness, to James Duke of Migvie. One for 1907–8 lists two bags of dust (particles of meal and husk) bought in December and March (3/6 each), $1^1/_2$ quarters of corn dried and bruised (1/6), 1 boll of meal (16/-) and four quarters corn cut (1/-), and two quarters seed corn. Dates range from December 1907 to May 1908, indicating the custom of half-yearly payments. The second account is for June to August 1908, and is for two bolls of meal (17/- each), four cwt cut barley (4/- each), three bags of dust (3/- each). It was paid on 16 December 1908. The system of half-yearly payments to the miller, blacksmith, joiner and to servants was the order of the day, and runs through the Buskhead Farm Cash Book (1885–95) also.

The pattern of work on a Glen farm in the nineteenth century does not differ too much from that of the end of eighteenth century. Mr W.A. Stewart, born at Buskhead in 1902, provided Greta Michie with the daily and seasonal routines on a Glen farm at the end of the nineteenth century. It is likely that he gleaned this information from his parents and older neighbours, and we cannot discount the possibility that routines were not so different by the time he reached adulthood around the time of World War I.

Daily Routine

Rise at from 5 to 6 a.m.
The men feed the horses, while the women go to the byre.
Breakfast before 7 a.m., then the men go out to work. This goes on until 11 a.m.
Dinner at 11.15 a.m.
Start again at 1 p.m.
Go on until 5.30 to 6 p.m., with mid-yokin' at 3 p.m. during harvest etc.
The horses are fed before the men and fed again between 8 and 9 p.m. and bedded down for the night.

Seasonal Routine

January – February	Ploughing. Get the dung out.
March	Ploughing. Started to sow.
April	Finishing sowing. Lambing.
May	Got in potatoes and turnips. Lambing.
June	Odd jobs. Cutting peat. Cutting hay late in month.
July	Getting in the hay. Thinning the turnips.
August	Harvest. Men who could be spared might go to the hill to the shooting. Sheep sales.
September	Sales of stirks.
October	Potatoes towards the middle of the month. Grubbing stubble. Sometimes the harvest continued into November or later.
November	Much the same, and got in turnips.
December	Stubble ploughing.

These tasks were, of course, all weather dependent. The one major difference in eighteenth- and nineteenth-century farm routines was the shooting.
The fact that men could be spared to go to the shooting in August is further
evidence that the Glen was entering a new economic pattern in the nineteenth
century.

The increase in the size of farms and the loss of country craftsmen had been
largely economic, for the state of agriculture in the second half of the nineteenth century does not seem to have been nearly so prosperous as it was in the
first half, when it was still benefiting tremendously from the stimulus of the
Improving Movement.

There was still a great deal of common hill. For example, common ground
was shared between Buskhead, Turnabrane and Corhairncross, and a man named
Robbie Duncan was shepherd. He went so long to each place, according to the
number of sheep. Gradually, marches became fairly clearly defined, and the
common ground was lost. In the second half of the century, the average place
had 250 ewes, one pair of horses, several cows, a pig or pigs. The 'nesty new-
fangled' machinery was coming in. Probably the average amount of arable
land varied from 30 to 60 acres, at least twice what it had been in the early
part of the century, according to the inventories.

There was no one single cause for the exodus of people from Glenesk. Entering into a radically different economic pattern resulted in changes in land use
which saw many farms suppressed or thrown down. Machinery replaced manpower on the farms. Added to this was an agricultural recession in the last
quarter of the nineteenth century. Burning local lime became uneconomic.
Foreign markets were against the local farmers, especially in wool and grain
prices, and the Glen could no longer support a growing population. All of
these factors meant that people had to leave the Glen. There was also the call
of adventure, the chance of making money, and the attraction of a new, indus-
trial world. Yet, as many Glenners would agree, there is something about the
person who stays.[5]

---

[5] A. Fenton, Two Scottish Day Labourers' Day Books. In B. Larsson and J. Myrdal, eds. *Peasant
Diaries as a Source for the History of Mentality*, Nordiska Museet, Stockholm, 1995, 26–32.

12

SUMMER GRAZING AND ILLICIT STILLS

An essential link between higher and lower ground in the annual cycle of activities, based on the principle of making the best use of resources, was the summer exodus of man and beast in May and June to the fresh pastures in the hills, until the return in August. This allowed resting of the lower-lying grazing areas and let the crops grow unmolested. Such seasonal movement has now ended in Glenesk, as elsewhere in Scotland, and in many parts of the world where the co-existence of high and low land led to the evolution of the system. Although there is no longer a general exodus of people and beast to fresh pasture in summertime, as late as the mid-nineteenth century this ancient custom of transhumance was prevalent.

The shieling system was not just peculiar to the Highlands and Islands, but once formed part of many lowland villages, for example in Angus and the Borders. This system was displaced much earlier in the Borders than in Highland Scotland. The great monasteries in the Border regions had trade links with the Continent which saw great quantities of wool transported to Flanders through the ports of Berwick and Musselburgh.[1] As the emphasis shifted from cattle to sheep in these areas, hill grazing was developed instead and there was no need for stock to be taken to summer pastures in the same manner. The shieling system survived much longer in the Highlands and Islands chiefly because the emphasis remained on cattle. One reason for this was that the Highlands had a good trade in the export of cattle to England in the seventeenth century.[2]

There are still traces of this movement to summer pastures. On shelves of flatter ground, under the lee of a slope or rock face, with a burn nearby, the foundations of numerous shieling huts can still be traced. Place-names ending in -*shiel*, and -*ary*, from the Gaelic *airidh*, are indicative of shielings, examples in Glenesk being Arsallary and Burn of Deuchary, John Cobb's hut being in the vicinity of the latter.[3] Known examples of 'shiel' names are the Shiel of

[1] A. Fenton. *Scottish Country Life* (1976), Tuckwell Press, East Linton, revised edn, 1999, 133.
[2] ibid, 133.
[3] ibid, 130.

Mark, the Shiel of Branny on the Braid Cairn, the Shiel of Logan, three-quarters of a mile from Loch Brandy on the rigging of Green Hill, the Craig of Doune Shiel on the pony path above Effock at Bader Filly, the Shiel of Saughs on the Lethnot side near the head of Effock, John Cobb's hut between Lethnot and Keenie on Wirren, the Goats House on the Slates just above Gleneffock lambing parks and John Gordon's house in the Lee Wood. There are also many unnamed sites in the vicinity of the Lee Wood, in the Cowiehillock Plantation, also in Glen Mark, up the Unich and elsewhere.

The ancient place-name, the Rowan, may not be named after the rowan tree. It is in an area where, in the old days, women, children and the elderly migrated in the summer months with the livestock, leaving the able-bodied men behind to cut what hay they had and attend to other heavy duties. The day when people and stock located to the shielings almost had a holiday atmosphere about it, with the whole community participating in readying and transporting all the stock and necessary goods to the summer pastures. The men carried the timbers, ropes and various tools required to repair the huts. As for the women, they spent their time at the shielings carrying on many of their normal household duties, but in a different setting. Generally, although not uniform throughout highland Scotland, women would take with them to the shielings such items as dairy equipment, spindles and distaffs for spinning wool, while collecting roots and herbs for making dyes. This allowed the preparation of yarn for winter weaving to be done.[4] All would return in August to help with the harvest. There are, of course, so many marks of occupation on the Rowan over the centuries that shieling activities do not account for all that can be seen. Nevertheless, evident foundations of shieling sites and little fields are still visible.

Various types of shieling hut have been identified in Glenesk, and some of the sites may be medieval or older (Fig.12.1). An evolution can be observed from the oval or circular foundations that mark a former beehive hut, often with a smaller cell attached, to the four-sided form that evolved in the eighteenth century, sometimes with a second room (equivalent to the earlier cell) built as part of the main structure. These later huts were rectangular and about 29 feet (8.8m) long by twelve feet (3.6m) wide, with rounded corners and sometimes with two compartments.[5] There was often a smaller hut nearby which served as a store for such things as milking equipment, milk and cheese.

Some idea of the appearance may be got from Johnny Gordon's house. It is a stout rectangle of stone, nineteen feet long by twelve feet wide, with a narrow door two feet three inches wide and a small square window. In the back wall are two recesses, one of them one foot square, the other one-and-a-half feet by

[4] ibid, 137.
[5] ibid, 132.

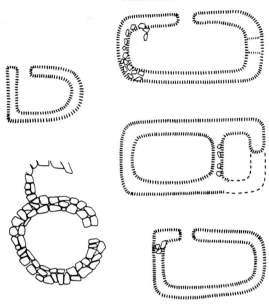

Fig 12.1   Diagrams of shielings near Lochlee. From A. Fenton. Scottish Country Life *(1976),*
Tuckwell Press, East Linton, revised edn. 1999, 132.

one foot, such as are found in all Scottish shieling huts for holding the milk
vessels and other equipment. Standing out into the room and sloping back at
the top to merge with the wall, is a stone-built fire-place. This hut, however,
was not built by the tenants but by the laird, Fox Maule, Earl of Dalhousie, in
1854, on the site of a former shieling hut. He appears to have kept to the
shieling hut tradition in the general dimensions.

   The building is named after John Gordon, the last occupant. According to
local tradition, he refused to leave, and only came down to the township of
Glenree two days before his death in the 1850s. The end of the tradition,
however, is represented by the Shiel of Mark, which was occupied by a stalker
until recent times, and had furniture inside it. Johnny Gordon's house and
some of the foundations are amongst trees, while others can be seen on a bare
expanse nearby.

   Shieling huts generally occurred in groups, and were located near streams
and lochs, which supplied water and trout. Occasionally, single huts may be
found, but these are usually sited on a smaller, less accessible piece of grazing
land.[6] Often these mounded ruins can point to long continuity of use, although
just how long is difficult to assess.

---

[6] ibid, 140.

Though the use of shieling huts lies outside human memory, they were well-known to Alexander Ross, poet and schoolmaster in Lochlee (1699–1784). From his poem *The Fortunate Shepherdess*, we get a lively glimpse of an interior with all its bustling imagery and activity:

> On skelfs a' round the wa's the cogs were set,
> Ready to ream, an' for the cheese be het;
> A hake was frae the rigging hinging fu'
> Of quarter kebbucks, tightly made an' new.
> Behind the door a calour heather bed,
> Flat o' the floor, of stanes an' fail was made.
> An' lucky shortly follow'd o'er the gate
> Wi' twa fu' leglins, froathing o'er an' het;
> Syne ream'd her milk, an' set it o' the fire;
> An' bade them eek the bleeze, an nae to tyre;
> That cruds, their weamfu', they sud get on haste,
> As fresh an' gueed as ever they did taste.[7]

The grazings were not necessarily remote and at high levels. They were more often comparatively low down, not too far from the settlements. Seventeenth- and eighteenth-century sources such as Edward's Map 1678, Roy's Map of 1755 and the Old Statistical Account in 1792, indicate a degree of afforestation that would have helped to provide shelter for humans and beasts.

Some idea of earlier numbers of stock can be got from seventeenth-century Testaments. These indicate considerable numbers of sheep and cattle, with a sheep to cattle ratio of five to one. In fifteen holdings there were 754 sheep, 157 cattle (including oxen) and 28 horses. These figures refer to the better-off places, whose occupants were of sufficient status for their stock and grain to be recorded on their death, but the stock of the numerous sub-tenants and cottars must not be forgotten. Lochlee is known to have had 74 such tenants in 1716, and each holding would have had a stock of about ten animals.

In earlier times it may be that sheep and cattle mingled at the shieling sites, though it is noteworthy that in 1641 complaints made by the Laird of Edzell, David Lindsay, on behalf of himself and his tenants, referred to the damage done by large numbers of 'brokine hielandmen' who carried away great quantities of horse, sheep and other plenishings. Curiously, cattle are not mentioned. In 1647, compensation amounting to £20,000 Scots was awarded by Parliament (see Chapter 3). In March 1649 the new Laird, John Lindsay, appealed for compensation because the rebel army under James Graham had

---

[7] M. Wattie, ed. *The Scottish Works of Alexander Ross.* (Scottish Text Society), Edinburgh and London, 1938, 82.

long been encamped and quartered on the lands of Edzell and Glenesk, burning the corn in the stackyards, and killing and driving away the cattle and
other animals, so that all the lands of Glenesk, worth 9,000 merks in annual
revenue, were lying waste because the tenants had not been able to cultivate
them. It may be significant that the Highlandmen took the sheep, presumably from the hills, and the rebel army the cattle from around the farms. The
Laird had not only to do without dues from his tenants in the meantime, but
had also to replenish their stocks and other requirements.

By the eighteenth century, following the Union, the demands of trade led
to a more concentrated use of the hills for cattle. Before the introduction of
Blackfaced sheep in the 1760s, the Glens of Unich, Lee and Mark were occupied in the summer by herds of black cattle. The Rev. John Pirie remarked
that after the Blackface invasion, cattle were grazed in the summer only in
Glen Unich.[8] In the 1790s, the stocking in Lochlee was 9,200 sheep and lambs,
130 goats, 192 horses, and about 600 black cattle – i.e. there was now a sheep
– cattle ratio of about fifteen to one. The horses and black cattle were small. Of
the sheep, about 6,000 were blackfaces, and over 2,000 were a cross between
blackfaced rams and the native white sheep, the true breed of which was thought
to have vanished by this period. The sheep pastured in Glen Lee and Glen
Mark, whilst Glen Unich was set aside for grazing around 300 black cattle in
June, July and August, the glen-keeper receiving 1/6 sterling a head for looking
after them.

Thus the hill-grazing, in the modern sense, of sheep and cattle came to
replace the older family-based shieling system, due to the pressures of changing
economic patterns which were introduced by landlords. This also included the
later development of deer forest and grouse moors.

The cattle were taken and sold at various markets and trysts, such as the
major ones at Crieff and Falkirk. Nearer at hand there were cattle and horse
fairs at Trinity (Taranty), St Catherine's Fair at Kincardine and later at Paddy's
or Palady Fair at Fettercairn. Others were at Glenesk and Edzell proper.
According to local tradition there was one at Glencat behind Baillies, but the
chief was Whittle Fair, held at the Fair Hillock on Craig Soales which is to the
west of Mile Cairn, halfway between Blackcraig and Tarfside. Later the fair
was held at Balhangie Inn, now the farmhouse of Cairncross. As a child, Mrs
Skene of Turnabrane was at Whittle Fair in 1855, probably in July, and
remembered the crowd of people drinking and speaking. At the time of horse
fairs, the Kedloch was a busy inn. Mrs Christison of Auchronie could remember as many as 40 horses stabled there on their journey to these fairs. Until
1517, fairs were illegal if held outside burghs, but Whittle Fair seems to have

---

[8] *The Old (First) Statistical Account of Scotland,* XIII, Angus, EP Publishing Limited, Wakefield,
1976, 432.

been an ancient tryst, designed for the disposal, before onset of winter, of beasts that could not have been fed on the short commons available prior to the introduction of root crops and artificial grasses.[9]

Some arrangements had to be made, however, for the tenants' stock. This took the form of a common hill to which the sheep went in summer, till well into the nineteenth century. The farmers sent their sheep to the hill there as regularly as they now send hogs for wintering. One shepherd tended all the sheep on the north side of the water, and another those on the south. Each man looked after about 8,000. The shepherd who herded in the summer months between Lethnot and Keenie, before the fences were put up, lived in John Cobb's hut in the Wirran, according to the late John Crowe, one-time schoolmaster at Waterside, whose father had herded sheep on the south side. Further details were given in a letter by James Stewart, 'Jimmie Buskie', of Buskhead:

> The common hill in the North was all the high ground west of the Tarf and above Craig Brawlin, Currie Duff and Kirnie and Garthead shared by Saughs, Aikenstock and Kirnie with Broad Cairn at the back. David Ross was the last shepherd that lived in Shiel of Braney. The common hill of Berry Hill was shared by Boddam, Corhairney, Turny and Buskie (Buskhead). They shared a common herd. Whiggie (Whigginton) had the right to summer a number of sheep on the Kirn hill.[10]

Where there is wholesale movement of animals, water becomes important. Great herds of cattle had gone through Glenesk by the Mounth roads from Aberdeenshire across to Lethnot and thence to the fairs. Resting places beside water were essential, probably used by traders and marauders alike. Some of these wells are St Colm's Well at the head of the Fir Mounth Road, Docken Well on Glentennet Road and Queen's Well in Glen Mark, all situated near Drove Roads. These hill tracks were used by highland drovers bringing their herds south to the Trinity Tryst on the Muir of Brechin, the first lowland market for the distribution of these cattle.[11] The following is a list of wells and their locations:

1. Drousty's Well	Slightly west of the House of Mark garden.
2. Medicine Well	At Bathie, near Dalbrack Bridge.
3. Greenesken	In Arsallary (used for Innes christenings).
4. Docken Well	On Glentennet Road.
5. Queen's Well	Formerly the White Well. Glen Mark.
6. Tod Cairn Well	On the Mudloch.
7. Tillgarrie Well	At Corhairncross, near the waterside below the Yattan.

[9] ibid.
[10] Letter from James Stewart, Buskhead, to Greta Michie, 21 November 1976.
[11] A.R.B. Haldane. *The Drove Roads of Scotland*, Birlinn, Edinburgh, 1997, 131.

8. Butter Well	Behind Blackhills.
9. Thravers Well	On the face of Garlet.
10. Linten Well	Back of Blackness.
11. Gairmont's Well	Up the brae from Broomknowe.
12. Bothy Howe Well	Craig Soales (supplies Tarfside).
13. Well at Clashinnie	On right hand side from the end of the old road at Blackness.
14. St Colm's Well	At the head of the Fir Mounth Road.
15. Wallee	The spring where the grain was soaked at Crosstyle.
16. The Well of Our lady	Parish of Edzell.
17. The Well of St Laurence	" "
18. The Well of St Dristan	Newdosk, about a mile from the old church-yard, in a field called 'Piper's Shade'.

The shieling grounds and wells were not only used for the summer grazing of animals, or for thirsty drovers and their beasts. They were also the scene of more illegal activities, namely the illicit distilling of whisky. The Malt Tax of 1725 which led to riots in Glasgow, spread a taste for whisky, which could be made without benefit of excise more easily than ale. Smuggling was rife, and the smugglers were popular. A professional smuggler could clear, free of all expenses, 10/- per week, which enabled him to keep a horse and an additional cow. The illicit whisky distilling industry was considered to be responsible for a rapidly increasing population because the necessary assistance of a wife could not be dispensed with and hence early marriages became general. One has to be cautious with such 'statements', as there is no way of proving them. Similarly, the abolition of such distillation is often cited in census returns as a cause of depopulation, but this is probably given more importance than it deserves in this respect.

Whisky bothies were usually situated far into the hills with good water available. Hulled six-row barley has been found on the floor of the Whigginton corn kiln, when it was excavated, and elsewhere. It is strange how corn-kilns, numerous as they are in Glenesk, have been lost to memory, and are not mentioned in the *First Statistical Account* of the 1790s. Below is a list of whisky bothies in Glenesk. There may have been many more, but these are the ones that have been identified:

One behind Townhead of Cairncross
One behind Glencat
One behind Kedloch (with three fireplaces)
One at the back of Garlet
One on the Rowan (Hill of Migvie) at Clashinnie

One at Stylemouth
One up the Mark, far beyond White's Pool at Fashieloch
One above Glenlee
One at the back of Carlochy of Lee
One at Badabae in Arsallery
One up the Turret Burn (Ladyholm)
One up the Shank of Wirren
One up the White Burn
One at the Latch

At the whisky bothy above Glenlee, one can still see the wells for the water going through. The water disappears underground and reappears at Glenlee (the house) and that is why the whisky bothy remained undetected. When the whisky was ready at the Latch, a stone was placed in a certain position so that people should know.

Whisky was taken across the hills in packets (panniers). Warning signs were used if the gaugers were at the foot of the Glen. Gaugers tapped with iron spikes for hollow places in their search for illicit stills.

The apparatus used in distilling was the copper pot, the head (or lid), the copper pipe or pipes called the shoulder from which the real whisky dropped, the worm, and the container in the ground. All this equipment was expensive. Mrs Stewart at the Spital was caught distilling whisky and she said that if they did take or destroy the kettle she would throw a 'stane at their heids, because it wisna hers'. The boiling was generally done in the bothies in the hills, and two servant women were employed for the boiling during the time of the smuggling. They boiled the pots with white 'cowes' (branches). An illicit still head was found by James Moir, gamekeeper, in 1967, while he was grouse driving. The still head was made of copper and had three pipes instead of one, which made it operate six times faster than was legal, plus the fact that the head itself should have been twice as large. On to the pipes had been fixed the 'worms' through which the distilled liquor descended to the container on the ground. The still head was found half a mile away from a whisky bothy, far beyond Townhead in the Bothy Howe, where the ruins of the building can be seen and where there is also a good spring well. This still head is on view at the Glenesk Museum.

As well as illicit stills and whisky bothies, there was also a number of inns in Glenesk. There was Tarry Inn, in the Ardoch woods; the Alehouse of Mark (Drousty); Glencat and an alehouse at Dalbog. The present farmhouse at Cairncross was formerly the Balhangie Inn, but it has been much altered. In the near vicinity are several corn kilns, and a brewhouse is recorded in the sale of lands to Lord Panmure in 1714. The last innkeeper at Balhangie was named Smith. Thereafter, from 1854, it was the Ground Officer's house, and gradually, the old unit of Cairncross was restored as the surrounding crofts were taken over. A descendant of the Smiths informed Greta Michie that the drovers stopped at Balhangie and filled their sporrans for the journey with balls of oatmeal rolled in whisky. The informant also said that if toddy was wanted by the freemasons, the whisky was heated in the copper kettle. If the whisky was too hot, it was cooled with the same, as it was regarded as sacrilege to do otherwise.

There had been a great deal of whisky distilling in Glenesk, and many stories have been told about it. Mrs Reid of Auchmull's grandmother, Mrs Paterson at East Migvie, had to sit on the hole when the whisky was being brewed. At Badabae in Arsallary, an exciseman knocked at the door and asked for something to warm him on a cold night. The wife gave him a drop of whisky, which he offered to pay for, as this was the way to catch her out. 'Na, na sir, that wadna be richt. I wadna dae that', she said. On his departure he laid down a gold piece, but the wife had the better of him. 'Thank you, sir', she said, 'It's far ower guid o' ye. But haste ye back anither day'. When he did come back, he told her that he was to carry out a search. Said she, 'Ye're rale welcome to dae that, sir. Ye can ca' every bit o't, but dinna wauken ma bairns'. Pointing to the kitchen bed, she said, 'They're a' in there, sir'. Apparently, she had hidden the whisky in the bed and fooled the exciseman into thinking that her children were asleep there.

Those caught distilling whisky faced a heavy fine, so ways had to be found to avoid detection. In the 1850s, the tenant at Kedloch, who may have been Peter Copland, was caught distilling whisky, and had to sell out to pay his fine. Martha Duke was herd lassie to a farmer in Arsallary, who said to her, 'If ye see a strange man fan ye're in the hill herdin' the kye, throw yer stick an' gar yer dog bark!'. This would serve as a warning of approaching excisemen.

These are just a few stories about the whisky distilling and no doubt there were many more. The illicit whisky trade could be quite profitable for those engaged in it, but it is highly unlikely that one could support a family from the proceeds. Any money made from whisky distilling only supplemented the family income, allowing them to indulge in a few extra luxuries. The trade in illicit whisky was not a major factor in the retention of population in Glenesk, any more than its abolition was a major cause of depopulation.

13

SPORT AND GAME

Sport, or hunting, is not just a manifestation of nineteenth-century estate policy. Hunting has been a pastime on the Glenesk estate for hundreds of years, and enjoyed by many visitors to the Glen, as this letter, dated 19 February 1587, from Mr William Scott of Edinburgh, to his good friend Sir David Lindsay of Edzell, at Invermark, demonstrates:

> This day, about sax in the morning as I araise furth of my bed, the chirping and singing of sparrows and other busy burdies, the foreflearis of Springtime did call to my memorie the happy estate of landward, and then immediately lukand to the north, I did remember on the plesant walees of Mark and Ley, the white hills and mountains that compassis them, in special Craigmaskaillie, Laire, Cairne, Craig of Doon and Montkene, albeit presentlie enviroint with their whyte winter robes, yit before I visit thame, soll be deckit with thair grene fragrant May garments ... no forgettand the bar (on) of Invermark, for the schowittis of Montkene to be raised at Willie Wolfiss tail will furneis mony michtie peremptoris (defences) aganis the bar of Invermark ... I have ane plaid and trewis riddie agane the fyftene day of Aprile nix to come ...[1]

On a later date, 15 May 1587, William Scott again writes:

> I man remember your M.ship of ane puncheon of wyne which ye aucht me for finding ane stane on the water of Mark, and adverteis us of the special time quhan we sall cum (and if ye will have wolf hunting this yeir or nocht), for be goddis grace, except the Spainzie arme stay me I sall be thair.[2]

Shooting and hunting was not a commercial enterprise on the estate in the sixteenth century, and these activities were confined to the Laird and his friends. Sport of this kind was not seen as a way of generating income and was for pleasure only. William Scott's letters refer to wolf hunting. Wolves were widespread throughout Scotland at one time, but they were persecuted because of their threat to livestock and were hunted to extinction by the eighteenth century. Perhaps Scott's query regarding wolf hunting reflects the fact that the number of wolves must have been in serious decline even at that time. Although

[1] Crawford Inventories, Box 1.
[2] ibid.

153

organised sport was not established until the nineteenth century, there were strict regulations in place against illegal hunting. There are references in the Dalhousie Papers to gamekeepers and watchers in 1789, regarding the unauthorised destruction of game. The following letter was written by the estate factor, John Spencer, to Lady Dalhousie, and is dated September 14, 1789:

> I had the honor of your Ladyships letter of the 27th last month. I am sorry the Muirfowl sent were so much spoilt ...
>
> I gave particular instructions to John Duke the gamekeeper, to enquire of all the gentleman if they had liberty and from whom, to shoot game. Messrs Montgomery and Campbell, the Lord Chief Baron and Advocate's Sons told him they had your Ladyship's liberty, the others of whom there were no less than twenty, gave no answer, But in general that they were to shoot; more Birds were killed this season in Glenesk than ever was known in any two seasons before. It will be absolutely necessary some steps be taken next season to prevent the killing of the game ....

Also in the Dalhousie Papers is a list of persons who took part in the Glorious Twelfth on 12 August 1789, in Glenesk. There are quite a few titled gentlemen in this list, the majority of whom would have been friends and acquaintances of the Laird. These persons would have been there by invitation only. It is unlikely, at this early stage, that the guests would have paid to participate, but contacts, business or otherwise, could have been made during the duration of the shoot, and may even have been the purpose behind inviting certain people. If nothing else, it certainly was a form of social bonding, and one should not forget the prestige that such events would add to the estate's, and its heritor's, image. Assuming that these are the men to whom John Spencer is referring in his letter to Lady Dalhousie, it is difficult to conceive that such a large group of gentlemen would have been shooting game on the Glenesk estate without the prior knowledge or permission of the Laird. Such a large body of visitors would have required lodgings in the Glen, and the landowner would certainly have been aware of the presence of so many distinguished people – assuming that he were not abroad at the time:

> List persones names gone to shoot game in Glenesk Aug 12, 1789

Sir David Carnegie	Captain Montgomery
Captain Jo. Carnegie	Mr Thornton
Chas. Greenhill	Mr Watson
Admiral Digby	Mr Guthrie of Guthrie
Admiral Elliot	Mr Gray
Mr Elliot	Mr W...... Minister, one who Lord Dalhousie peremptorly discharged
Mr Robertson Scott	
Mr Adam Gillies	Major Turnbull
Mr Hercules Taylor	Mr Cruickshank
Lord Chas. Townsend	Mr Strachan Jarvie
Mr Montgomery, Son to L. Chief Baron	Dr Stevenson, Arbroath

What the letter from John Spencer to Lady Dalhousie does convey, is the sense of urgency that game is being over-hunted and the recognition that the shootings must somehow be managed in a way that would give numbers a chance to recover. Legislation was already in place regarding the unauthorised killing of game, as an Act of Parliament, passed in 1621, and contained in an Interdict against poachers in 1814, testifies:

> It is statute and ordained that no man Hunt nor Hawk who has not a Plough of Law in Heritage under the pain of One Hundred Pounds. And by an Act of Queen Ann's Parliament, twenty fifth March One thousand seven hundred and seven, Chapter Thirteenth. It is inter alia enacted. That no fowler or any person whatsoever should come within any Heritors grounds without leave asked and given by the Heritor with Setting Dogs or Setts for killing Fowls – and if any common Fowlers shall be found in any place with Guns or Setts having no licence from any Nobleman or Heritor, they shall be sent abroad as Recruits. And moreover by Act of Parliament of the thirteenth King George the Third, Chapter fifty fourth, it is enacted that any person not qualified to kill game who shall have game in his custody without the authority of a qualified person, shall be liable in a penalty of twenty shillings sterling. That neither of Alexander Duke, James Duke or John Duke, residing at Dalhestnie in the Parish of Edzell, or Francis Duncan at Migvie in the Parish of Edzell, are possessed of a qualification in terms of the Act One thousand six hundred and twenty one; Or have the leave and licence mentioned in the act one thousand seven hundred and seven; nor are qualified and have authority agreeably to the Act George the Third.[3]

The Act of 1621, more or less, excludes all but the landowner of the right to kill game. The Dukes and Francis Duncan were probably penalised for their misdemeanours. Under these terms, however, it seems even more inconceivable that twenty or more gentlemen intent on shooting game, could descend upon Glenesk on a Twelfth of August without the Heritor's prior knowledge or permission. All concerned probably had the necessary Plough of Law in Heritage and were, therefore, qualified to shoot game. What is clear, is that even at this period it was recognised that muirfowl numbers had to be protected. An advertisement to this effect was posted in the nineteenth century:

Preservation of the Game

> As the Game on the Estates of Glenesk, Lethnot, Edzell and Navar has been very much destroyed for some years past, and as the late severe winter has killed great numbers of them, the Earl of Dalhousie finds himself obliged to take every method possible to preserve these grounds for the ensuing season and as he is not to shoot himself, or to allow any of his Gamekeepers to shoot, he hopes that his friends will join him in the resolution of sparing the Game upon these grounds for this season. Other persons beside the ordinary Gamekeepers are appointed to preserve the Grounds, and a premium will be given for the discovery of such as shall counteract the purpose of this advertisement.

---

[3] NAS GD45/18/2353 *Extract Petition, The Honourable Wm Maule against Dukes and Others.*

Poaching remained a problem for the estate despite the threat of legal action being taken against those caught committing such an offence. For some, such a threat seems to have been no deterrent whatsoever. On 24 December 1833, a Bill of Suspension and Interdict was raised by the Rt Hon. William, Lord Panmure, against James Gordon, his two brothers Francis and Peter also of Ballater, John Paterson, shoemaker at Ballater, Andrew Cumming, Coriebeg, Andrew Lamond of Ardoch, Alex. Davidson, John Gow and Duncan Stewart – no fixed abode. The hill grounds in the parishes of Edzell, Lethnot and Lochlee, abounding in game, have, 'been infested by a gang of poachers of the most desperate character'. In a sworn statement, William Wilson, gamekeeper to Lord Panmure, and James Michie, assistant keeper, related how the accused had turned their guns on them when challenging the men about the illegal shooting of game on the Panmure estate. One of the accused was also alleged to have kicked William Wilson. These men flouted the law consistently. Indeed, two of the poachers interdicted by Lord Panmure, Frances Gordon and John Paterson, had also been interdicted by Lord Airlie. The authorities were dealing with a very organised gang of poachers. Even though the above poachers were banned from entering the grounds of the Panmure estate, under any circumstances, Lord Panmure's legal representatives complained bitterly that these men were still able to organise groups to poach in their stead. This particular group had been raiding from 12 August onwards. The Interdict against them, to stop shooting and hunting, was granted on 27 December 1833. This gang, however, were recurring offenders. The same poachers were still at it, and an Interdict was granted (extended) on 27 January 1834. Again the current Interdict was extended on 22 October 1835. Eventually, on 1 December 1836, a 'Petition and Complaint ... for His Majesty's Interest' was made. The Interdict had been made perpetual, but the poachers still persisted. Parallels can, perhaps, be made between these raids by men from over the Mounth with those bands of 'Highland caterans' who frequently harried the Glen in bygone days. By the nineteenth century the raiders were interested only in taking muirfowl, rather than cattle and 'other plenishings'.

The scarcity of grouse is a problem not only associated with the nineteenth century. Even in the 1990s, numbers were low, and some locals believe that this condition is of a cyclical nature, with feast followed by famine. The following saying is attributed to one local man, Davie Stormonth, former head stalker to the Earls of Dalhousie at Invermark in the early decades of the twentieth century: 'The grouse are like the broom. Calm for twenty years, stay for twenty years and go away for twenty years'.[4] A Grouse Book is kept by the Keeper, in which is recorded the number of young that have been reared, as

[4] Christina J. Mackenzie. *Glenesk. An Ethnological Study of a Community in Angus*, Honours Dissertation, School of Scottish Studies, University of Edinburgh, April 1992, 46.

well as those birds that have been killed during the shooting. The most grouse shot in one day stands at 512 brace from the Rowan and 375 brace off the Leg of Moss, a record which belongs to one Colonel Stirling, sometime in the 1930s.[5] A good day's drive now would be in the region of 40 – 50 brace.[6]

Grouse shooting. The horse on the left has panniers for carrying the shot birds off the hill. Two of the men in the photograph are James Eggo and George Caithness. Date unknown. G1/11/13A.

As a sport, organised grouse shooting was rare in Scotland until the 1880s. It was fairly general in England before it had been considered north of the border. The new railway networks allowed English sportsmen ease of access into Angus.[7] The demand for deer stalking increased as the price of wool and sheep fell in the latter part of the nineteenth century and great efforts were made by estates to attract the affluent sportsman north. Organised sport brought a great deal of money into the estate, and many famous people visited the Glen to shoot. In 1992, the let for shooting grouse was £450 per day or £3,000 per week.[8] One frequent visitor was Horatio Ross, recognised as the foremost rifle shot of his day, first visited Invermark in 1869. He became known as the finest deerstalker Scotland had produced.

---

[5] ibid, 47.
[6] ibid, 47.
[7] E.B. Dobson, Angus. In L. Dudley Stamp, ed. *The Report of the Land Utilisation Survey of Britain*, Geographical Distributions Ltd, London, 1946, 550.
[8] Mackenzie, op. cit. 45.

Archibald Stewart loading for M. Achille Fould at a butt on the Rowan Hill. Stone butts such as this were unusual. Date unknown. G1/31/2.

The earliest Scottish attempts at driving were at Moy, Inverness-shire and Dalnaspidal, Perthshire, but they were not very successful. Butts, used by shooting parties as camouflage, were also in use earlier in England than in Scotland. The butts, which are constructed, generally, of turf, heather and grass sods, need to be maintained, and in July it is the keepers' responsibility to repair and, if necessary, rebuild those which will be used during the coming shooting season.[9]

Before the introduction of butts, shooters walked in line and used setters and pointers which, if one was walking upwind, stopped on finding the scent of a grouse. In a letter dated 1 July 1844, Duncan Michie tells A.G. Roberts of a red and white setter bitch that might be good for hunting.

Into the spring there is the heather burning, and it is the gamekeepers who do this job now. The draining and burning of heather keeps it young and encourages the grouse population. There exists a rhyme which is reputedly to do with the burning of the heather and is as follows:

> Haud the fyr amo' the heather
> An' no' lave twa tae sing thegither
> Send them a' tae hell thegither
> In a haze wi' tar an' tow.

[9] Mackenzie, op. cit. 49.

Some of the heather burnings were quite large, and evidence survives from George Michie papers relating to fires, probably dating from the early twentieth century. It is not clear if all of the fires mentioned were controlled burns or not. One particular burning was the Bog of the Haugh fire, the length of which was 1,450 yards and was, approximately, 420 yards wide and covered some 120 acres. Millden moors were carefully managed and this is shown by the consistent size of bags obtained over a period of years. Between 1929 and 1935 the average numbers of grouse shot was 5,000 brace per season. In the 1934 season, 7,400 brace were killed.[10] With this kind of decimation, it is hardly surprising that there is a problem with declining numbers. More recently, the grouse have suffered from disease, thus reducing the population even further.

D.W. Hanton, centre, pouring some refreshment from his hip-flask during a grouse-shoot. Late nineteenth century. C.12882.

Humans are not the only hunters of game. The *New Statistical Account* of 1845 informs us of how foxes had been very destructive of estate land. However, by the mid-nineteenth century, 'hunting and other means of destruction had much reduced their number'.[11] Foxes and wildcats destroyed great

---

[10] M.F.M. Michie, *Studies in the History of Glenesk: Sport*, Glenesk Museum, 50.
[11] *New Statistical Account of Scotland:*Forfar and Kincardine, XI, WM. Blackwood and Sons, Edinburgh, 1845.

numbers of grouse, although the latter were not considered to be as big a
pest as the fox, long regarded as vermin by farmers and landowners and still
exterminated as such. There is also a suspicion among people in the Glen
that protected species such as Eagles and Peregrine Falcons are being treated
as a form of winged vermin and are also being exterminated. Rabbits are also
a big problem, as they cause a great deal of damage to crops and young trees.
It is the gamekeepers' responsibility to control the rabbit population. Some
local men, Angus Davidson and Ramsay Guthrie, remember as young boys
being paid threepence for every rabbit they killed, and receiving £1 for
eighty.[12] Even today, a game dealer from Brechin visits the Glen regularly
and those people who have game for him signal this by hanging a white flag
outside the house.[13] The current rate for rabbits is fifty pence for one, and
some of the retired gamekeepers shoot them in order to supplement their
income.[14]

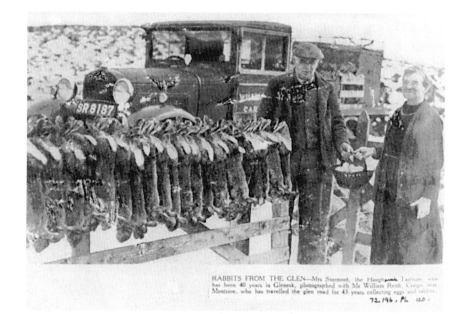

RABBITS FROM THE GLEN—Mrs Stormont, the Haugh, Tarfside, who
has been 40 years in Glenesk, photographed with Mr William Reith, Craigo, near
Montrose, who has travelled the glen road for 43 years collecting eggs and rabbits.
72.196 . Ph 120 .

*Mrs Stormonth, the Haugh, Tarfside, who has been 40 years in Glenesk, photographed with Mr William
Reith, Craigo, near Montrose, who had travelled the glen road for 43 years collecting eggs and rabbits.
Between the Wars. Glenesk Museum.*

[12] Mackenzie, op. cit. 47.
[13] ibid, 47.
[14] ibid, 47.

While grouse shooting eventually took off at the end of the nineteenth century, the emphasis at the beginning of that century was very much on deer forests. Lord Panmure set apart four farms, Inchgrundle, Kirkton, Glenlee and Invermark, and other lands totalling about 50,000 acres and paying a rent of between £400 and £500. Nothing was wanted to make a superb deer forest except the deer. Archie Campbell came as trustee to Inchgrundle and in 1853 the ground was cleared of sheep.

During the preceding spring, several deer calves had been obtained from Lord Breadalbane and some from Lord H. Bentinck. A few died during the winter of 1853, but 24 healthy animals survived. The deer rapidly increased to about 230 in 1854. In the first season, which lasted eight days, four deer were killed. In the Retreat, a set of antlers in the front hall bears the inscription, 'Found by the Forester in Glenmark, 1853'. Later, deer were sent from Glenmark to New Zealand, where they again flourished. They were taken out by John Ewan, a native of Brechin who had many Glenesk relatives, and who was later knighted.

Early in the nineteenth century those who came to shoot grouse in Glenesk stayed mostly in farmhouses. At one time there were two staying at the Kirkton, while one stayed at Inchgrundle and slept in a box bed. The farmer and his wife slept in the other box bed in the same room. As time went on, landowners realised it would be worth their while to organise the business and let their shootings. Gradually, splendid shooting lodges with fine kennels and other

Millden hunting lodge. Part of the building is now the oldest in the Glen still used as a lodge. 1975. G1/12/2A.

accommodations were built. The first shooting lodge in Glenesk was
Gleneffock, although Invermark Castle can be regarded as the earliest hunting
lodge in the Glen built by the Lindsay lairds. The Retreat was also a shooting
lodge, built by Captain Wemyss in the 1840s, and extended three times.
Invermark lodge was built by Lord Panmure in 1854. Part of Millden is now
the oldest in the Glen still used as a lodge.

On the hill, the Shiel of Logan, situated on the Green Hill near Loch Brandy,
was often used by ponymen waiting on stalking parties working that part of
Invermark deer forest. The last to live in it was Davie Stormounth of the
Haugh. His job was to keep the sheep out of the deer forest, and to turn in the
deer if the wind was in the right direction. He was also to assist the stalker of
the 'Sooth Beat'. For fuel at the hut, logs were sawn and split and carried there
in panniers. Davie Stormonth is reported to have had two collies, Moss and
Sharp, to stop the Clova sheep from trespassing. Interestingly, regarding dogs,
Duncan Michie thought that the rules and regulations should instruct all those
in Glenesk without sheep or cattle, except shepherds out of employment, to
put away or destroy all dogs they may have. He also believed that all tenants
and shepherds should keep their dogs in at night. His first statement is rather
contentious, but no one could really argue against the logic of not letting their
dogs out at night, as Michie's chief concern was for the welfare of the sheep on
the hill.

Heather is a bone of contention between shepherds and gamekeepers, and is
important to the livelihood of both shepherd and gamekeeper alike, but for
different reasons. Gamekeepers manage the moors in order to maintain grouse

Stables of Lee was a hill bothy used for stabling horses at stalking. Date unknown. G1/7/8.

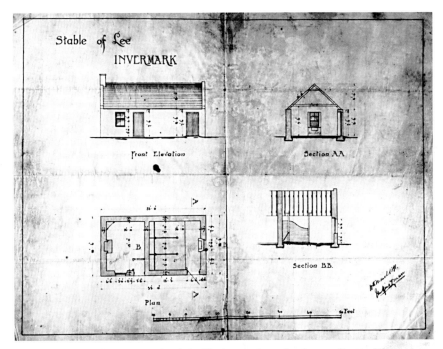

Stable of Lee
INVERMARK

Front Elevation   Section AA

B

Section BB.

Plan

Feet

The plans of Stables of Lee, Invermark. The building was modernised with cement flooring. The horses were stabled in section A, the right hand part of the building. 1896. C12848.

stocks, which, in effect, keeps them in a job. The conflict arises because the keepers blame sheep for eating heather, which adversely affects grouse stocks, and, consequently, blame shepherds for allowing their flocks to graze the heather on the shooting lets. At one time, agriculture was the main occupation in the Glen, and this clash of interests highlights the damage done to the age-old agricultural/ecological balance of the Glen, set in motion by the entry of the estate into a radically new economic pattern in the nineteenth century. Although there is a genuine conflict of interest, shepherds and gamekeepers do work together at shearing time.

While the shootings brought a lot of money into the estate coffers, there was still a large outlay in terms of Gamekeepers' wages and expenses connected with the shooting lodges, as evidenced in a report for the period 1 September 1874 to 31 December 1874, by Robert Stocks, Factor to the Earl of Dalhousie:

Shooting: Keepers/Watchers wages. Gannachy Shootings, November 18, 1874.

Paid Andrew Grant, Keeper at Gannachy, wages from 28 July to 11 November at £22.10/- per half year: £13.10/-.

Paid James Gordon, watcher Gannachy, wages from 28 July to 23 November, 17 weeks at 15/-: £12.13/-.

Paid Patrick Gold, watcher Gannachy, wages from 28 July to 23 November, 17 weeks at 15/-: £12.13.[15]

Invermark Shootings. November 22, 1874

Paid John Mitchell, Deer Stalker, wages from 28 July to 22 November at £22.10/ - per half year: £14.14.8.

Paid Robert Christison wages from 28 July to 22 November at £19.10/- per half year: £12.15.4^1/$_2$.

Paid Donald McPherson(?) wages from 28 July to 22 November at £18.10/- per half year: £12.2.3^1/$_2$.

Paid Wm. McGregor wages from 28 July to 22 November at £17 per half year: £11.2.8.

Paid James Mitchell wages from 28 July to 22 November at £13 per half year: £8.10.3.

Much of the shot game was sold to dealers. On 3 November 1874, the estate received £135.6/- from Alexander Pitcathly, Game Dealer in Perth, for game sold off Edzell Ground in October. The same dealer also paid £42.6/- for game from the Invermark Shooting.[16]

Much maintenance work was also required on the lodges, their grounds and the roads which led to them and on to the hill. The following is a sample of the seasonal work required to keep the lodges and the shootings operational:

Expenses Connected with Shooting Lodges. 1874

Sept. 22   Paid David Low, casting peats for Invermark lodge: £6.12/-.
            Paid David Low for clearing carriage road: £1.16/-.
            Paid David Low for cleaning walls at Retreat lodge: £1.5/-.
            Paid James Watt for work on roads, Invermark: £1.4.9.
            Paid Jas. Christison 5 days for work on roads, Invermark: 15/-.
            Paid Arch. Stewart 7 days for work on roads, Invermark: £1.1/-.
            Paid John Jolly 8 days for work on the roads, Invermark: £1.4/-.
            Paid David Low 1 day filling gravell Gleneffock bridge: 3/-.
Nov. 10   Paid J.D. Scott & Co., to repair fences at Invermark: £2.9.9.
            Paid John McIntosh expense of beaters at hunts on two different days: £18.18/-.
Nov. 22   Paid Rev. Walter Low, Lochlee, half-year's rent of hill: £10.
Dec. 8   Paid Chas. Middleton & Sons, plumbers account for Invermark.
            Paid Wm. Black & Sons, Carpenters, Brechin a/c for Edzell lodge: 5/6.

Management

Nov. 22   Paid Duncan Michie, Ground Officer, Lochlee, wages from 28 July to 22. November at £22.10/- per half year: £14.14.8.[17]

---

[15] NAS GD45/18/1788, *Account Charge and Discharge of the Intromissions of Robert Stocks, Factor to the Earl of Dalhousie, 1 September 1874 – 31 December 1874.*
[16] ibid.
[17] ibid.

The needs of the estate during the shooting seasons were varied and many. For the most part, it seems that local workmen were employed to carry out the various tasks which needed doing. The one exception is that carpenters from Brechin were used for work on Edzell lodge. This is not to say that there were no longer any carpenters residing in the Glen, though it is recognised that there was an exodus of tradesmen from the area during the last quarter of the nineteenth century.

Much of the work on roads involves clearing the roadside drains of winter debris. The work which John Jolly and others carried out in 1874 would have involved repairing, improving and upgrading the access road to Invermark lodge, and firming up the hill paths used by the ponies carrying the panniers.[18] Nowadays, students are recruited for the shooting season to carry out this work.

The outdoor staff at Invermark. G. Bigg, G. Christie, W. Lowden, H. Low, J. Lowden, R. Walker, J. Campbell, R. Christison, J. Anderson, G. Low, J. Stewart, J. Davidson, R. Jolly, C. Jolly, J. Gibbs, E. Gold, G. Crockett, R. Christison, J. Mitchell, John Mitchell, J. Leighton, D. Stormonth, W. Davidson. Some of the names are missing. Early 1900s. G1/9/27. Per. Mrs John Milne, Laurencekirk (formerly of Mangie).

[18] Mackenzie, op. cit. 49.

As the above examples demonstrate, a gamekeeper's tasks were many and varied, with one retired keeper stressing that there is 'mair tae keepering than a gun – there's the spade tae.'[19] The gamekeepers' year is quite full, with March, April and May being the only months outwith the shooting seasons. The gamekeeper's calendar is: Hind culling in June/July; Stag culling – mid-July/February; Pheasant shooting – October/January, and Grouse shooting from mid-August to mid-October.

In the twentieth century, the Glenesk estate has been broken up, although the Earl of Dalhousie and Lord Ramsay are still the largest landowners in Angus, with 47,200 acres.[20] Their estate now consists of Invermark from Tarfside up. The shooting rights of Millden were acquired from the Dalhousie estates in the 1950s by the Duke of Roxburgh. However, Millden is now the property of the Millden Estate Limited, and with 18,700 acres this makes it the third largest estate in the county. The proprietors of Gannochy are Derald H. and Mrs Ruttenberg, and with 16,800 acres, this makes it the sixth largest estate in Angus.[21]

After a day's deer-stalking. Invermark, with the old Lochlee church in the background. W. Lowden, D. Stormonth (Head Stalker), J. Gibb. 1917. C.12902.

---

[19] ibid, 45.
[20] A. Wightman. *Who Owns Scotland?* Edinburgh, 1996, 38.
[21] ibid, 39.

As the Millennium begins, changes in land use and amalgamation of farms are still of concern to many people in Glenesk. Other issues which concern critics of sporting estates include the frequent change in ownership, the under-utilisation of valuable land, and the fact that, in many cases, they are uneconomic. In his book, *Who Owns Scotland*, author Andy Wightman quotes Sir John Stirling-Maxwell, Chairman of the Departmental Committee on Deer Forests in 1919:

> It may be true, I believe it often is, that a deer forest employs more people than the same area under sheep. It certainly brings in a larger rent. From a purely parochial point of view it may therefore claim to be economically sound; but from no other. It provides a healthy existence for a small group of people, but it produces nothing except a small quantity of venison, for which there is no demand. It causes money to change hands. A pack of cards can do that. I doubt whether it could be said of a single deer forest, however barren and remote, that it could serve no other purpose.[22]

There is an argument that land is under-used in Glenesk. Certainly, there is now very little cropping done in the Glen. The estate does not want to encourage cows on the hill as it is thought that this interferes with grouse breeding.[23] There are now only two shepherds in the Glen, when formerly sheep were an important part of the Glen's economy. Even in the 1930s there were as many as nine shepherds in Glenesk. Now there are three head keepers and eight under-keepers: Albert Taylor is head keeper at Invermark; Dennis Caithness is head keeper at Millden, with Greg Anderson as under-keeper; Fred Taylor is head keeper at Inchgrundle, with Billy Walker his assistant; other under-keepers are: Ronnie Hepburn, the Chalet; Sandy Bertram, Dykeneuk; Andy Malcolm, Milton; Sandy Duncan, Ardoch; Jim Grant, Auchintoul; Graham Fraser, Greenburn. Many former farms can be recognised in this list, which demonstrates the extent to which much former agricultural land has been made over to grouse moors and deer forest.

Critics argue that sporting estates do inhibit rural development, and there is no doubt that changes in land use are responsible for much of the out-migration from Glenesk. There is a conflict of interest between estate policy and those in favour of agricultural development, i.e. farmers and shepherds, but it seems that, for the time being at least, they will have to co-exist as best they can. It is fitting, perhaps, to leave the last word to Peter Copland, formerly of Kedloch, who penned these (prophetic?) lines either just before or just after he emigrated to the United States between 1850–5. Three verses are quoted here:

> Your glen a desert will become
> No fields of corn you'll see
> The deer, the roe, the grouse and hare
> inhabit will Lochlee.

[22] ibid, 172.
[23] Mackenzie, op. cit. 44.

Your landlord though a worthy man
and highly praised by thee
must find a place where deer can roam
and chosen has Lochlee.

Then up, rise up, both old and young
Example taken by me
Rise, cross the sea to Canada,
Sing farewell to Lochlee.

14

HEARTH AND HOME

The ruins of the croft of Whigginton lie on the south side of the North Esk, a mile beyond Tarfside and a field's length from 'Whiggie's Ford' across the water. The nearest inhabited houses on the east and west are Buskhead and Kirn (Drumgreen), although, in time past, there were numerous houses in the vicinity. The last tenant was Jess Cattanach, who died there on 28 January 1919. Her people had farmed the croft for generations. She was a great character, much painted and photographed, and her memory was still green after half a century. The long life of the last occupant and her independent character, the isolation from modern developments, and the interest of the tenants in the preservation of the ruin, have all contributed to this contact with the past which Whigginton can provide.

No record of Whigginton prior to 1636 has yet been found. In August 1636 William Chrystie made his will. He left estate valued at £625, a substantial sum at that time. In the ground, 5 bolls of black oats and 1 boll of bere had been sown. The extent of the holding in 1636 is unknown but, in 1895, Whigginton was a croft of eight acres with pasture for 80 ewes, including commonty, to which Whigginton continued to have the right as long as it was a holding. This would not nowadays be considered a viable unit, yet comfortable living seems to have been possible in the seventeenth century.

In 1967 a small corn kiln for drying grain was recognised and excavated by Professor Alexander Fenton. It is tucked into the west bank of the stream beyond most of the ruins. It goes five feet into the ground, and when four feet had been dug, seeds of small oats and bere were discovered, all of them charred. The floor was of clay, and the carefully built stone walls take the shape of the bottom part of an egg, with an entrance flue, along which heat is carried.

In the *Old Statistical Account* of 1792, there is no mention of corn kilns, but nearly every Glenesk farm had a similar structure. Tenants were thirled to a particular mill, that is, bound to grind their grain there for payment of certain multure and sequels. Multure was the quantity of grain or meal payable to the miller or by the multurer to his tacksman, whereas the sequels were the small quantities given to the servants (knaveship, bannock, lock or gowpen). Thirlage implied the upholding of the mill, repairing the dam-dykes and lades, and bringing home the millstones. There the obligations ended. The tenant had every right to dry his own grain. Corn kilns may have been in use in comparatively recent times, but no one alive in Glenesk had heard of them until the search for them began. From New Zealand, James Dunbar, born at Garthead, Glenesk, wrote in 1904, 'The horrors and anxieties of a rainy harvest in Glenesk still haunt my imagination'. Frequently, the corn kilns face the prevailing wind from the east. They were liable to catch fire, if carelessly watched, for the drying floor was of straw laid over wooden laths. For this reason, an entrance flue of a reasonable length was needed, but not so long that it would dissipate the heat.

The ruin of a substantial house in the vicinity of the corn kiln may have been William Chrystie's 'awin dwellin' house'. Unfortunately, the surviving testament from his will does not detail the house plenishing. The spaces for timber crucks, probably six pairs, are clearly seen on the north wall. There are remains of others of the kind at Arsallary and Turnabrane. The age of this house is unknown, but the sloping lintel over the east gable fireplace is reminiscent of similar lintels in Invermark Castle. The back wall has had to be strengthened by a buttress at some period in its existence. The kitchen end probably had a wide 'hangin' lum' of wood, such as is still remembered at Turnabrane in the late 1960s.

Around this house are many other ruins, one of which, Whiggie's Bucht, has a low type of door for letting animals in and out, and several others, one of which had been a byre. Near the later house, also a ruin, are other outbuildings. Below this is a lime-kiln of the stokehole variety, with a ramp up to the bowl above the furnace where the lime-stone was deposited. This is a common type dating from the late eighteenth century. It is likely that this later house was built for or by the Cattanachs. James Cattanach married Margaret Christison in 1785. A room is built on to the west side of the house, and it is likely, from the construction of the back wall, that this had been part of the original design. As Margaret Christison's father, James, died in 1793, the room could well have been for him. It is possible that the single room may be a late addition, though there is no clear trace of abutment at the back, and may have been where Jess's grandparents lived, along the lines of a 'Granny flat'. It had been customary to provide accommodation for the old folk, or for the young couple. The good stone fireplace within the wall still exists, and there is a window in the back wall as well as in the front one. There is evidence of a straight-jointed abutment at the front, though this is not clear on the rear wall.

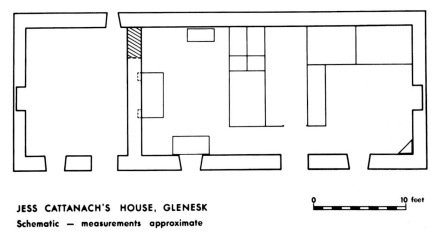

JESS CATTANACH'S HOUSE, GLENESK
Schematic — measurements approximate

0 _____ 10 feet

A diagram of Whigginton. The main house is partitioned by various pieces of furniture, with the smaller room built on to its west side. The kitchen area occupies the left part of the main house, with the hanging lum set against the left gable. C3915.

Migvie limekiln with an underground potato pit to its right. C12877.

The ruins of Whigginton, surveyed by Alexander Fenton in 1968, can still provide us with enough detail to build up a picture of how the house would have looked when habitable. There is a strong possibility that the building dates back to the end of the eighteenth century. The stonework of Whigginton is well squared and door checks were of quarried and shaped stone. The side walls now stand to six feet six inches high approximately. The inner gable still stands to about eleven feet three inches. The window sills are two feet ten inches up from the ground, and the height of the window itself is 2 feet 6 inches. The but-end and the single room have gable fireplaces, with nice breast stones.

Gleneffock

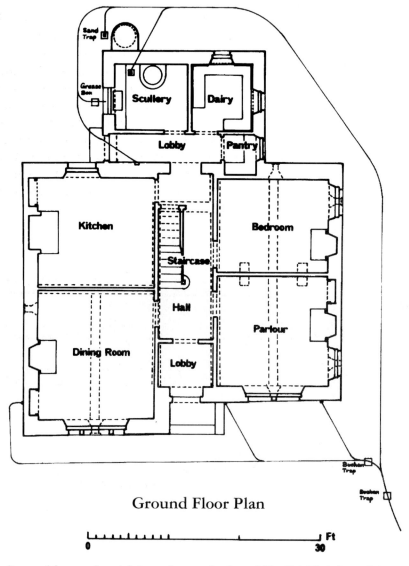

Ground Floor Plan

```
0                              30  Ft
```

A diagram of the more substantial nineteenth-century farmhouse of Gleneffock. The bedroom, dining room and parlour all have fireplaces, and the kitchen its cooking area. C18198. Drawn by C Hendry NMS.

Below Jess Cattanach's house is another group of buildings, including a dwelling house, which Jess's house may have replaced. This earlier house had its roof supported by crucks and some wall slots for crucks are still visible. The spacing of the remaining slots suggest that there had been six sets of crucks. The stones of this house were clay mortared, as was Jess Cattanach's house. In contrast, the ruins of Whitestone farm show that the stones were not clay mortared. The walls were built of roughly shaped and unshaped stones, and a mixture of clay, straw and chopped up heather was used as luting in the crevices between the stones.

Before the advent of slate, most of the houses in the Glen would have had thatched roofs. In a 1906 photograph of Whigginton, the thatched roof is a notable feature. According to James Stewart of Buskhead, wheat straw was used generally in the thatch. The tools used in thatching included a long ladder, a graip and a round stick about four feet in length which was used to beat the straw into position. The graip was for laying the bunch of straw on the roof from the top of the ladder. The type of wooden graip found in the thatch at Buskhead is one of only three known in different parts of Scotland, though this suggests that its use was much more widespread at one time. It is striking in that it is parallel in form to Scandinavian graips, used for muck. The Glenesk graip is in good condition. It measures three feet two-and-a-half inches long by ten inches wide, and has three prongs.

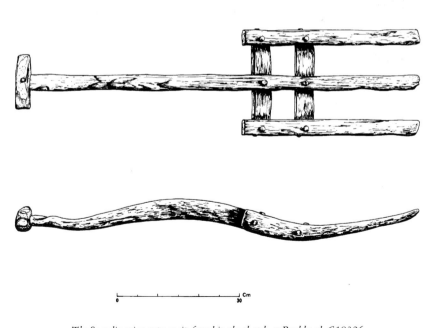

The Scandinavian type graip found in the thatch at Buskhead. C18326.

James Stewart of Buskhead with the graip. 51/9/4. A. Fenton.

The thatchers started at the eaves on the right hand side of the house. The thatch was laid in strips, with the straw overlapping about a third of its length until the easing was reached, then the ladder was shifted over an equal distance and work started on another strip. It was knitting the two strips together that showed the thatcher's skill, because if it was not done properly, in time, a hollow developed, letting in the rain. After the roof was thatched, easing boards were laid along the edge of the roof to which the esparto rope was tied. Ropes were put right over the roof twelve inches apart, then cross ropes were laced round the upright ones twelve inches apart until the whole roof was covered. Finally, the edge of the straw was trimmed to give, in James Stewart's words, 'a gie tidy roof'.

Mrs Elizabeth Christison at York Redoubt, wearing a shirt of hard-wearing wincey cloth. The hangin' lum on the left gable served the kitchen area, while the stone chimney was situated in the best room. A wooden or metal spar, known as a 'runce' runs a little above the eaves to keep the thatch from lifting in the wind. Early 1900s. Glenesk Museum.

The Beadles' house beside the former Free Church (now Maule Memorial Hall), opposite Cairncross cornyard. There is a thatched wooden lean-to at the gable. On the left is a well-built peat-stack. 1893. Glenesk Museum.

Buskhead, with James Stewart as a boy in foreground. On the left is the remains of the old house and on the right is the new house with its slate roof. About 1910. C3408.

Another example of a stone built farmhouse at Burnfoot with a byre attached. The door of the byre may have been where the extension was joined onto the main house. Late nineteenth century. G4/3.

The farmhouse at Milton of Lochlee has stone-built chimneys with chimney pots. The house has been designed so that the attic area can be used for rooms. Another innovation is the fine porch. Date unknown. Glenesk Museum.

HEARTH AND FUEL

Before the hangin' lum, fires had often been in the middle of the room, and smoke escaped via an outlet in the roof as in highland black houses. As yet, no evidence of this has been found in Glenesk. Opposite the built-in furniture, Whigginton had its 'hangin' lum', that is, a chimney fixed against the wall, and standing out into the kitchen. The outlet was the width of the wall from the gable. It was made partly of stone and clay or lime, and partly of wood. In Glenesk, materials for such chimneys varied. The house at Dykeneuk contained the last hingin' lum in the Glen, and it was still in use in 1968. The canopy was three feet seven inches across, and had a depth of 22 inches. It stood on little jambs. The lum was rounded on the wall, to keep the flame going up. In 1854, Dykeneuk is described in the Lochlee Rentals as 'West Migvie House', and J.M. Davidson retained the name 'West Migvie'. There was more wood about the Migvie lum, not surprisingly, as the Davidsons were the local joiners. The same kind of wooden canopy was still being made as late as 1850–60. The all-stone fireplaces came later, after 1850. The Whigginton links, for supporting the kettle and pots, can be seen in the Museum. They were suspended from a 'rantle-tree', a cross-bar in the chimney. The swey that could be swung in and out came along later.

The hangin' lum at Migvie, with Mrs Duke sitting by the fire. The hooks hanging from the ceiling were used to smoke or dry food. Note the pictures used for decoration. Date unknown. C13142.

Will Stormonth's house, with the chimney built into the gable end. The fireplace is raised above the level of the floor. The pot chains are hanging from a swey. Note the electric light bulb hanging from the ceiling. Early 1970s. 4/22/11. A. Fenton.

By the eighteenth century, the fire sat on a rounded stone and there were hobs at the side. Peat and sticks were extensively used, and peat cutting was one of the season's occupations, taking place in May and June. So long as family farms persisted this was economical, but when workers had to be paid the cost of peats became dearer than coal. Moreover, the peat mosses close at hand became used up, and the good peat is now less accessible. Peat fires were banked at night so that in many places they did not go out as long as a certain family was in occupation.

*Peat-cutting, possibly in the Townhead of Cairncross area. George Michie is holding the flachter spade.
Note the peat barrow lying behind the spade. 1890s. Glenesk Museum.*

There was communal peat cutting at Westbank (Cock's Hillock). No payment was made, and there were several rules. The bank had to be bedded
properly, that is, the top turf was stacked and re-laid in the bed after the peat
was removed to prevent large holes being left. Drainage had to be good, to
prevent stagnant water which was dangerous to animals.

Two people were required, one to dig, the other to load the barrow. The
bank was four feet wide and no more so that the barrow could be easily loaded.
The bank was divided into four widths and the peats were five inches in width.
A flanged spade was used to keep the peats square. First, the rutting spade was
used to cut the ground, then the turf was turned with the flachter spade, the
surface divots being removed until the moss was reached. If the moss was deep
enough, one cut in from the briest (banking or breast). If not, then the doon-
cuttin' method was used. The top-most layer was always cut from the top
(doon-cutting). This seems to have been the common method in Glenesk.

When the banking method (cutting from the breist) was used, the spade was
pushed into the peats so as to slacken the whole length before dividing it into
normal sized peats. The peats were then lifted into the peat barrow, with twenty
peats to the barrow and twenty barrows to the cartload. They were wheeled into
the blair (drying area) and laid out singly, not touching, and ten days later were
collected into small bundles or rickles of ten–twelve peats, and left till they were
scroggit (well-dried) and hardened on the outside, the rain hardly touching the
rickles. They were put in larger bundles, taken home and stacked. The time for
cutting the peats was between the sowing and thinning of turnips.

Driving the Peats - Dinnertime - June, 1888

Stylemouth, 1888. Behind left, are the steadings of Westbank. In the picture are Diddlin' Davy, Mill of Auchronie, the Christison brothers, three summer visitors to Auchronie, Young Nannie, Old Nannie (Mrs. Agnes Davidson and her daughter), occupants of the house.

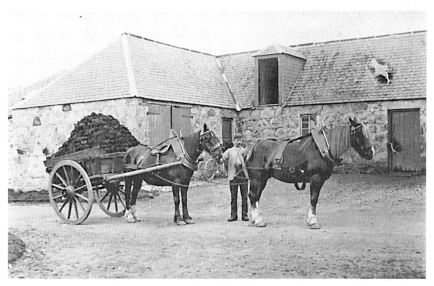

Horseman George Strachan transporting peats. Note the bicycle leaning against the wall behind him. Date unknown. Per Miss G.F. Michie. C6763.

FOOD

All of the cooking utensils were made of iron. There were pots, girdles, frying-pans, kettles, of all sizes. The pot-oven, with its lid, was a useful utensil. It was placed on the fire and covered with glowing peat, so that the heat was evenly spread. In such ovens the housewives cooked and baked with great success. If broth was being made, an 'overlay' was placed below the lid to keep the pot from boiling over. The muckle pot was for days when a great deal of water was used, for example, when the pig was killed. The girdle, hung on the cleek, was in more or less daily use for a family. Bannocks of oatcakes were fired on the girdle on one side and finished on an oval toaster in front of the fire. There were two kinds of bannock, the thick ones with fat in them, and those as thin as a sixpence, without fat. Girdle scones and drop scones were also favourites. Jess Cattanach liked bannocks. 'They hail the stomach', she used to declare. There was also the brander and spurtle, all of a kind known in a wide area and used over a long period of time. Although there were tea-kettles in grand houses in the late seventeenth century, ordinary kettles do not appear to have been in every household until one hundred years later.

The interior of Whigginton kitchen with its hangin' lum. The lower sides of the chimney consist of white-washed stone, and the pot over the fire is hanging from a 'rantle-tree'. A bannock spade is hanging on the chimney above the fire. The crook and the links, plus a cast-iron pot, are now in Glenesk Museum. The photograph, probably taken by J.D. Ross in September 1906, won first prize in a Loudon competition, under the title 'Declining Years'.

The kitchen fire at the Baillies. Bannocks are being cooked on the girdle, which is attached to a swey. Some bannocks have been placed on the floor level toaster to harden off them. Note the bannock spade standing in front of the kettle. 1930s. Glenesk Museum.

Often, a ham or salmon was smoked in the lum. There was, of course, plenty of food to be had if one ignored game laws. It is well known that farm servants used to stipulate that they should have salmon only three times a week. The 'saut backit' (salt box) also hung in the lum to keep the salt dry. Jess also kept tobacco in it for her friend Mrs Christison, widow of a Chelsea pensioner, who lived on the other side of the ford, and enjoyed a smoke.

Other common foods were brose, sowans, kail, hares and rabbits, venison in season, milk, butter, cheese and eggs, fowls, skirly, tatties and dip, tatties and butter, stovies, milk broth made with rice and onions, broth proper, dried fish, trout and birse tea (with a 'bristle', a little whisky in it). In some houses the teapot sat at the fire the whole day. It was said that 'the pig made a hearty house', there was so much one could do with it. It could be roasted, boiled, fried, made into potted head, while the bones helped with soup. There was also offal and black and white puddings. At the pig killing there was activity in and out of doors. It was an important occasion. Pigs were generally kept until they were about 30 stone in weight, to get the full benefit of them, although they tasted better at half the size.

Moss dinners were often used when peat-cutting was in progress, and were so called because they could be taken out to the site.[1] Moss dinners were fairly

[1] P. Thomson. *Take One Glen: Recipes From Glen Kitchens*, Standard Press, Montrose, 1973, 166.

quick to prepare. The most common ones were milk barley and steepies. The former was barley boiled in water, to which milk was added, then salt or sugar to taste. Steepies was bread soaked in milk and sprinkled with sugar, which would be taken with soup.

Jess Cattanach used a plump (plunge) churn when she had a cow, and a wooden tub for making the butter in. She must have used the mid room as her milkhouse, for Whiggie slept in the room off the kitchen. After 1850 she had a cheese press of the all-stone variety, with the square press, now at Cairncross.

There had been plenty of work to do when the place was a croft, and the Cattanachs had a servant in 1851, according to the *Census Returns*, but Jess was earning her own living at this time at Auchronie. The daily routine had included rising at 5 a.m., going out to milk and returning for breakfast. As there were no horses at Whigginton, Whiggie had employed his time before breakfast possibly feeding the hens.

FURNISHINGS

In the 'room' at Whigginton was a corner press situated between the fireplace and the window, and in it Whiggie kept the whisky. There was a little black grate and opposite it were two box beds. The room was lined with books, some of which are in the Museum. According to Mrs Johnston, who was very well acquainted with Whigginton, as she lived at Buskhead, Jess's house was well furnished. The kitchen was bare but the room was very comfortable. In the crevices of the dyke outside some fragments of very good dishes and glass have been found. In the Museum is the red and white diamond pattern cotton bedcover which Greta Michie remembered seeing on Jess's bed in the kitchen when she lay ill. She always wore a woollen bonnet. Jess Cattanach was a big woman, six feet tall, and wore men's boots and shoes. She used to build dykes, clip sheep, and cut the grain with a heuk. She was the last person to use the spinning wheel in the Glen, and it was the muckle wheel she used. She used to spin the wool and knit stockings with it. Unfortunately, by the turn of the century, the Blackface wool was coarsening as the original strain of white sheep disappeared. One customer of long standing, Mackie Smith of Dundee, wrote to say that his feet had been so chafed by the wool that he could not renew his order.

The muckle wheel is now rarely seen, and only in the Highlands of Scotland, Wales, Ireland and parts of Canada. It arrived in Scotland by the sixteenth century, and was used for weft yarn, the warp being still made on the spindle. By the 1770s they were mostly superseded by a treadle wheel, but some people preferred the large one. The spinner used to go out into the lobby and wind the wool round herself, so that she could bring it back without ravelling. The muckle wheel in the Museum came from Mr J.M. Davidson, Dykeneuk. On two spars are the two wear marks of fingers, one for spinning and one for winding, when one went in the opposite direction. The Dykeneuk wheel is known to have been in use at Dochty in Glenlee by Mr Davidson's great-grandmother, Ann Ennerdale, in the eighteenth century.

The main house at Whigginton had two rooms and a very small place entered from the lobby, where Jess had a chest of drawers containing the will. A door led through from the kitchen to the extra room. There was built-in furniture consisting of a box-bed and a double press. The colour of the wood was the result of the application of linseed oil, turpentine and beeswax. A trap door in the kitchen, near the fireplace, led up to a narrow garret, a corner in the roof of the house. After Jess Cattanach's death, this was found to be full of spinning-wheels and suchlike. In the older houses the entire kitchen wall opposite the fire consisted of movable furniture, which was the property of the occupant, and could be removed at a flitting. Many of these houses were really one long room divided into compartments by fittings. The furniture in the ordinary tenant's house would have been simple, and the ruins of cot houses are too small for them to have contained more than the essentials. The following list of the contents of Burnside of Arsallary in 1865 is probably typical of most households in Glenesk in the nineteenth century:

Kitchen
Two Fir tables
Plate rack with dinner ware
Two ladles, masher (for potatoes) and three caps (bowls)
Two milk pitchers
Two flagons
Tea kettle
Lantern and two tin jugs
Knife board (for sharpening)
Five pots and boiler
Seven chairs (old)
Form (old)
Old bound bed and press
Two pails
Two smoothing irons and a piping iron
Box with horn spoons
Two candlesticks
Crook bellows and Tongs
       Total value of the above was £2.8.4d.

South Room
Eight day clock
Two bound beds and presses
Fir table and presses
Six chairs
Tea crockery in press
Three tumblers and three glasses
1 dozen Knives and forks
1 dozen Britannia metal spoons
2 dozen   "   "   Tea spoons
Small mirror
Tea tray
Eight volumes of old books
Clouty carpet
Grate and fire irons
     Total value of above £7.2.5d.

The Middletons flitting from Tirlybirly to Edzell. The family would have taken all the movable furniture from the house, including the box-beds, kists and presses. Note the mattresses on the right hand cart. It would have taken a few more cart-loads to complete the flitting. c.1908. Glenesk Museum.

BEDDING

There was plenty of bedding, blankets and sheets. The bolsters and pillows were sometimes of feathers and sometimes of chaff.

The typical Glen farmhouse of today is a comfortable stone building probably dating from the late nineteenth century. Although there is usually a modern annex containing kitchen premises, the outside appearance of such houses has changed very little. One of the main front rooms is the living room, while the other is 'the (best)room'. Between is usually a mid-bedroom and a staircase. Upstairs are two large bedrooms and either a bathroom or a smaller bedroom between. All permanently occupied houses now have bathrooms.

In the early part of the twentieth century, the average house was fairly uniform in its basic design. At the back door there would have been a small scullery and milkhouse. The kitchen usually had a stone-slabbed or concrete floor, although in the nineteenth century, the floor would have consisted partly of hard-beaten earth and partly of stone flags. The country kitchen windows of such houses usually had nine panes and did not open. There was generally a black grate, with a swey, an oven on one side and a water boiler with a brass tap on the other. Sometimes, where a hot water system had been installed there was a range. These black grates shone with daily polishing, and the steel parts were rubbed with sandpaper until they were like mirrors. There were also the older kinds of fireplaces, such as the low fires with granite jambs and lintel and a hearth where the teapot stayed comfortably warm, and also low fires with a canopy. Most of the rooms in the house had a black grate.

Most early twentieth century kitchens had a dresser. This was not the Welsh dresser, but the ordinary kitchen dresser. Above the dresser was frequently either a dish rack or shelves with handsome plates and jugs for decoration. The walls were either white-washed or wood-lined. Opposite the fire was generally a bed recess or else a proper box bed. Here the maid usually slept, if there was one, but if not, the farmer and his wife occupied these comfortable sleeping quarters. On the same side as the bed was either a large pantry with a door leading from the kitchen, or else a huge double press.

The house of Cosie Howe, built by Robert Gibb in 1850 but now a ruin, is interesting as it is a fine example of a late nineteenth-, early twentieth-century house, recorded by Greta Michie. To the left was a good-sized kitchen, with a window both to the front and the back, the latter very small. The walls were white, the ceiling wooden, with the beams concealed, the latter being treated from time to time with linseed oil, turpentine and beeswax, as was the box bed and large press which made up one side of the room. The bed had curtains, but sliding doorways were customary. The fireplace had a high mantelpiece, on which the brass rail was brightly polished, and was used for drying or airing clothes on. The water was carried from a nearby well, and the pail and wash-up table and basin stood in the little window recess, with a dish rack on the adjoining wall. The floor consisted of stone slabs. The custom was for the parents to sleep in the kitchen. On the other side of the lobby was 'the room', with two box beds and a fine chest of drawers. Between this room and the kitchen was the mid room with a box bed and another chest. The house also had a low loft. Outside there was a shed where Mrs Gibb could put on a fire and heat the water for washing. There are many similarities between Cosie Howe and Jess Cattanach's house.

Before World War I, American clocks were popular, often sitting on their own on a small shelf. Grandfather clocks were common, and stood in the lobby. In the best room there was generally a black marble clock, or a clock under a glass globe.

Lighting was supplied by paraffin and candles. There were lamps of various kinds, including those which were suspended from the ceiling, or standing lamps with one or two burners. Most houses had small lamps either for hanging on the wall, keeping the bathroom warm in frost or for taking upstairs. Byre lanterns progressed from candles to paraffin lighting.

Before the advent of paraffin and tilley lamps, one of the most common forms of lighting would have been the crusie lamp. They were constructed of two, often shell- or leaf-shaped vessels, generally made of iron. The lower vessel was fixed, while the upper one was attached on a ratchet so that it could be tilted forward, allowing all of the oil to be used. Any overflow was caught in the vessel below. Generally, rushes were used as wicks, and the oil would have been in the form of animal fat.

The best room was reserved for special occasions. The wallpaper was usually of good quality, and there was either a Brussels carpet or good inlaid linoleum with rugs, often of the Brussels type. The furniture was of light oak or of good mahogany. Mahogany chairs with rounded backs were popular, and large couches of various shapes and sizes, including the chaise longue, were common. Most households had a sideboard and a corner cupboard. The table was large and frequently of the extending type. On special occasions it was covered with white damask, on which was laid the finest table ware. From the beginning of the nineteenth century at least, and until comparatively recently, christenings, weddings, and funeral services were held in the 'best' room, no doubt spreading out into all of the house and, so far as weddings were concerned, perhaps moving into the barn for dancing.

CLOTHING

There were various interesting customs regarding clothing. Men slept in their grey shirts or 'sarks', and women tucked their skirts up when working, to keep them clean. Women wore a cotton bonnet, which was used to keep the sun off the face and neck. Shawls and plaids were common. There were travelling tailors who used to make clothes for boys out of their father's old suits. The farmers wore their cord breeks and waltams (straps around the legs), the game-keepers the district tweed, and the thatchers and stone-breakers their knee pads.

John McIntosh, who was shepherd at Baillies for over 20 years. The breeks are of the Dalhousie tartan. Early 1900s. Glenesk Museum.

Many people in Scotland wore stockings and often no shoes, although it was the custom in Angus to wear simple footwear called 'Forfar Brogues'. Greta Michie heard from an old man how his mother used to walk over the hills barefoot on a Sunday, with her boots slung over her back, until she saw the church in sight and then she put them on. Several people related similar stories. The dislike of footwear lasted into the twentieth century. Duncan Michie, Greta's brother, was expected to wear boots by his parents, but he hid them in the morning in a wild rose bush at the roadside beside Loch Giseney, and he collected them again in the afternoon.

There is a large collection of costumes on display in the Glenesk Museum, some dating from the eighteenth century. A beautiful gown, dating from 1750, was presented to the Museum by Lord Forres. It belonged to an ancestor of his who was a farmer's wife at Brigton, St Cyrus. Most of the costumes in the collection are women's dresses, mainly wedding and ball gowns, such as Minnie Lindsay's ball frock, dating from 1908, which was made at a class at Tarfside. Most of the costumes are in very good condition, and are still eye-catching today.

With the advent of modern amenities, there has been a tremendous disposal of older domestic furnishings. It is one of the reasons for the large Museum intake year by year. That, and an awareness on the part of the Glen people of the historical importance of a collection which shows a way of life which will not return.

15

PEOPLE AND PLACES

In her younger days, Jess Cattanach used to walk into Brechin with her butter and eggs, over the hill by Lethnot. Actually, the road to Whigginton was a mere track originally, but it was a right of way. As she started on her journey she would have passed by houses on the Leyhillock, now long forgotten.

Greta Michie's relations, the Fairweathers from Dundee, came to know the Cattanachs. About 1880, Alexina Fairweather and her brother, James, had travelled from Dundee and had lost their way to Drumgreen. They landed at Whigginton, knocked on the door, which was opened by an old man. They asked if this was the road to Drumgreen and he said: 'Ony wey's a road here. Come in'. This was old Whiggie, John Cattanach, brother of Jess. All the time he was entertaining them in the room, Jess was frying ham in the kitchen. Jim Fairweather produced a newspaper, and you would have thought it was gold. Not to be outdone, Old Whiggie went to the corner pressie and produced the whisky bottle. This was difficult for the visitors as they came from a teetotal household. Jim whispered to Alexina: 'You'll hae tae tak it. I'm ower young'. She did and that began a great friendship.

Jim Fairweather and his brothers used to come to Whigginton for holidays. They slept in the room and went fishing every day. When they came home, Jess fed them on cockerels. One day she said: 'The cocks are a' dune. Will hens dae?'.

John Cattanach did all his work with a box-barrow. He used to bring his hens' meat from Tarfside in this way, taking help from anyone he met on the road. Whiggie never had a horse. The Mitchells of Turnabrane did the horse work, while Rob Middleton at Tirlybirly on the other side of the water built the stacks. When John Cattanach went to the ghillying at Invermark, Jess saw to the harvest. At Whigginton, as in many other places, sprots in the bogs used to be cut as bog hay, and were used for thatching houses and stacks, and for covering potato pits. Bog sprots are tougher than rushes which break up readily.

When John Cattanach died there was a roup, but the furniture consisted of fixtures. The Stewarts of Buskhead acquired the arable ground and one third of the hill. The rest, including the commonty, went to the Dunbars of the Kirn.

Greta Michie recalled her memories of Jess Cattanach:

> She was very kind to children, had parties for the young Stewarts, gave children 3d out of a tin in which she was keeping the pension money she was unwilling to take, washed my frock when I blackened it on the pots. She had children's picnics. When I attended Tarfside school, my mother used to call for me at a quarter past three in the afternoon, once every three weeks, and together we visited Jess. The experience left a lasting impression on me. This was between 1911 and 1917. I also visited her in 1918, shortly before she died.

Jess Cattanach died of a cerebral haemorrhage after falling out of her box-bed in the kitchen. The executors were Archibald Stewart of Buskhead and Joseph Dunbar of the Kirn. The Will was found in the mid-room chest of drawers, and according to custom it was not examined until after the funeral. There is no stone in either churchyard to commemorate the Cattanachs or the Christisons of Whigginton. Perhaps the original one has sunk below ground level. Were a stone to be raised, a suitable inscription might be: 'The last of the old style of Glen crofters'.

Jess Cattanach with one of the Dunbars from the Kirn. About 1915.

Jess Cattanach at the 'stroop' for water. The spout was an cast-iron mould-board, made at Arbroath Foundry, of a plough. The mould-board is now in Glenesk Museum. About 1915 C.12876

The jingle 'Thow, Low, Christison and Kinnear', provides the Glen names commonest in the nineteenth century. These, and others, not completely gone from the district, are found in documents of the sixteenth century. In 1543, a Court of the Barony of Glenesk was held at Dalbog. The names mentioned include Christison, Kynnear, Hech, Nockall (Nicoll), Davison, Guthre, Archibald, Smart, Donaldson, Fyndlo, Ross, Brabonar (Bremner), Carncross, Laue (Low), Tailor, Will, Wilkie, and Anerdaill. The last, usually spelt Ennerdale or Inverdale, has disappeared from the district but not from the stock. At the Baron's Court of 1543, Henre Annerdaill, with several others, was fined for cutting wood at Dalbog. In 1482, John Annathirdale had the third part of the Mill of Ennerescondy with the mill lands of the same. In 1716 and 1759, the Ennerdales are recorded at Dochty in Glen Lee. Some of the Glen people can, therefore, be said to be 'aulder than the laird'.

A family tree shows the descendants of Peter Grant, joiner, Dykeneuk and Ann Ennerdale, a daughter of David Ennerdale of Dochty, which is a holding a mile beyond the head of Loch Lee. Their daughter married John Davidson, joiner at Dykeneuk, and a descendant of theirs, J.M. Davidson, was the last resident estate joiner, and one of the promoters of the Glenesk Museum. The muckle wheel – for spinning – in the Museum belonged to Ann Ennerdale. Among other families with Ennerdale inheritance were, or are, the Christisons of Glentennet, the Donaldsons, who were at Greenburn, some of the Caithnesses, the Mitchells of Turnabrane and the Mitchells of Auchintoul.

Jess Cattanach posing for the photographer with her muckle wheel (normally, the wheel would have been kept inside the house). About 1915.

Auchintoul farmhouse was built in 1897, although the site is an old one. This was, originally, Wester Auchintoul. In 1835, James Mitchell became tenant of Wester Auchintoul, on a 19-year lease. In 1854, both East and West Auchintoul were let to John Pirie on a 19-year lease, commencing Whitsunday 1854. When John Pirie died in 1899, his brother James retained only the house at East Auchintoul. George Strachan became farmer. He was a very hard worker and greatly improved the farm, even recreating fields overgrown by trees. His wife was Jean Michie and they had two sons, Victor and Duncan. The former, who died in December 1966, aged 69, was a farmer of Milton of Lochlee. Duncan had been farmer at Auchintoul, but retired for health reasons in 1971. He came to Auchintoul when only a few weeks old.

In 1854, John Pirie took over Easter Auchintoul from his father, Robert, who was living there in the 1830s. At that time the latter was a gamekeeper with Lord Panmure. Previously he had been schoolmaster at Lochlee, and his father was Rev. John Pirie, parish minister. John Pirie died in 1899, and his brother, James, retained the house at Easter Auchintoul until his death in 1917. For a time the Guthrie family lived in part of the house.

By 1925, Mr and Mrs Duncan Strachan were living there, and they continued to do so until the death of Duncan's father, George Strachan, in 1942, when they moved to the farmhouse. Since then, Mudloch Cottage, as it was by this time called, has been let as a holiday home.

Mrs Mitchell, Betty Stewart, lived at Inchgrundle. Her husband, James Mitchell, was the estate shepherd, and the couple brought up their family at Glen Mark in the thatched house which has been replaced by the present one. Queen Victoria lunched there. It was probably on the occasion of the Queen's second visit in 1865 that James Mitchell was one of the men who went to the shoulder of Mount Keen to meet the royal party coming from Balmoral.

In the summer the Mitchell children walked to school at Tarfside. In the winter they stayed at Cairncross. John Mitchell, for a time, assisted as schoolmaster. He had a wide store of knowledge, and became an authority on the treasures of the ground.

In 1854, Invermark Deer Forest was created by Royal permission. Archibald Campbell came to Inchgrundle in that year as head stalker, and remained in that position until 1872. When he went to Gleneffock, he was still in charge of the Forest for two years. John Mitchell succeeded Archie Campbell in 1872, and went to Inchgrundle. He was a stalker on the Invermark estate for fifty years, and died in 1933 in his 90th year. One stalker, Willie McGregor, lived at Glenmark, and the other stalkers lived at Inchgrundle. The Mitchells occupied the West house, and Reverend Dr Guthrie the East. James Mitchell Jr became head gamekeeper on Invermark. His son, John, became head gamekeeper at Millden, retiring in 1970.

As well as the name Kinnear appearing on the Baron Court of 1543, the signatures of Thomas Kinnear, Inchgrundle, and David Kinnear, Auchlochie (Westbank) appear in the Forfeited Estate Papers in 1716. From 1768 to 1780, the births of the Kinnear family in Boddam, behind Keenie, are recorded in the Episcopal Register. From this last branch were descended the Dukes of Dalhestnie and Migvie, and in the Museum is a nursing chair used by five generations from one Martha Kinnear in Boddam onwards. It was presented by Miss Minnie Lindsay who died aged 85 in 1964. She was a direct descendant of the Kinnears of Boddam, through her grandmother, Martha Kinnear, Mrs Duke of Dalhestnie.

At the same time that William Kinnear tenanted the Boddam, another William Kinnear was in Holmhead and Knappiegreen. The latter was married twice, and of the five children from his first marriage, only his son John is known to have married and had children. At the beginning of the twenty-first century, their descendants are still in Edzell and district. In 1805, William Kinnear's eldest daughter, Agnes, married John Mitchell in Turnabrane, and from this family are descended the Skenes, Caithnesses, Cuttlehaugh Birses and many more.

There were many Christisons in Glenesk. For many years the cottage of Mangie was the home of Mrs Christison, whose husband had been farmer at West Aucheen. Now, the house is let to visitors during the summer months. It was last permanently occupied by Miss Agnes Gold, who died in 1950.

Mrs Christison, whose maiden name was Margaret Gibb, died at Mangie in 1933, aged 78. With her stayed her daughter, Mrs Menzies, and grand-daughter. Mrs Christison's other daughter was married to James Duncan, farmer at Ardoch, on whose ground Mangie was situated. Charles Duncan, their only child, was born in 1906 and farmed at Tigerton, Menmuir. Eventually, James Duncan moved to Drumcairn, Lethnot.

The house at Tirlybirly was built for a family named Birse, and was later occupied and named by a Chelsea Pensioner, Charles Christison, who died in 1886, aged 74, at York Redoubt, Lochlee. Charles Christison enlisted in the Black Watch in 1836 and went through all the Crimean War. The Museum holds a collection of letters which Charles Christison wrote from the Crimea and he named most of his family after battles of that war. Charles was born at Eastertown of Glentennet in 1812, and later married Elizabeth Clark.

Charles was probably the uncle of Mary Christison, who was also born at Eastertown of Glentennet and was a well-known character in the Glen. Mary and her blind mother (Isobel Ingram) lived for some time at Tirlybirly, before they moved to the East House (Turnabrane) around 1910–12, where Mary's mother died. Mrs Christison was a friend of Jess Cattanach, and it was she for whom Jess kept the tobacco in her saut-backet (salt box). Mary went to live with her sister, Jean, in Airneyfowl, Glenogil, and died there in 1931. Tirlybirly was occupied by a Miss McGregor, who was tenant until the place was destroyed by fire in the 1920s.

The name Jolly has been associated with Glenesk for a long time and their story could not have been told so fully had not a deed box been discovered in an Arbroath attic during World War II. The Jollys claimed French ancestry, but no proof can be found. The name Jolly (or Gellie), however, appears in the record of a Baron Court held at Dalbog in 1474, and continuously from then onwards in Testaments, parish and family records. Descendants and connections of the Jollys still living in the locality, and others in possession of a short family history written by a Mrs Elizabeth Beattie, owner of the deed box, have helped to piece together some of the family history, and to contact relatives all over the world. The name Jolly now no longer exists in Glenesk.

Margaret Wallace was tenant of Holmhead, Dalblae and Wellford, having got a nineteen-year tack on 20 November 1766, for a money rent of £9.10/- sterling per annum. She married John Low, son of James Low who had a tack of half of Shanno, and the tack was extended in John's name. In due course, she bore a daughter, Jean, who was destined to be progenitor of descendants who were to pioneer lands far beyond her ken.

Jean Low married James Jolly, a neighbouring crofter, who was also the Glen miller. They enjoyed only a few years of married life. When her husband died, Jean was faced with the problem of how to fend for herself and four young children. At Easter 1769, William, Earl of Panmure, agreed to transfer the tenancy of the mill town and mill lands of Aucheen to the young widow.

Willie Glass after he had moved to Tirlybirly. His clothes, with collared shirt, are the attire of a retired, or semi-retired man. 1928. Glenesk Museum.

Money was a scarce commodity in rural Scotland in the eighteenth century but two legacies helped to solve Jean's initial difficulties. Both were family bequests but she acknowledged them with legal exactitude on 'stampt' paper, and then placed the parchments beside the tack in her deed box.

The first document, written by Alexander Ross, Notary Public, Poet and Schoolmaster of Lochlee, acknowledged a settlement for 300 merks left to Jean by her father in 1771. The second is a legal agreement. A bachelor brother died in 1775, leaving an estate of £30 sterling. Jean made a pact with her surviving brother, and it is interesting to note that in this, and in all subsequent documents, she continued to use her maiden name. 'I, Jean Low, hereby oblige and bind me, to pay thankfully and with content, a yearly free annuity of "One pound, Ten Shillings sterling", during all the days of his lifetime to my surviving brother, David Low, in place of the Principal of "Thirty Pounds Sterling"'.

For an annual rental of £13 sterling and subject to certain conditions, Jean and her young family occupied 'the Mill and Mill town of Aucheen, the mill lands thereof, and astricted multures of the same, together with the houses, biggings, yards, pasturage, and whole parts and pendicles thereof.' The conditions were that she should 'bind and oblige' herself to:

1. To improve and meliorate the land, manuring, liming, marling, straightening and adjusting the marches, where necessary.
2. To plough up all baulks amongst arable land, and to sink all stones taken out, where practicable, before the end of the first 12 years of the Tack.
3. To enclose the space with the stone dykes, sufficient to keep out horses and black cattle.
4. To drain wet and marshy ground, and to divide the enclosure into lesser ones, if so ordered.
5. To fence and plant in one or more places contiguous to the houses on the farm, half an acre of ground, to care for and preserve the trees so planted, and to plant more in place of such as may decay within the first 8 years of the Tack.
6. To plant, thin and cut trees, at the direction, and for the use of the Earl, and to destroy none on her own behalf.
7. To take in, and improve one tenth of an acre of waste ground yearly during the nineteen years of this Tack, and to clear the same of stones.
8. To furnish yearly, if required, for the use of the family residing at Brechin Castle, twelve good hens fit for killing, for immediate use, for which she will be allowed out of her rent money, sixpence sterling for each hen so delivered.
9. To furnish one man and horse, two days yearly for performing such service as shall be required for building and repairing of Churches, bridges, manses, schools, and other public edifices. Also to pay to the Schoolmaster at Lochlee, yearly, the customary proportion of the Schoolmaster's salary.

Jean hired two servants, one to work part-time in the mill, the other full time on the land. Within nine years, existing arable land was improved, baulks levelled, stone dykes built, fields drained and enclosed. The shelter belt of trees was planted contiguous to the farm buildings, and an acre of waste ground was wrested from the surrounding muir. The meal and barley mill flourished.

Jean's sons grew to manhood, and Jean Low decided to re-marry (James Mollison, tenant in Craigendowre). The Tack of Aucheen was legally transferred to her son James Jolly, and this document, with his mother's signature dated 1778, was deposited in the family deed box and retained at Mill of Aucheen. Over the years other documents, letters and bills were crammed inside the old box. Then it was packed away and forgotten, till the attic was cleared out in the twentieth century, by which time her descendants to the eighth generation were scattered over Canada, America and Australia. Possibly not one of them ever heard of the hardy lass who trod the Braes of Angus years before.

In 1893, the Beadle's house was beside the former Free Church, now Maule Memorial Church, opposite Cairncross cornyard. Although only the foundation is now visible, lilac trees, roses and honeysuckle still bloom in the old garden. A saugh (willow) taken from the bottom of the garden grows profusely at Cairncross.

Cairncross farmhouse, previously the Ground Officer's house, was formerly an inn, facing 'down the Glen', and was known as Balhangie Inn. The Smithy was at Mid Cairncross (Midtown). Nether Cairncross, the name which Greta Michie's grandfather took, was below the road, as were other numerous ruins, the foundations of which have been forgotten.

The oldest known photograph of Cairncross dates from around 1864–70, but, in the Estate accounts for 1854, there is a description of repairs being carried out, and stones being carted away. The oldest part of the farm seems to be the back. When a bathroom was installed in 1905, a three-feet wall was found in the centre of the house. Originally, a straight stair with steps and ropes led upstairs from the kitchen (it is now a large cupboard). The back door had a double door with a chain and iron pin. All the doors in the back part had snecks. Behind the kitchen was a long outshot called the cellar. It then became the larder and the milkhouse.

For long, the farm of Cairncross was in the tenancy of the Michie family. Duncan Michie (1810–86), formerly of Strathdon, farmed Cairncross until his death in 1886, when it was taken over by his son, George. Originally, Duncan Michie went to the Drum in 1839 as gamekeeper, and his beat was Glen Mark. In 1852, he became head keeper at Invermark, and in 1854, Ground Officer, when he moved to Nether Cairncross, built on the site of the Balhangie Inn. As neighbouring holdings fell vacant he acquired them, so partly recreating the ancient holding of Cairncross. George Michie also retained the post of Ground Officer, which his father held, until it was discontinued in 1906. In 1904, George Michie married Alexina Fairweather, and they had two children, Margaret (Greta) b. 1905, and Duncan b. 1908. George Michie was well known as a fiddle player, and this was his chief interest beyond the farm. The

Glen was famous for its fiddlers. One of them was Willie Littlejohn, one of the band who played at Balmoral for Queen Victoria. Willie's son, Robert, was also recognised as a good fiddle player. It is related that a Glenworthy described a concert in the 'grand style' as 'no' worth a scart o' Geordie Michie's bow'. When George Michie died in 1924, the farm of Cairncross was continued by his son, Duncan, who later added Glentennet and Shinfur to his holdings.

George Michie, Greta Michie's grandfather, playing the fiddle in his Sunday best clothes. The whole family were good musicians, and music played a vital role in the life of the Glen. 1869. Glenesk Museum.

Greta Michie at three years old and her brother Duncan, a few months old. Note the wheels on the finely carved wooden high chair. 1908. G1/23/23A.

Duncan Michie was regarded as a pioneer in the improvement of hill sheep grazings, and he reclaimed a lot of land on his holdings. By progressive re-seeding, he created almost 200 acres of good grass and clover, which ran for two miles over the heather. Duncan Michie died in 1963, and his wife, Susan, became tenant of the farm of Cairncross. They had no children.

In the nineteenth century, before the Michies moved there, the Drum was occupied by the Stormonths. The Drum had at one time been a township, and numerous foundations of buildings, some of them dwelling houses, are still visible. Traces of ridge and furrow cultivation lie in the vicinity. The house was said to be the highest in the county, standing at 1,100 feet above sea-level, and is protected from high winds by the Drum Craig and Wood. Nearby is a dyke, apparently pre-nineteenth century, which encloses a large area of ground. It can be traced around the back of the water-works and across the water above Invermark Castle, reappearing at the Drum Wood, coming down and crossing the river and continuing above the House of Mark.

The Drum is mentioned in the Lochlee Register of Baptisms from the 1630s to the 1680s, the names being Christie, Egoe, Thow and Innerdale. When the estate was sold in 1715, the Drum must have been included either in the Kirkton of Lochlee or Drousty. In a list of subscriptions in aid of the Government in 1798, the names Tosh, Crockat, Birse and Innerdale are mentioned.

From the Drum, an equally good view can be obtained of Glen Mark and of Glen Esk proper. With its breathtaking view, Mrs Michie was justified in saying she never 'wearied' there. The Drum was a small farm before most of its ground became Invermark policies.

Wood Cottage, which came to be known as Cosie Howe and is now a ruin, was built around 1850 by Robert Gibb, stonemason, on the grounds of the farm of Ardoch, which was tenanted by his father. He built it for his bride, Mary Deakers. She became a well-known character in the Glen, and lived in the house until she died in 1918, aged 92. There are five photographs of her and her husband in the Glenesk Museum. The house continued to be occupied by their daughter, Jemima, who died in 1941, aged 69. From 1944, it was allowed to fall down.

The house at Turnabrane was built in 1782, to replace a building possibly two hundred years older, which was eventually used as a shed. There has been a house at Turnabrane for 400 years, although the name Skene only became associated with the farm in 1896. George Skene tenanted Turnabrane in the 1960s, and his widow was still there in 1970. George Skene's paternal grand-mother's family, the Mitchells, also tenanted Turnabrane, certainly since the eighteenth century, and the connection could possibly go back earlier through the Smarts.

When the house was built in 1782, it had a cruck framed roof with wooden pins. It was turfed, with thatch on top. When the roof was removed in the

Mrs Gibb (Mary Deakers), age 92, standing outside Cosie Howe built by her husband, Robert Gibb. The black dress and bonnet indicate that Mrs Gibb is a widow. c.1918. Glenesk Museum.

early twentieth century, a small powder horn was found, which is now in the Museum. In the bedroom above the kitchen were two box beds, one of which is also in the Museum. It is built in the sixteenth-century Dutch style, and would have been in the earlier house which was replaced in 1782. Apparently, the Skenes were in the habit of telling ghost stories. They were fond of telling a story about a drunk man who woke up in a box bed and in his fear shouted: 'Buried, buried, by God, buits an' a".

Mr & Mrs Charles Skene, Margaret.
George, James

A family portrait of the Skenes of Turnabrane. The men are wearing gaiters (sometimes termed 'queetikins' in the North-East). Note the heather besom on the left. Early 1900s. Glenesk Museum.

Stylemouth was a farm on its own, probably till around 1860. As previously noted, it is said to have been the last place to 'ca' oot muck fail'. There are numerous details of life at Stylemouth. The old parsonage at Stylemouth was occupied for about 25 years, 1780s–1810, by the Rev. Peter Jolly, Episcopal clergyman, and thereafter for over a century by the Davidsons who farmed the holding at Stylemouth, now included in Westbank which has been amalgamated with Auchronie. Old Nannie and Young Nannie (Mrs Agnes Davidson and her daughter) were well-known. Old Nannie died in 1919, aged 91, and her daughter emigrated to Canada.

One evening, when coming up from Tarfside with the newspaper on his way to Westbank, Jim Skene was passing Nannie's door and heard the concertina being played. He knocked, then ran to the window, and saw Young Nannie heave her instrument into the box bed. She was shy about her playing.

Around New Year, there used to be a party for the Stormonths. Nannie 'aye keepit a bottle'. At Christmas she received iced cakes, shortbread and suchlike, and she invited the Stormonths to eat 'that stuff'. It was held in 'the room'. Her best dishes came out for the occasion. Young Nannie took them to Canada with her, along with her axe. On one occasion Nannie gave Davie Stormonth a drink of Clensel in mistake for whisky.

David Stormonth, head stalker at Invermark for many years, and his family. Early 1900s. C13140.

Mary Christison, as an old woman by 1920, said of Arsallary: 'Aye, I mind eichteen reekin' lums there'. The list of units coming under the name, some marked on the Ordnance Survey map and some not, covers Arsallary itself and Arsallary school; Burnside, also called Betwixt the Burns; Badabae, and the whisky bothy there; Kirny; Stoneywell with two houses; Garthhead or Garthead, Dykefoot; Greenesken (Green Erskine); Tillicoulter; Blackhaugh; Turnamuck, between Stoneywell and Garthhead; Stripeside; Shade; Whitestane, with three houses, including a shop; Couternach and Braidlees; and Boghead.

Arsallary was tenanted by the family of Innes of Fordoun, and the Innes Papers constitute one of the most interesting collections of papers in the Glenesk Museum Archives. According to the *Extract of Matriculation of the Arms of Innes of Fordoun*, the Innes family were tenants in Arsallary from about 1684. Walter Innes, First in Arsallary, had possession between about 1684–1720. His son James was tacksman there, 1736–58, the tack being renewed in 1758. Next in line was his son, James. On his death, his son, John, who died in November 1838, took over. He married Margaret Edwards in Blackcraig of Glenesk, and their son, David, who died September 1865, kept up the tradition of linking Glen families by marrying Martha Christison probably of the Croft, Townhead.

David and Martha had a son, William, who died in 1926, described as 6th in Arsallary, and there followed David's William, who was followed by his son William, born in July 1923. William's son Robert was in Arsallary till 1934. All these Inneses lived at Burnside from about 1684. It was said that when Robert Innes gave up his tenancy in 1934, the fire had not been out for 250 years.

Burnside was renovated in 1907. The single-storey, thatched dwelling house was given upstairs rooms and the downstairs windows remain smallish, but the house is roomy. The work was done by William Littlejohn of Corhairncross. It was his son, Alexander, who took over Burnside when the Inneses went out. It is the only standing house in Arsallary now, and is used as a holiday cottage.

Mr and Mrs Birse of Cuttlehaugh, which was situated below the road and now a ruin, were another example of the remarkable longevity bestowed upon many people who lived in Glenesk. Mrs Birse was a Mitchell of Turnabrane. Her husband, Andrew, came across the hill from the forest of Birse, at the age of sixteen. He had with him the Gow (Smith) tartan plaid of hard material now in the Museum. The type of cloth used and the herringbone selvedge suggest a mid-eighteenth century origin. Mr and Mrs Birse celebrated their golden wedding anniversary in 1898, and, ten years later, they celebrated their diamond wedding anniversary. A new house was built at Cuttlehaugh by Stewart Porter who lived there with his family until the 1950s. In 1970 it was occupied by Hugh Ferrier and his wife. Hugh Ferrier's mother was a Gibb of Cosie Howe, and Mrs Ferrier's grand uncle was Andrew Birse. In Autumn 1976, the Ferriers moved to Little Balloch. Mr Ferrier died in April 1977, and his wife in 1978.

Another nonagenarian in Glenesk was Mr David Lowden, a shoemaker to trade. His wife was Jean Proctor. He died in 1913, aged 96, and his wife died seven years later aged 84. The Lowdens tenanted Greenburn Croft. The house originally had a thatched roof, but that has long since been replaced, and is occupied during weekends and holidays. David Lowden's son, James, lived almost as long as his father, reaching the age of 93 when he died in 1939. James Lowden was the Glen postman in the days of the horse and trap. In 1895 or 1896, Glenesk was hit by one of the severest snowstorms on record. The Glen was cut off from the Thursday to the following Monday by huge snowdrifts. James Lowden was caught in this storm at Tarfside while delivering mail. The mailcart stuck in one huge drift about a quarter of a mile from the Post Office. He unyoked the horse and left the cart, which remained there for thirteen weeks. He had gone back to look for it the following day but he could not find it, the cart being completely drifted up. He was tenant of Tarfside Farm, which his son Gilbert, and grandson, Gilbert Jnr, also farmed. Gilbert Lowden Jr now lives at Druids Knowe in Glenesk, having moved from Tarfside farm some years ago. He is a member of the staff at the Glenesk Museum, and

Mrs Birse of Cuttlehaugh at her knitting. She is wearing a bonnet similar to that worn by Jess Cattanach, and oval steel-rimmed spectacles. Early 1900s. Glenesk Museum.

is a keen local historian with a vast knowledge of the Glen's history. James Lowden's grand-daughter married Ramsay Guthrie, who still lives in the Glen.

Another son of James Lowden, William, died in 1891 from blood poisoning. He was a shoemaker like his father, and he had his shop in the west room of the house at Heatherbank, Tarfside. His wife was a Stewart and her mother a Donaldson of Greenburn. Mrs William Lowden died, aged 99 years, in 1949. Their two daughters both married into the Caithness family. One of the daughters, Jean, married George Caithness, and she died at Heatherbank, Tarfside in 1968, aged 93 years. Her sister, Lizzie, married Pat Caithness.

In the nineteenth century, Alexander Caithness emigrated to New Zealand with his family. It is alleged that he had been seven times to New Zealand and back. His eldest son visited Glenesk in 1958, at the age of 81, and contacted his relatives, one of whom would have been James Caithness, son of Pat Caithness and Lizzie Lowden. James Caithness, (whose school memories are recalled in chapter 10) was the postman in Glenesk for many years, and still lives in the Glen today.

The farm of Baillies was home to the Campbells for 72 years, from 1873–1945. Archie Campbell was the first head stalker at Inchgrundle, coming from the Black Mount in Glencoe, Argyll. Campbell went to Gleneffock in 1871. There is a fine photograph of the old fireplace at Baillies, taken in the 1930s when Andrew and John Campbell, along with their sister Lizzie, were tenants. The old fireplace has now been replaced by a modern one.

Interesting early forms of the name Baillies, are 'Bailzie' and 'Bellie', lacking the final 's'. In November 1612, Johne Schand in 'Bailzie' died, and the inventory of his possessions was made and presented twelve years later, though said to refer to the time of his death. The total value of his stock was £312, his grain stock was £245, and the contents of the house were valued at £263. Clearly, Johne Schand was a man of some substance. He was also a man who could be called upon for defence when the need arose, for listed among his possessions were a sword, a shooting bow with bag of arrows, a pair of pistols, a steel bonnet and a pair of 'plait slewis' (metal sleeves).

Between Kirn and Whigginton lies Tillybuckle, where the buildings are fairly numerous. It was at Tillybuckle that Greta Michie's father, George, was initiated into the mysteries of horsemanship. The Coplands flitted from the Leyhillocks to Tillybuckle. They thought 'Tillybuckle an awfu' bra hoose, efter the ither ane, for it had windows'. Leyhillocks had only holes, without panes of glass, into which divots were stuck at night.

Leyhillocks lay between Whigginton and Buskhead, but was mostly higher up the hill. There had been a community there of at least three to five houses. Jess Cattanach remembered being sent to a dressmaker there. Either subtenants or cottars had occupied these houses. Similar dwellings continue at regular intervals as far as Tillybuckle.

The holding of Dalbrack is marked in maps of the seventeenth and eighteenth centuries. In 1716, James Campbell lived in Dalbrack, and, in July 1753, David Campbell in Dalbrack is mentioned in the will of John Innerdale, late of Kirn, as owing him £5. By the mid- nineteenth century the Stewarts tenanted Dalbrack. In 1854, William Stewart's heirs had a 19-year lease from Whitsun 1846.

In 1961, a Pony-Trekking Centre was set up at Dalbrack by Mrs Nancy McIntosh. It was a highly successful venture, though it closed following an illness suffered by Mrs McIntosh in 1976. The trekking stock amounted to 18–20 trekking ponies in summer, catering for fifteen guests at a time. In 1970, Dalbrack had 1,800 acres of hill ground and 26 acres arable. The farmer, Gordon McIntosh, had 400 ewes and two milk cows and their followers. The farm is still tenanted by the McIntosh family, and Mrs Muriel McIntosh is the current curator of the Glenesk Museum.

Glenesk has had its fair share of characters in the past and none more so than David Stewart (1843–1919), known to Glenners as Diddlin' Davie, who was noted for wearing a lum hat. Davie's mother was the old woman in Irvine's painting of a cottage interior. He was born at Turnagob, and his mother did not allow him to go among other boys or to school until she was forced to do so. She allegedly kept him in bed for three years, and no one saw him. When Davie grew up he worked at Auchronie. He was also Kirk beadle and gravedigger. Sometimes he did not dig deep, and when he came on an old coffin, he put all the wood behind the stove to dry and then keep the fire going. He went down to Corhairncross or Turnabrane every Sunday or thereabouts. He was fond of the girls and when he was drunk he used to follow them and cry about them. He fell in love with every maid that came to Auchronie, but he was quite harmless. One letter he wrote to a maid who had left Auchronie read as follows: 'Dear Isobel, I love you very well'. This was repeated right down to the bottom of the page.

When the old-age pension started, Davie walked to Tarfside, drew the pension and bought chocolate for the maid at Auchronie and any other young women coming home. Occasionally, he would walk down to Whigginton to hack (chop) sticks for Jess Cattanach.

He thought he was a Mason, because he got into the Ball once. The Masons regarded him as a nuisance, because he went to all the meetings and was refused admittance. However, when he got a bottle he cleared out. Apparently, he was fond of the drink.

Mitchell, the vanman on D.C. Knowles's van, used to stop at Gleneffock every week overnight. Davie had gone down one evening demanding drink and was refused. However, he waited until all had gone to their beds, climbed on top of the van and drank himself senseless.

George Skene, who was just a laddie at the time, recalled the occasion when Davie was found lying in the house at Auchronie, dead drunk. John Christison put Davie in a wheel barrow and wheeled him home. George was following behind and asked John what he was going to do with Davie. John Christison replied: 'Bury him', and George was broken-hearted. In the Museum is a study in plaster by Ernest Lang, entitled, 'Diddlin' Davie', a gift from an anonymous friend.

DIDDLIN' DAVY, last
occupant of the
house at Mill of

Diddlin' Davy, last occupant of the house at the Mill of Auchronie on the Branny Burn. He died in 1919. Glenesk Museum.

Mary Smith, who lived at Skelly and was known locally as Mary Skelly, was another well-known Glen character. She later moved to Tirlybirly. At Skelly there is now only one house standing, and that is the former schoolhouse which later became the shepherd's house. There are, however, traces of several houses in the vicinity.

Mary Skelly was recognised as a very good-looking woman, and though she had highly respectable relatives, she dressed in rags. She once went over the hill to Aboyne, carrying her cat. When the cat became unmanageable she put it on a rope and led it. She carried an alarm clock in her 'jacket' and wound great lengths of grass rope around her legs for leggings, with a pair of men's wheeling drawers underneath the rope. She earned her living by gathering knot grass, going to the turnips and other outside work. In the field it was said that she looked just like a scarecrow. Mary Skelly was a favourite of Dr Campbell at Keenie, where she was allowed to stay until Skelly fell down. It was then that she moved to Tirlybirly.

Mary 'Skelly' (Smith) at work in the turnip fields. Early 1900s. Glenesk Museum.

Perhaps the most unusual 'gaein' aboot body' was John MacGregor, known to people as the 'Blind Fiddler'. It is believed that he was blinded by an explosion in the quarry where he worked, though judging by his peregrinations it is not clear if he was completely blind or only partially sighted. Shunned by his sweetheart, he took to roving through the highways and byways of Scotland, ranging as far as Braemar, Glenshee and Dunkeld, accompanied by various collies, his only companions over the years. Many a night he slept in the quarry at Gleneffock. According to Miss Minnie Lindsay, the Blind Fiddler used to take soup at the seat in front of the window at Migvie. Then he used to play on the fiddle and sing 'The Lass of Glenshee'.

A very tall man, he always wore a kilt of MacGregor tartan, and his outer garment was an old Highland cloak. Miss E. Davidson, who once lived at Migvie, recalls that the Blind Fiddler got tea and a piece at almost every dwelling in the Glen, and he once received an E-string for his fiddle at her house. He died at Kirriemuir Almshouse on 27 December, 1916, having been found unconscious on a roadside in the parish of Kingoldrum.

Vagrants were frequent visitors to Glenesk, and an amusing tale is told of an Irishman named Nathaniel Cochrane. He had trained for the Ministry but his eyesight failed and he travelled the countryside with a boxie and a few odds and ends. He was going up by Inchgrundle, when he met the Laird who was going shooting. 'Don't go to Invermark Lodge', said the Laird. Nathaniel replied: 'There's no need to go to Hell when you've met the Devil by the way'.[1] The Laird was highly amused by this remark and sent word to Nathaniel to call at Invermark Lodge, where he got something to eat and something to put in his pouch also.

Travellers, or tinkers, also passed through the Glen. In the Museum are some very fine-made tinker pieces. There is a tinker's lantern, found in the thatch of an old house at Greenburn, as well as other pieces of tin work, mainly milkhouse utensils. There are also staved vessels with 'feathering', made by tinkers, and an old basket or two. The making of horn spoons was another of their trades, though this practice was not restricted to tinkers. Also in the Museum is a tinker's anvil, left at Auchenreoch, where the Glenesk carrier used to live. The carrier had a horse and vehicle and would transport goods to and from the Glen which people otherwise may not have managed, for example, a new dresser from Laurencekirk. The story goes that on the occasion of a tinker's wedding, a candle was lit on the anvil, and the happy couple had to jump over it.

Several tinkers were found dead in the Glen. One was found dead lying in the Burn of Glenmark. He had a broken leg. Dr Campbell of Keenie was called up to certify the cause of death. John Davidson, uncle of Will Stormonth, was present and helped to bring the body down. Another, Thomas McQueen, who had been going about the Glen a good deal, was found dead in a bog below Westbank, where he had been lying for some six weeks.

John MacGregor, the 'Blind Fiddler'. He was a resplendent figure in his MacGregor tartan kilt. Note the piece of rope dangling from his fiddle which was used to loop the instrument round his neck. c.1910. G1/25/2A.

There are many other stories about these wanderers, all part of the story of Glenesk, but sadly disappearing as people have moved away from the Glen, and many of the older generation have passed on. Therefore, with so few left at present, where once there were many, it is desirable to record the former way of life before the contacts are all gone and the mode of life lost to memory. This chapter can by no means be a comprehensive account of folk and places in Glenesk, but perhaps it gives a flavour of the Glen, its people and their lives, those who are long gone and their descendants who remain. It is well-nigh impossible to give details of every farm or former township in Glenesk; however, a comprehensive list of recognisable sites of houses, former dwellings, mills, etc, compiled by Greta Michie, can be found in Appendix 1.

Tarfside before the removal of the 'Blue Cairn'. Left: Heather Bank and Post Office; Middle left: Masonic Lodge; Middle: Elm Cottage; Middle right: School and Schoolhouse; Right (to left of house): Blue Cairn; Right: Dalhousie Cottages. 1892. Glenesk Museum.

Tarfside Post Office and Grocery Store. David Moir is seated to the right of the door. The sign reads 'David Moir, Grocer, Licensed to Retail Tea & Tobacco'. Early 1900s. Glenesk Museum.

With continuing out-migration, and with many former homes in Glenesk now being let as holiday cottages, there are fewer and fewer people left to pass on the old stories which help keep old traditions and memories alive. These stories and memories give substance to a community, and help instill a sense of place and belonging within the people who make up that community. Wherever the small community is lost or is breaking up, the anecdotal treasure trove which it fosters begins to vanish, and people and places fade away and are, in time, forgotten.

The cage across the North Esk to Turnabrane which was removed in 1909 following a fatal accident. This is on the site of the present 'shaky briggie'. Date unknown. Glenesk Museum.

Maggie Stewart, Mrs Stewart and Mary Ann Stewart buying in winter supplies. 1913. G1/30/34A.

NOTE

1. This remark is only one of many well-known 'sayings' in Glenesk. Below is a list of sayings and proverbs compiled by Greta Michie, some peculiar to the Glen alone.

1. As the auld cock craws, the young ane learns.
2. Changes are lichtsome and fules are fond o' them.
3. There's aye some water far the stirkie droons.
4. Lairn young, learn fair, learn auld, lairn sair.
5. It's a' guid that's gotten oot o' an auld thing.
6. Fules and bairns shouldna see half-dune wark.
7. Better a toom hoose than an ill tenant.
8. A gaein' fit's aye gettin'.
9. A burnt bairn dreids the fire.
10. Ye canna tak the breeks aff a Hielandman.
11. Slow at meat, slow at wark.
12. It's an ill thaw that comes fae the North.
13. Broken breid maks hale bairns.
14. Set a stoot hert tae a stey brae.
15. The evening brings a' hame.
16. A fat soo's aye creishy.

16

POPULATION CHANGE FROM 1700

When Lochlee was disjoined from Lethnot in 1723, there seem to have been 400 examinable persons in the parish. An examinable person was one old enough to be examined in the Catechism, and though the age varied at different periods and places, it tended to lie between six and twelve years old. A number of non-examinable people, therefore, has to be added.

When Alexander Webster produced his 'Account of the Number of People in Scotland' in 1775, he gave the figure of 686 for Lochlee. This was composed of ten Papists and 676 Protestants.[1] In part he may have been depending on the number of examinable persons, using an arithmetical conversion to work out a total, but it was only with the first Census of 1801 that anything like precision became possible.[2]

The Rev. Mr John Pirie's account of Lochlee in 1792 gives a smaller number, 608, though this was a little more than the figure of 600 he specified for 1766. The 1792 figure consisted of 178 men, 237 women and 193 children below twelve years of age. There were 10 per cent more women than men.

Records provided by Pirie for 1784–92 show the following pattern:

	Births	Marriages	Deaths
1784	17	7	13
1785	17	6	12
1786	13	8	13
1787	14	6	11
1788	15	1	13
1789	20	6	9
1790	13	5	3
1791	12	2	8
1792	10	4	13

Averaging out over the nine years, we get 14.55 births, 5 marriages and 10.55 deaths; that is there are nearly three times more births than marriages,

[1] J.G. Kyd, ed. *Scottish Population Statistics*, Scottish History Society, Edinburgh, 1952, 48.
[2] M. Flinn, ed. *Scottish Population History from the 17th Century to the 1930s*, Cambridge University Press, Cambridge, 1977, 61–2.

and just over twice as many deaths. The late eighteenth-century pattern, there-fore, showed a slow but definite increase in population.

These figures can be compared with those for Lethnot, recorded for 1781–90. Births averaged 13.5, marriages 5.7 and deaths 8.8.[3] There were fewer births, more marriages and fewer deaths than in Lochlee, which, by implication, seems to have been a somewhat better favoured area.

The Rev. Mr John Pirie observed in 1792 that the people had a strong attachment to the place and seldom left it. Nevertheless, agricultural advances and higher wages in the Scottish Lowlands had exerted a drawing power on the young men since the 1770s. This is what made the apparent difference between the numbers of women and men in the parish.[4]

The day-to-day needs of the parishioners in the late eighteenth century were met by a small number of tradesmen: four wrights, four tailors, three weavers, two smiths and one shoemaker. The wrights and smiths were not fully occupied by their crafts all the time, and also ran small units of land, keeping a few black cattle and sheep. Textile needs were limited to coarse woollen cloth and some sheeting, though the making of these provided full-time jobs. The shoemaker produced or rather repaired coarse black leather shoes, called Forfar brogues, readily available in Brechin and Forfar and at the markets in the neighbourhood.[5] Though these fourteen tradesmen served over 600 people, many others would have had the ability to carry out some of these jobs themselves, as in all rural communities. Nor was there anything to stop anyone from going to or employing tradesmen from neighbouring parishes, if they so wished. The people were described as respectable and regular in their lives on the whole, though dram-drinking had lately become more frequent.[6]

By the census of 1821, there had been a decline in population to 572, and to 553 in 1831. This latter drop was said to be due to the stopping of smug-gling, that is, trading in illicit whisky, during the preceding four years.

By the 1830s, there were 120 families giving an average family size of 4.6. Of these, 60 were engaged mainly in agriculture, and eight pursued trade, manufacture or a handicraft. There were thirteen unmarried men, including widowers, over 50 years of age, and thirteen unmarried women, including widows, over 45. Births, deaths and marriages averaged over the previous seven years stood at fifteen, nine and five respectively, not very different from the situation in 1792. A high number, 150 or 27 per cent, were young folk under fifteen. Only 25, or 4.5 per cent, were over 70.

The Rev. David Inglis considered that the people were remarkably clean in their houses and persons. Their food was plain and substantial, and they

[3] *The Old (First) Statistical Account of Scotland:*Angus, XIII, EP Publications, Wakefield, 1976.
[4] ibid.
[5] ibid, 361–2.
[6] ibid, 368.

enjoyed the necessities and many of the improving comforts of life. Living standards were clearly rising. The people were praised for their kindness to strangers, including the beggars who came to their doors.[7]

The number of people has continued to decrease, typifying the general depopulation that has characterised Highland glens.

Population Table: Lochlee			
1755	686	1881	359
1766	600	1891	343
1792	608	1901	326
1801	541	1911	295
1811	521	1921	282
1821	572	1931	198
1831	553	1951	155
1841	622	1961	130
1851	615	1971	
1861	495	1981	
1871	424		

These figures, translated into the form of a graph, show a fall and rise between 1750–1850; then the drop which was very steep between 1860 and 1880, somewhat less steep from 1881 and 1950, stable again for the following decade, and after that sinking slowly again. Reasons varied in different places, but in Glenesk the factors related primarily to farming. In the late 1700s, the attractive power of higher wages in Lowland Scotland pulled young men out of the Glen. Measures against illicit whisky distilling had a small effect in the 1820s. The major factor, however, was the seemingly inevitable changes from mixed farming to a more exclusively sheep farming economy, and the gradual reduction in numbers of holdings allied with an increase in size of those that remained. Emigration to other countries took place. Small farms, organised in groups as identifiable farming communities, were eroded and replaced by individual farms that could manage with smaller work forces. As time went on even two such farms came to be managed by one farmer, who maintained one in grass. Five such double units existed in Lochlee in the 1940s, and again fewer workers were required.

The steady decline in population has continued through the twentieth century. In 1967, there were 126 permanent residents in Glenesk, which means that almost four-fifths of the population has gone since the publication of the *New Statistical Account* in 1845.[8] There were 47 permanent houses and 49 other dwellings in the Glen in 1967, 34 of which were occupied only in summer or at weekends.[9] Compare that total to the 128 houses accounted for in the 1841 census.

[7] *New Statistical Account of Scotland*, 1833, XI (1845), 194.
[8] *The Third Statistical Account of Scotland*, The County of Angus, 1977, 163.
[9] ibid, 163.

The main causes of depopulation are the same as those which have affected other isolated, highland areas, mainly the attraction of the towns, want of employment opportunities, an increase in the size of farm units, mechanisation and the lack of amenities.[10] The lack of employment opportunities is reflected in the number of tradespeople in the Glen. The last joiner, who was also the undertaker, retired in 1951. Tradesmen from Brechin and Edzell now serve the Glen, while professional undertakers in Brechin organise funerals.[11]

By 1992, the population of the Glen was 120, only six fewer than in 1967, which gives the impression that the number of inhabitants has stabilised. However, there is a large ageing population, many of whom are single, and there is also a disproportionate ratio of adults to children.[12] A breakdown of the population in 1992 shows that there were 53 men, 41 women and 27 children, which, incidentally, is the same number of children as 1967. In 1833, there were 150 children in Glenesk.

Attending High Schools outside Glenesk also plays a role in out-migration. Until the 1950s, children attending High School in Brechin stayed in lodgings during the week and were driven home for the weekend. Now pupils are driven to and from school every day, which means that they actually spend more time in the Glen. Nevertheless, it could be argued that attending high school in Brechin introduces pupils to the attractions of town life, with the risk that they then 'lose their native attachment'.[13] Young people then move to the cities to pursue further education, and there is rarely a chance for them to return home to their native glen and find employment with their new-found skills.[14]

A survey revealed that there were 97 properties in Glenesk in 1992, one more than in 1967. Of that total, 49 were under-used, with 33 properties being used as holiday homes, (one fewer than 1967), five serving as accommodation for seasonal employees, and a further seven lying empty.[15] The other 48 house the permanent population of Glenesk. There were eleven tenant farmers whose rent is reviewed every three years, calculated by the numbers of ewes that they have, which, in 1992, ranged from £4.50 to £6.00 per headage.[16]

Many of the 128 houses mentioned in the 1841 census now lie in ruins, and some places, such as Glencat, have been empty for more than a century. Piles

[10] ibid, 164.
[11] Christina MacKenzie *Glenesk. An Ethnological Study of a Community in Angus*, Unpublished Honours Dissertation, School of Scottish Studies, University of Edinburgh, 1992, 38.
[12] ibid, 22.
[13] *Third Statistical Account*, Angus, 164.
[14] MacKenzie, op. cit., 25.
[15] ibid, 31.
[16] ibid, 32.

of stones are all that is left of once thriving communities, such as Glenlee, where over twenty families were living in the early nineteenth century.[17]

> The bracken's creepin'
> Whaur the sheep aince fed,
> A staney rickle is the ancient hame,
> Scarce ony soul can find it.

[17] *Third Statistical Account*, Angus, 164.

17

LEAVING THE GLEN:
NEW HOMES ABROAD

JAMES AND ROBERT JOLLY, PIONEERS IN CANADA

In the middle of the nineteenth century a flood tide of emigration carried thousands of young Scots to undeveloped lands, far beyond the seas. Letters sent by two brothers from Canada to Scotland over a century ago tell how they got on.

James and Robert Jolly were born and reared in Glenesk, descendants of Jean Low and James Jolly, miller of Glenesk. Their earliest known paternal forebears were reputedly French Huguenots who fled from France to Scotland to escape religious persecution, but no evidence to support this story has come to light so far. Family legend avers that two Frenchmen landed at Aberdeen and wandered over the hills, into quiet Glenesk. An empty stretch of heath, known as the Muir o'Aucheen, became their home resting place. In time the land was leased to them by the local landowner. The descendants of the two Frenchmen developed and worked the lean and hungry muirland, and during that time they also built and operated a meal and barley mill.

The original mill house was a stone and clay bigging, with heather thatched roof. It consisted of a but and ben, separated by a small dairy. The upper loft was roughly raftered, and provided sleeping accommodation. Here in the nineteenth century lived James Jolly, the Glen miller, his wife, five sons and three daughters. From November to April, the miller's bairns, girls as well as boys, were regular fee paying pupils at the nearby school. From Beltane onwards, they joined their elders on the land, and worked to ensure survival through the hungry winter months.

The family at Mill o'Aucheen was perhaps slightly more fortunate than some of the crofting neighbours. It was taken for granted that the meal girnel could always be refilled. If the family seldom feasted, rarely did they go hungry. As the miller's sons grew to manhood, they worked hard and well, but they never earned much money. The lack of an adequate reward at home soured them, so they looked elsewhere for a decent living. Little regular work was available, either within or outside the Glen.

The question of emigration was debated. James and Robert Jolly weighed up prospects at home and abroad, and finally decided to emigrate. Steerage fare to Canada, £3.10/-, was just within their means.

Their first letters from 'the rich Province of Ontario' reached Glenesk during the Crimean War. In August 1855 James Jolly wrote: 'I expected letters before this time but the post does not come across the Atlantic so regular as usual, on account on the mail packets being employed for war purposes'. 'I believe I will never be in Glenesk again, but I often think of my old acquaintances therein. Send as full an account as you can, for it is only by letter that I can know about them'.

In 1856 he continued:

When I wrote you last year I did not like Canada at all. Now I like it so well that if anyone were to offer me a free house and five pounds a year in Scotland, I would not take it, for I can soon have 100 or 200 acres of land which yield me more in one year than I could ever get in three at home. I believe the working man is more independent in Canada, for here he can make his own soap and sugar, and grow many things that cannot be grown at home. To my mind, Canada is a country which offers many and great advantages to a poor man, especially one able and willing to till the soil. I have not had to work so hard as a ploughman in Scotland. I believe that to be the most slavish life on earth and worst paid. Here wages are good and work is steady. In sawmills and flour mills a man can earn about half a crown a day with board and washing. Harvest work is well paid. Sometimes the wage rises to as much as 10/- a day. Food prices are moderate. Beef is 4c to 6c a pound; Pork 3c to $3^1/_2$c; Butter is 1c per lb and eggs 8c a dozen. When I first came to Canada, I could have had land as low as 4/- per acre. I knew a man who bought 200 acres of land for 400 dollars. He built a rude shanty and worked on the land for a year. Then he sold 100 acres for 600 dollars and so was left with the other 100 acres, the shanty and 200 dollars profit. Who could have won so much in Scotland? I admit such chances are rare now. At the present time I have a 100 acre offer in a peopled part. I do not know if I shall take it, as I would be hard up for years to come, and the working man is so well off that I think I would be better for some years that way. I have travelled a great deal and come in contact with people of every nation, and every clime, men of all colours, and all kinds of characters, and more than once, I've come through the furnace of affliction and paid the smart for trusting to the honour and honesty of those who were lacking in either commodity.

Still later James Jolly wrote:

You will be glad to know we have bought a farm. The cost is two thousand, two hundred and fifty dollars. We have got that amount on a ten years loan, and will have a struggle to get it paid. At the present time we are fit and strong, but we don't grow any younger, and we are well aware that time is fleeting and strength does not endure.

Robert Jolly's story was similar at the beginning but it ended differently. Incidentally, he was one of the few nineteenth-century emigrants who re-visited Scotland. Early in 1864 he wrote:

Your letter carried me back to days that are past. It wafted my thoughts over the lone Atlantic and reminded me of the sacred ties of Home. In fancy, I once more crossed the threshold of home, and for a time bade adieu to my troubles in the wilds of a foreign land. Once more, I took my seat in the happy family circle, by the blazing peat fire, free from care. In fancy, I again became the lighthearted laddie of twenty years age, and with my youthful associates, I footed it with elastic step over the Row-in-Hill, among the bonnie blooming heather. And now I shall proceed to give you some account of myself. I have never regretted coming to Canada for I have never lacked work, and have bettered my condition considerably. After seven years hard labour and rigid economy, I am now if not on the road to wealth, at least in a fair way of arriving at independence. At various times and seasons I have worked on the land, in saw-mills and in flour mills. Lately I have found employment and satisfaction in the mercantile business with a Scotchman named Hector Morrison. He intends leaving this district towards the end of the year, and in company with an Englishman, I intend taking over the business. The stock consists of cloth of all kinds, groceries, crockery, ready made clothing, hardware and boots and shoes to the amount of eight or nine hundred pounds stg.

August 1864 saw Robert Jolly back in Glenesk for a fleeting visit. He revisited every corner of the Glen and renewed many friendships, before returning to Canada to keep troth with Hector Morrison. Both James and Robert Jolly lived out the rest of their lives in Canada.

James Jolly's Canadian saga of emigration began with regret that the Packet Boats were not sailing regularly owing to the Crimean War. The story ends with a dramatic sequel which occurred towards the end of Hitler's War.

In 1944, a tall young airman dressed in Royal Canadian Air Force uniform visited Scotland during his service leave. After persistent inquiry the young man managed to contact one of his great grand uncle's descendants. Rather diffidently he introduced himself: 'I understand you are related to me?' Though completely taken aback by the claim, the personable Canadian was invited to explain the relationship in greater detail. 'My name is Bill Vallance and I come from Ontario. Perhaps I'd better show you some family photographs'.

The airman produced his wallet and handed over a snapshot. 'This is a photograph of my mother. Before she married. Her name was Annie Jolly. Her grandfather, James Jolly, left Glenesk for Canada about 1854'. The family link, tenuous for many years, was firmly forged once again.

JOHN JOLLY, PIONEER RANCHER IN THE USA

In the 1950s some American tourists visited Glenesk for the first time. The visitors, sheep and cattle ranchers, came all the way from Colorado, with three objectives in mind. They wanted to see the Glen where their forebears had lived and they hoped to find relatives still resident in the Glen. They also wondered if anyone still remembered their father John Jolly, who had emigrated to the States in the eighties of the last century.

All their hopes were realised one summer day, when the sun smiled through an occasional smirr of misty rain. The Glen, encircled by rolling hills, just like the foothills of the Rockies, fulfilled every expectation. The ranchers' expert eyes viewed the green pastures, the brawling brown river, the flocks of hardy black-faced sheep, the herd of black and highland cattle, and found all alike good.

On the Muir o' Aucheen, where their father had herded sheep years before, they glimpsed a present day shepherd in the distance, complete with crook and collie. At Tarfside, they met a former Glen gamekeeper. His memories coloured the past, and made it come alive. 'Of course I knew your father. In fact, when he came home in 1893 he asked me to go back wi' him to Colorado. He painted a picture o' life on the prairies that made me rarin' to go. However, I was only sixteen then, and my mother wouldna' listen'. The thread of the reminiscence changed. 'Have you ever met General Eisenhower?' 'No'. 'I have. He and General Bedell Smith shot over the grouse moors here, just after the war.' Pawkily he added: 'Had I gone wi' your father to Colorado, I might have had to handle mair siller the day, but I would never have met General Eisenhower or General Bedell Smith'.

Still farther up the Glen, the visitors met relatives, who convoyed them to a neighbour's home. The neighbour, a sprightly lady of eighty, had known John Jolly when both were 'in their daft days'.

> Fine I mind your father. A bricht young spark he was, when I kent him. Aye ready for a ploy! Ae Hallowe'en, he and a like minded crony cam' to our farm town. They wheedled the young lassies into lendin' them frocks and hats for guisin'. Then each armed an outsize lidded basket and off they set to sing for their supper at the nearby crofts. They cam' back wi' their baskets crammed fu' o' shortie, biscuits, and cheese and currant loafie. Nothing so common as scones and bannocks for them that nicht. The old lady paused and sighed. 'To think that happened mair than sixty year syne. To me, it seems like yestereen'.

What prompted John Jolly to leave Glenesk? Perhaps his early years and his heredity offer some explanation. He was the youngest son, in a family of six, but he was only twelve years old when his father died. Older brothers and sisters scattered in the search for work, but John stayed on in the Glen, doing all sorts of odd jobs. By the time he reached his early twenties, he realised that casual labour was dirt cheap and led nowhere.

His maternal ancestors had been hill sheep and cattle farmers, and John felt he had a natural bent for stock raising. But what hope had a penniless Glen laddie of acquiring either land or stock in nineteenth-century Scotland? The unknown, outside world beckoned too, for news came to Glenesk from emigrants in every corner of the globe.

The letters that interested John Jolly most came from Colorado. Men whom he knew and whose judgement he trusted wrote that the vast prairies of mid-west America were wonderlands for stock raising. They declared that Colorado wanted men who were willing to work hard and well, even though they possessed no capital. Wages were high on the sheep and cattle ranches, and moreover prospects for ambitious emigrants were excellent. The Government offered land holdings to pioneers with good records, and capital loans could also be obtained over an agreed period. This followed a very familiar pattern of emigration in nineteenth-century Scotland. Letters sent home from family and friends extolling the virtues of their new homeland, especially the offer of cheap land, were often the catalyst for many emigrants. Many people probably did not want to leave their homeland, but conditions and circumstances must have been bad enough for people to even contemplate emigration. When John Jolly left Glenesk in 1887, he was accompanied by the elder of the Stewart brothers, Jack, also from the Glen. When he returned to Scotland in 1893 to find a bride, the other Stewart brother, Jim, went to Colorado with him in 1894. According to his grandson, the Stewart brothers were boyhood friends of John Jolly.

In 1887, John Jolly decided to try his luck. He borrowed £20 from his mother and set off for Colorado. For six years he gathered ranching experience in various sheep and cattle outfits, working for two Scots, Alexander Simpson, though descendants of John Jolly say it was David Simpson, and Ebenezer 'Scotty' Robinson. They paid him $15 a month, out of which John managed to acquire a small flock of his own. John Jolly's grandson believes that his grandfather had possibly worked for David Simpson in Scotland, and that it was he who persuaded John to emigrate to Colorado.

Under the first Homestead Act he applied for and was granted 160 acres of rich native grassland. Homestead laws changed, as the authorities realised that 160 acres of this dry land was not enough for a family to live from, so it was doubled to 320 acres. Because the land was so dry it could be purchased at $1 an acre. The land was watered only by salty or alkaline springs. Rain and flash floods provided the only other sources of water. Catchment dams, constructed of earth, were built to hold rainwater, and are still used today. For as long as John Jolly lived here, he hauled water from Deer Trail in barrels or tanks for domestic use. The territory where Red Indians had once hunted herds of buffalo, became a sheep and cattle ranch area. He filed his claim in 1891, and in 1893 John Jolly returned to Scotland to marry his sweetheart, but that lass had married someone else. Instead, he married Jean Howe Henderson on 13 December 1893, returning to Colorado early in 1894 with his new bride.

The young couple's first home was necessarily primitive. For a few years they lived in a hillside house – half under ground, and half above ground – where four of their children (Mary, Margaret, Jeannie and John) were born.

About the turn of the century a more substantial homestead was built, which became the headquarters of the Jolly ranch. Life was extremely hard on the prairie and the family endured much hardship and heartache. The 'Plains', known to early travellers as the 'Great American Desert' were vast and lonely, prone to violent storms, drought, flood and extremes of temperature. In summer the plains of eastern Colorado can bake in temperatures of 100 degrees, the fierce heat drying up the creeks, exposing their bone-dry beds, leaving the earth cracked and dusty under the hot sun. In Winter, the temperature can drop as low as -30 degrees centigrade, accompanied by the biting Prairie wind. It was no place for the faint-hearted pioneer.

The Jolly ranch was a few miles from both the small railhead town of Deer Trail and their closest neighbour. Deer Trail is a small town in eastern Arapahoe county, situated on the Union Pacific Railroad, 56 miles east of Denver. It lies at an altitude of 5,180 feet and stock raising and farming are the main industries. The town's claim to fame is that it held the world's first rodeo competition in 1869. At the time of John Jolly's death in 1944, the population was 485.[1]

In 1900 the children contracted diphtheria, and the disease claimed the life of eight-month-old Jeannie. The nearest medical help was fifty miles distant. John Jolly carried her on horseback to a doctor in Fort Morgan, but she died on the journey. Of the four children who were born in the hill-side house, only one survived into adulthood and even his life was blighted by tragedy. Mary died, aged nine, in 1904 and Margaret died in 1912, just short of her six-teenth birthday. John, the eldest boy, was kicked on the head by a horse while an infant and was mentally handicapped as a result. Another child, Maria, died in 1908, aged two months. Margaret died in Denver where she had been sent to attend high school. While there she contracted scarlet fever and her parents never saw her again. Margaret, Mary and Maria were buried in a little family cemetery on the ranch. Many years later the headstones were moved to the Evergreen cemetery in Deer Trail, but the bodies were not exhumed. The little mound where the girls were put to rest was cemented over. It was not until the summer of 1999 that John Jolly's grandson, on visiting the site, discovered that the girls' names along with their dates of birth and death had been inscribed on the flat slabs. The smallness of the little grave mound set amongst the vastness of the plains seemed to symbolise the struggle, heart-break and hardship endured by many early settlers.

A combination of loneliness, stress and watching four of her daughters die young, was too much for Jean Jolly. According to her grandson, John, she tried to commit suicide. Jean Jolly swallowed some rat poison, but had a change of heart and took some medication which induced vomiting, thus saving her

---

[1] *Colorado State Business Directory*, Gazetteer Publishing Company, Denver, 1943, 255.

life. One can only imagine the emotional and physical strain she endured, living in such isolation and under such conditions. She must have suffered badly from homesickness in those early years, 5,000 miles away from Scotland and the comfort of family and friends. She never returned to her native land. Further tragedy struck the family when the oldest son, John, aged 32, drowned after stepping into an ice-covered cistern at the ranch.

The Jolly's had six other children, five boys – Dave, Charles (Carley), Jim, Robert (Bob), William (Hap) – and one girl, Elizabeth. All five boys became good stockmen, and their father helped four of them acquire their own ranches, while the fifth remained on the home ranch. His grandson, also John Jolly, remembers his grandfather as being a very stern man and related the following story as an example of his austerity:

> We were being babysat by Aunt Lizzie. We had an old phone which had five lines on it, including the old Jolly ranch. We were real fond of Aunt Lizzie, she was just like her mother, Grandmother Jolly, good fun to be with, and she asked me if I would like to call Grandma Jolly on the phone. And I'm real enthused about it, because I'm gonna get to visit Grandma, because we loved Grandma, we really liked to correspond with her. So we dragged the chair up by the phone. I got on the chair and rang one long and two shorts, and Grandpa answered the phone. And he said, 'Who is this?'. And I said, 'Well, it's John Jolly'. He said, 'The hell it is. This is John Jolly over here'. I didn't say anything, of course. He then asked me, 'Well, what do you want?'. And I said, 'Nothing'. He said, 'Well, why don't you hang up the goddam phone and leave it alone then'. And that was his idea. Phones were for business and not entertainment. And I didn't go near that phone probably for six months after that. I wouldn't answer that phone for nothing.

The grandson also admitted to being frightened of his grandfather:

> I was scared of him. He was pretty demanding. He and his boys were alike in this respect. If they didn't give you hell, you knew you were doing pretty good. And they never commended you. But they gave you hell when things went wrong ... They had the coldest ... [to his brother Gene], do you remember how, when them guys would look at you, and they would just freeze you in your tracks. And they were all five like that. The five of them boys and everyone of them, they'd look at you, you knew you'd been looked at.

John Jolly believed that his sons should be doing something responsible at all times. He was a hard taskmaster, but perhaps he had to be in order to be a success and to survive. When it was light enough to work, then everyone should be up, as John Jolly wanted to utilise all the daylight hours. Even as children, all of them, including Elizabeth, were proficient in most aspects of ranch work. At the tender age of eight, Elizabeth and her younger brother, David, were sent out to tend sheep camps. This was a lot of responsibility for such young children, as it often entailed setting up a camp and having it in a liveable condition when the sheepherder arrived. There were thousands of sheep on the Jolly ranch and, as teenagers, the Jolly boys often found themselves in charge of up to 3,000 sheep each. Large sheep sheds, up to 300 feet long, were built on various locations throughout the ranch.

The wool of the Colorado sheep is much shorter than that of Angus sheep, and in his early days out west, John Jolly experienced difficulty in determining whether they had been shorn or not. The sheep were predominantly Rambouillet, because it raised good wool. They used a lot of black-faced or Hampshire bucks (rams), because they produced a much better feeder lamb. The blackface were always sold. They were never kept on the range because they were more inclined to trail and run around. Blackfaced sheep were forever raiding haystacks or open granaries and were considered a nuisance. In winter, Rambouillet bucks had a lot of wool especially on their face, which would grow over their eyes causing them to become 'wool blind'. Nearly every winter they had to have their faces sheared in an operation known as 'facing'. Wedder lambs were sold every fall, and ewe lambs were kept.

In summer, when rounding the sheep up from the different pastures, the herder was often out for days at a time, so large was the area covered. On these occasions, the herder lived in a sheep-wagon. Constructed of wood and mounted on wheels, the wagon could be moved from pasture to pasture. It contained a stove, some provisions, and accommodation for one person. The wagon was for summer use only, as it was not built to withstand the rigours of the Colorado winter. When moving flocks, one had to train the sheep to graze rather than trail. If the flock moved fast, they made trails in the ground and would tramp out more grass than they would eat. All of John Jolly's sons were tough about that, and would have no hesitation in firing a herder if he allowed that to happen.

There were also stationary camps which were more like winter camps. There was a small shack for the herder to live in, a corral for the sheep and quite often a shed in times of bad weather. One person stayed out in the shack all winter. The shack was two or three miles from the ranch house, and the rancher would check on the herder a couple of times a week, and take provisions out to them. The herder just hoped that he would not get bitten by a rattlesnake or become ill or develop toothache. A herder was with the sheep at all times, and they were corralled at night because of the danger of coyotes. Sheepdogs were used when moving large flocks. In the early days, Welsh collies were used, and Border collies were not introduced until the 1950s.

Not too many animals were lost to extreme weather. If there was a severe drought, for example, the sheep were sent to the mountains. On one occasion they were even taken to Laramie, Wyoming.

Sheep shearing began on 10 June. A crew was hired for this work, mostly consisting of men from New Mexico, Texas and Mexico. A crew of twenty could shear 2,000 sheep in a day. The crews stayed in the area for two or three weeks, working on different ranches, before moving on. Most of the wool was shipped east to Boston. Lambs used to be trailed to the South Platte River valley near Fort Morgan. It would take five days to trail the lambs 55 miles, with three or four men herding them.

John Jolly and four of his sons on the ranch near Deer Trail, Colorado, after the sheep shearing. Per John Jolly, Deer Trail, Colorado.

Although predominantly a sheep farmer, John Jolly did raise cattle. The first cattle they used were shorthorns, but, later, Herefords were introduced, which were considered to be far better range cattle. These two breeds were cross-bred, but eventually it was strictly straight Hereford. Most of the beef went to Denver in the early days, but in the 1930s and 1940s it was sent to areas closer to Deer Trail. John Jolly's grandson recalls his father, David, telling him about the 'light warfare' that took place between the sheep farmers and the cattle ranchers. The cattle owners had arrived in the area first, and resented the coming of the sheepfarmers. David Jolly also said that passing cowboys shot out the windows of the old dug-out house on several occasions.

John Jolly turned merchant as well as rancher, opening a store which became the oldest business establishment in Deer Trail. Initially, it was a man named G.L. Burton, who borrowed money from John Jolly to open the store. He asked to extend the loan in order to pay for the transportation of glass windows which were intended for the store. John Jolly suggested that he take over the building as Burton already owed him a lot of money anyway. Jolly realised that he could make substantial savings on his ranch by buying goods wholesale, therefore operating the store made good business sense. However, he extended credit to many people and when the store closed in 1942, he was owed $50,000 from debtors. He hired managers to run the store, and each of his sons, with the exception of John, managed the store for two years in place of attending high school. He considered it to be a good business education. A combination of factors, including rationing, forced the store to close in 1942. After John Jolly's death in 1944, the store was sold to a Mr Dischner. The store returned to the Jolly family when Wanda Jolly, wife of John Jolly's youngest son William, bought it in 1958. She ran the store for a few years, but then ownership was taken over by John Jolly's granddaughter, Dorothy Docherty and her husband, who operated it successfully for almost 30 years. The store now lies empty, its façade worn and dilapidated. John Jolly was also president of the Deer Trail State Bank, but resigned that post when the staff would not let him look at the books.

John Jolly acquired other property in Deer Trail, mainly through foreclosures because people could not repay their debts to him. He maintained one house in the town and kept it open year round. In the Fall of each year he would send his wife and the children to live in town, so that the children could go to school during the winter months. However, just as in Glenesk, come spring he wanted them home working on the ranch. The children received what education was available when they were not being utilised at home.

The diet on the ranch did not include a wide variety of foods. The family butchered their own beef and mutton, and had staples such as flour, lard and

Jean Jolly with her children outside the family's winter home in the town of Deer Trail. Per John Jolly, Deer Trail, Colorado.

eggs which they got from the chickens which they raised. Corn and pinto beans also formed a part of the diet. Because there were no refrigerators, the family used a lot of canned foods, and bought large quantities of dried fruit and jam. Meat was salted so that it would keep.

According to John Jolly's grandson, very little communal help took place in the first couple of decades after his arrival in Colorado. Neighbours were so far apart that it took half a day to get there, therefore it was just not feasible. It was not really farming country. Perhaps people would raise a few beans, or grow some corn for their livestock. By the 1940s, though, the emphasis began to change from livestock to cropping, and the Jolly boys used to help their neighbours thresh their wheat at harvest time. In the 1960s, wool prices fell and it was getting more and more difficult to find herders and shearers. Jim Jolly got out of the sheep business in the late 1960s and ran a cow-calf operation for the rest of his life. His two brothers, Carley and Bob, stayed with sheep for a little longer.

'On the land their God had given them', the pioneers celebrated their Golden Wedding anniversary. One Sunday in 1943 saw all their descendants and hosts of well-wishers at the Homestead. There they honoured and congratulated the unique couple whose story had become legend in their own lifetime. John Jolly had indeed travelled fast and far from his penniless daft days. His original borrowed capital of £20 had been miraculously transmuted into a vast ranch, extending over an area of 75 square miles – 40,000 acres. His flocks and herds were beyond number.

Over the years most of the land was sold off and, nowadays, John Jolly's ranch, eventually worked by the youngest son William (Hap), is owned by a family named Kalsevic, of Czechoslovakian origin. There are still a couple of ranches in Jolly hands. John Jolly's son Robert bought the Field Ranch near Hugo, which is still run by his son, Jay. In 1949, Robert bought the old Foote Ranch, also near the small town of Hugo, and that is now run by Tom Jolly. Another two of John Jolly's sons, Jim and Carley, bought the 35,000 acre Agate Ranch, which Jim lived on for the rest of his life. He and his wife had no children. Tragically, he was murdered on 10 December 1980. Several sections of his former holdings are run by Carley's family, as is the old Stone Ranch, which Carley operated.

Jim and Jack Stewart, who emigrated to Colorado with John Jolly, also became ranchers. Jack Stewart had a 20,000 acre ranch which John Jolly's second eldest son, David, purchased in 1936. Unfortunately, David's eldest son, John, lost his share of the ranch to unscrupulous business partners. Much of the former Jolly grassland has now gone under the plough, and there is a genuine fear among local people that over-intensive cropping may create another dust-bowl. Altogether, John Jolly and his sons controlled 200,000 acres at one time.

The Stewart brothers outside Jack Stewart's ranch near Deer Trail. Per John Jolly, Deer Trail, Colorado.

John Jolly became a highly respected rancher in eastern Colorado, eventually owning as much land as the present Earl of Dalhousie in Glenesk. Had he and the Stewart brothers remained in Scotland such opportunities would never have arisen. In fact, it would have been inconceivable. They made the most of the opportunities that came their way and succeeded where many others failed, though not without much suffering and personal loss.

NORMAN BEATTIE (MARGARET JOLLY'S SON). PIONEER FARMER IN THE AUSTRALIAN BUSH

When the Duke and Duchess of Gloucester were resident in Australia, official duty took them to Hyden, a new development area in the southwest. The local branch of the Returned Soldiers' League was on parade. As the Duchess passed along the ranks, she asked an ex-service man a casual question. On hearing the reply she looked again and smilingly observed: 'You are from Scotland, what part do you come from?'. 'My home is in Angus, within a bus run from Glamis Castle'. 'Would you like to go home?', asked the Duchess. League mates grinned as Norman Beattie, the loyal new Australian with the unmistakable Scottish accent replied: 'Just for a holiday'.

When the Kaiser's War broke out, Norman Beattie was only seventeen years old, but already a volunteer in the Territorial Army. Within a year he was driving heavy guns through the mud and blood of France and Flanders, and meeting service comrades drawn from the ends of the earth. On returning home, he, along with thousands more, found nothing but frustrating unemployment. During long spells of enforced idleness, his mind kept harking back to memories of Australian comrades in the Ypres salient. He recalled their tales of the vast, empty bush, and of the welcome that awaited white settlers in their sundrenched land.

By 1923, soured and disillusioned, Norman Beattie, refused further acceptance of 'the Dole'. Steady work he must have even though he had to travel ten thousand miles to get it. He collected his war gratuity, booked an ex-service man's assisted passage, and sailed for Western Australia. 'Why Western Australia?' he was asked. 'It's nearest home', came the answer.

Five weeks later he and a fellow Scot, Bob Purvy, whom he met aboard ship, stepped on Australian soil, strangers in a land of strangers. Within a week they were in the bush working, but at the end of three months hard labour, each was handed enough money to buy one pair of working trousers. They left forthwith.

His next employer, Mr L.C. Dalton, gave personal encouragement to the young emigrants, and sent a letter to Scotland: 'Norman, as you will know, is with me now. He is going to succeed, for he is a tryer, and I am interested in tryers. They are the sort we want in Australia'. After two years of profitable experience, Norman Beattie took an option on 1,100 acres of land in a wheat development area at Hyden, 350 miles from Perth. The Government Loan granted to pioneers extended over a period of 99 years. Lack of capital cramped progress, so, for another year, the emigrant remained an employee and saved steadily.

In 1926 Norman Beattie and his future brother-in-law Bob Dalton set out for the latter's home, to claim adjoining Land Blocks 98 miles away. They travelled all the way by horse and wagon, but, when nearing their goal, found their way completely barred by trees 50 feet high and two feet thick. Scattered patches of low scrub filled intervening spaces. They literally hacked and blazed a wagon trail through the last eight miles.

Water, or rather the lack of it, was to prove a major problem. There were no springs, and no underground supplies. Home-made catchment dams were constructed at an early stage, but over long periods rainfall was negligible. Seven miles away from the Block was a rock area of 200 acres and, here, pioneers collected what water they could in cans and buckets. In prolonged drought, this source failed and then pioneers had to travel 50 miles for adequate supply.

In 1928 Norman Beattie married Ava Dalton, his former employer's daughter. Their first self-built home was iron walled, tin roofed and dirt floored. Here, two of their three sons were born. During summer, temperatures often soared to 100 degrees and over, making the shanty furnace hot. With water at a premium, raising healthy children was a worrying nightmare. Their second house, made of mud and bricks, was built with the help of a casual workman.

It boasted four rooms and had a verandah all round. It was a really 'dinkum' bush home.

As the months and years passed, more and more land was cleared, seeded and cropped. While Norman Beattie felled trees, cleared scrub, carted water, tended stock, ploughed, sowed and reaped, his young wife burned fallen timber, watered stock, helped with the keeping of poultry to pay housekeeping bills, and cooked, cleaned and cared for her family. At first, visiting their nearest neighbours meant a journey of twelve miles, and personal shopping a trip of fifty miles. After four years came Red Letter Day. A local store was opened only eight miles away from the bush farm, named 'Angus'.

As the family grew, the schooling problem had to be faced. At seven and eight years respectively, the older boys were given push-bikes. Every school day they pedalled eight miles to learn the three R's and eight miles back. They sum up their youthful trails thus: 'We didn't know which were the worst, the scorching hot days or the nasty wet ones. It was a big job for young lads, but it certainly built up our leg muscles'.

There were occasional high days and holidays also. There was the memorable day when the family rose at 4.00 am and motored more than one hundred miles to greet the Queen and the Duke of Edinburgh. 'It was wonderful, we saw our Queen and how young and beautiful she is'.

The highlight of each year, however, came at Christmas when the family held open house. The spread of food and kindness at 'Angus' was proverbial. The temperature might soar to over 100 degrees, but traditional fare was ever welcome. New Year's Day brought picnics and a sports programme, and then once more it was back to 'auld claes' and pioneering projects, the overcoming of bush fires and dust storms, the control of pests like emus and dingoes, the patient waiting for rain to fill out the crops.

The year 1940 brought crisis. 1,000 acres had been cleared, but there was prolonged drought and finishing rains failed. The bank account was more than ever 'in the red'. Norman Beattie decided to cut his losses and admit defeat. Had the pioneers but known, success for the whole area was just around the corner. Hitler's war created boom markets for all farm products. The finishing rains came to the district with increasing and heartening regularity. Today – 36 years after its start – Hyden is a flourishing farming area.

Norman Beattie and his family started all over again on another farm. He never saw his work come to fruition, but lived long enough to glimpse the golden fringe of success. Today as his three sons watch wheat and oats come into head on their present farm, thoughts must sometimes stray back across the years to Hyden harvests, when the finishing rains failed, the crops shrivelled, and family hopes died. This account, presented here in digested form, was written by the late Miss Elizabeth Beattie, Arbroath. The original documents are now in Australia.

The Jolly story is typical of the experiences of many Glen families. Almost every family has relatives abroad who have emigrated, as well as those who went to England. The Museum provides a wonderful meeting-place, and through it many visitors from abroad have been re-united with their relatives. Indeed, relics of Glenesk have come from all over the world. The late W.D. Ross sent linen woven by his grandmother in Middleford, Glentennet, Elizabeth Middleton. W.D. Ross was a game warden in British Columbia. Many of his relations, the Dunbars, emigrated to Canada, USA and New Zealand. His uncle, James Dunbar, elder son of John Dunbar of Garthead, taught Greek in Otago University, Dunedin, New Zealand. James Dunbar was formerly Head-master at Portree in Skye, where he met his wife, Jane Fairweather, when she was appointed assistant there. They emigrated to New Zealand. Their two sons died tragically within two years of each other, one in a drowning accident and the other of double pneumonia. Both were regarded as brilliant medical students and there is a plaque commemorating them at Dunedin University. Members of another branch of the family are ranchers in the States.

In a case containing trinkets in the Museum is a little gold brooch in the shape of a thistle. This was sent to the late Miss Minnie Lindsay, the last Lindsay to live in Glenesk. She and William Middleton, the sender, were engaged to be married, but he had emigrated to the Yukon as a Prospector but never struck enough gold to send for her. On one occasion after a little success, he had the brooch made in Seattle.

Greta Michie was in touch with so many descendants of emigrants that she found difficulty in choosing examples. There are Christisons all over the world, although none of that name remains in Glenesk. The descendants of Helen Farquharson Smith, once innkeeper at Balhangie (now Cairncross), appeared a few years ago from Australia. A family bearing the name Glenesk had come over from Vancouver.

The name Lindsay has also disappeared from Glenesk, but, like the Christisons, not the inheritance. A marriage of a Lindsay with one of the Smarts established a double contact with the South. Helen Catherine Lindsay Smart's genealogical work has produced a family tree of the Lindsays and Smarts of Glenesk. The Smarts migrated to England, where Catherine's father entered the Church.

Three of the Skenes of Turnabrane emigrated to Canada in the early part of the twentieth century. James Skene returned after World War I to take over the farm of Blackcraig. Many Glen people went to British Columbia, and Alberta is also full of emigrants from Glenesk. It is strange how emigration seems to affect families from the Glen. One family has almost died out at home, but in Canada their descendants are like the sands of the sea.

In the Glenesk area, at the height of emigration, the main reason why people went abroad was want of opportunity at home and the chance to earn a living.

James Dunbar and his family in Dunedin, New Zealand. 1890s. Glenesk Museum.

There were better chances abroad and the call of adventure in the great unknown kept young men sitting round the fire discussing their problems far
into the night. There were also rebels who would rather emigrate than endure
existing systems at home. Many felt that they had no other option but to
emigrate. Amalgamation of holdings, appropriation of land held in common
and evictions for false reasons were all contributing factors. To his eternal
credit, it can be said that the tenth Earl of Dalhousie did all in his power to
arrest depopulation, spending much of his private fortune, inherited from his

mother, on the improvement of houses, steadings and general living conditions. The Edzell Arch is a monument of gratitude. Following Lord Dalhousie's efforts, population in Edzell parish did rise, but in Lochlee it decreased with the rate accelerating after World War II.

Although people emigrated to far-flung corners of the globe, the distances are not great in time nowadays. Through air travel, Christisons, Jollys, Dunbars, Farquharsons, Davidsdons, Skenes, Lindsays, Smarts, Stewarts and all of the others can come quite easily to the land of their forbearers. One day Greta Michie found a man standing at her door, a typical Lowden. 'Hello', he said and named her. He had come from Sydney. She knew his folk and his pedigree very well.

18

RECENT DAYS

When the Panmures were joined by marriage to the Ramsays of Dalhousie, two of the most ancient families in Scotland were united. The 2nd Lord of Panmure was the 11th Earl of Dalhousie (1801–74), who, in 1866, erected the Rowan Tower, a prominent feature of the Glenesk landscape, as a memorial to his brother who died without a male heir and thus ended the Panmure line. The House of Ramsay was seated at Dalhousie, Midlothian from a very early period. Sir William Ramsay is reputed to have signed the Declaration of Arbroath in 1320, and another William Ramsay was created the 1st Earl of Dalhousie in 1633.

In the present century the 14th Earl, Arthur George Maule Ramsay, married Lady Mary Heathcote-Drummond-Willoughby in 1903. Lady Mary Dalhousie fought to have a midwife installed in the Glen and after her appointment the first baby she delivered was born at Mudloch Cottage. He was named Ramsay Willoughby Guthrie in honour of Lady Mary's efforts and now lives at The Parsonage, Glenesk. The name continues in the family through his daughter, Sandra Willoughby Guthrie. (SA 1992/46). The 15th Earl, John Gilbert Ramsay, died unmarried in 1950 and his brother, Simon Ramsay, was until recently the 16th Earl of Dalhousie. John Gilbert inherited 140,000 acres but estate duties obliged the present Lord Dalhousie to sell 35,000 acres of the Panmure estate in Angus and 2,000 acres of the Dalhousie estate in Midlothian. Only Dalhousie Castle and its immediate grounds remain in Midlothian. In Glenesk, Dalhousie Estates have retained the grouse moor and deer forest of Invermark Estate. In his book, *A Pattern of Land Ownership in Scotland*, Robin Callander explains that the landowner in Scotland is a vassal of the Crown and within this system anyone who disposes of land they own in Scotland can retain an interest in that land. The process is known as subinfeudation and there is no limit to the number of times it is practised:

> At each stage, superiors can limit the extent of possession conveyed by reserving the rights to themselves and by imposing unlimited additional conditions and burdens on the vassals.[1]

[1] R.J. Callander. *A Pattern of Land Ownership in Scotland*, Haughend Publications, 1987, 13.

This explains how Lord Dalhousie was able to sell off parts of Glenesk and yet retain the Retreat building and Tarfside village. What had been Dalhousie land at the beginning of this century is now divided into three separate estates, The Gannochy, Millden and Invermark. The entrance to the Glen is off the B966, Edzell–Fettercairn road. The Gannochy, at the 'fit of the Glen' (16,000 acres) was sold by Dalhousie Estates to an American, Mr Ruttenberg, in 1981, and he administers the estate from London through his factor, Mr Elphinstone, at Edzell. Dalhousie Estates leased Millden Estate (19,000 acres) to the Duke of Roxburgh in 1963, but subsequently sold it to Grenfell Incorporated in 1979. It is managed from London by Mrs Duffield on behalf of Millden Estates Ltd. From the Millden Estate, Lord Dalhousie retained the Retreat building which houses the Glenesk Folk Museum, but not the Retreat shoot. He also retained Tarfside village which is the focus of social life in the Glen. The area at the top of the Glen, Invermark Estate (50,000 acres) has also been retained by Dalhousie Estates. They use Invermark Lodge during the shooting season. The estate is administered by the factor, Mr Richard Cooke, at Dalhousie Estate Offices, Brechin Castle where the family home is.

The Dalhousie family are well known and popular Glen visitors and since the 16th Lord Dalhousie has been an influence in the Glen for much of the last century, it is appropriate that an abbreviated biography be included. This information consists of excerpts taken from the Guard Book, *The Dalhousie Family*, at the Glenesk Folk Museum. Simon Ramsay, Lord Dalhousie, KT (1971) GCVO (1979) GBE (1957) MC (1944), Lord Lieutenant of Angus (1967–89), Lord Chamberlain to the Queen Mother (1965–92) and a Member of the Royal Company of Archers (who are the Queen's bodyguard in Scotland), was born on 17 October 1914 and educated at Eton and Christ Church, Oxford. He was a Major in the Black Watch Regiment (1936–39) and fought in the desert during World War II. He married Margaret Elizabeth Mary Stirling, daughter of the late Brigadier-General Archibald Stirling of Keir in 1940, and they have three sons and two daughters. The present heir is Lord James Ramsay, now the 17th Earl. Lord Dalhousie was a member of the former Angus County Council and was elected Unionist MP for Angus in 1945 (1945–50). He was the Conservative whip but resigned office when he succeeded to the title and estates on his brother's premature death in 1950. He was appointed Governor General of Rhodesia and Nyasaland (1957–63), and he has accepted many offices as Lord Dalhousie: President of the Victory League; Vice-President of the Royal Highland Agricultural Society; Chairman of the Scottish Country Industries Development Trust. He was Chancellor of Dundee University (1977–92), and he was the first Dalhousie to visit the Dalhousie University in Halifax, Nova Scotia since it was built in honour of the 9th Earl of Dalhousie who was Governor General of Canada 1819–26. He received an Honorary Doctorate LLD (1982), and was given a civic reception by the town of Dalhousie in Nova Scotia.

Lady Dalhousie was a former director of Highland Home Industries and with Lord Dalhousie she set up the Glenesk Trust in 1959 with the object of creating a community centre in the Glen consisting of a Folk Museum, a sales outlet for Highland Home Industries and a tea room catering for tourists at the Retreat. The Trust initiated classes for basketry, stone polishing, metal-work, weaving and tapestry. This is where Ross Robertson, son of Agnes Robertson who was the previous curator, was first introduced to weaving and he now has a successful career in textile design in America. When he began to show a keen interest, Lady Dalhousie arranged for him to spend some time on her sister's estate at Morar where weaving was done quite extensively.

Lord Dalhousie was also involved in the modernisation of farms and cot-tages in the Glen, part of which was to pipe water from the burns directly into the houses. It is said in the Glen that he was 'forced to by the Hill Farming Act (1946) and the Church of Scotland minister'. As part of the Queen's Silver Jubilee Trust (1977) Lord Dalhousie leased, free of charge, two cottages at Greenburn, Millden, to the Youth Organisations of Brechin. Her Majesty the Queen stipulated that the object of the Queen's Silver Jubilee Appeal was to help young people to help others and the Glenesk Cottage Project received funds from the Central Fund in London to carry out the conversion and exten-sive repairs to the cottages. They were completed in 1979 and every summer parties of Youth Organisations from Brechin, comprising able-bodied and disa-bled members, use the cottages as a base for outdoor activities. There is only one criticism of Lord Dalhousie in the Glen. He has not seen it as appropriate to build deer fences on the south side of the Invermark Estate although the north side is fenced. This leads to problems for the farmers when deer wander on to their fields, although legally they are entitled to shoot any deer which invades their crop. Lord Dalhousie's decision not to sell any estate properties is fully supported by his tenants. They will point out that only two cottages of the five sold by Millden Estate is permanently occupied by a family – the other three have become holiday homes. His decision not to allow fixed caravans on any of his properties has been met with reservation but it is accepted that the extensive development of tourism may damage the sporting estate. The relationship between Lord Dalhousie and his tenants in Glenesk was amiable and there is no reason to doubt that this will continue with his son James.

POPULATION

The decline in population is typical of the general depopulation which has taken place in the highland glens in Angus and Perth but according to Dr James Hunter in *The Making of the Crofting Community*, this is the opposite of the recent upward trend in other Highland areas such as the Western Isles, Argyll and Inverness-shire. Such a decline in population has several contributory factors and some of those can be applied to any Highland population. The education system sends pupils to nearby towns, in this case to Brechin, at an impressionable age and introduces them to the attraction of town life. Those who wish to pursue further education at a higher level must go to the cities and there is seldom an opportunity for them to return with their new skills. Mechanisation, which increases the scope of the work covered while maintaining unchanged labour requirements, is another consideration. As well as these common factors, Glenesk also has particular problems. The system of land-ownership and estate management does not allow for diversity of economy. Glenesk is struggling to survive as a Highland sporting estate and there is conflict between the rearing of game and the interests of the farming community. The farmers are unable to grow any crops because the uncontrolled rabbit population (and, in some cases, the deer) invade their fields. In order to make farming financially viable, the farmers have resorted to amalgamating farm units which has meant that there are fewer farms available to the rising generation.

FAMILY

When Glenners talk about 'family' they are referring to continuity of names, surnames and history in the Glen. The best illustration of the continuity of the older family names is the Grant/Davidson family tree, a fully researched record of which is in the Folk Museum at the Retreat. The informants on this occasion, Angus Davidson and his sister Isobel Low, belong to the oldest family still living in the Glen, the Davidsons and the Grants. Their great-great-grand-mother was born in 1768 at Dochty, a settlement at the top of Glenlee which is now a ruin. Their great-grandmother, Ann Grant, was born at Dykeneuk in 1796. Their great-grandfather, John Davidson, came from the Forest of Birse, Aberdeenshire, and married Ann Grant in 1826. Their grandfather, William, who was born at Dykeneuk in 1836, began the family tradition of being the joiner and undertaker in the Glen. He had eight of a family, one of whom was James, father of Angus and Isobel, who was born at Dykeneuk in 1887 and became the joiner and undertaker in the Glen. He married Margaret Robertson and had three of a family — Alexander (b.1925), Isobel (b.1927) and their brother Angus (b.1935) were born at Dykeneuk. Alexander emigrated to America in 1949 after World War II, and Angus and Isobel married their respective partners and settled in the Glen.

Angus and Ruth have a son and a daughter. Their son Grant has a haulage business in Aberdeen and lives in Portlethen, while their daughter, Isobel (Bea) Rawlinson, has recently come to live with her family at the House of

Mark, Invermark, which Bea runs as a Guest House. Her husband was a teacher at Brechin but was re-training to become a Reporter to the Children's Panel. They have three children, two at Brechin High School and one at Tarfside Primary school. Angus was very disappointed when his son decided not to follow in his father's footsteps and go into farming, but he is now reconciled to the fact and sees that his son has been very successful in what he chose to do: 'The pace of life here was too slow for him. He would have liked more mechanical farming, a bit more bustle about the place maybe' (SA 1992/44). Angus and his wife Ruth planned to retire in 1993–94 and at that time no family member was prepared to take over the tenancy of Gleneffock where they farmed. Isobel Davidson's late husband, Gordon Low, was a gamekeeper and they have three daughters who have settled in Perth, St Andrew's and North Wales. They love to come back to the Glen with their families for holidays, but none have settled in the Glen: 'I don't suppose they are that far away, what with transport the way it is nowadays, they're not that far away at all, but it would be nice to have them nearer ... maybe even in the Glen ... but it was not to be' (SA 1992/44). This is an update of a family whose history in the Glen can be traced back to 1769.

Two other families with long Glen ancestries can tell similar stories. Jimmy Caithness, whose family goes back to 1790, has a family of five and only one son, Dennis, is living in the Glen as Head Keeper on Millden Estate. Alistair Skene, whose grandfather was born at Turnabrane in 1868, has five of a family. His son Fraser is married and jointly farms Midtown and Blackcraig with his father. Fraser supplements his income by taxi and lorry driving at weekends. His daughter Valery and her family have recently returned to live at Muir Cottage. Valery works at the tea-rooms in Edzell and her husband is employed by Tayside Regional council at the Lochlee Water Scheme. This pattern of depopulation is repeated in many small communities and although the older families still have a representative of this generation living in the Glen, informants had mixed feelings about those who had left and those who had decided to stay or return. Alistair Skene sums up the ambiguity when he says that 'his two other sons can make more in one day working at the oil in Peterhead than Fraser can in a week' (SA 1992/45). Angus Davidson is worried about creeping materialism:

> My grandchildren can see on the telly and that, what other kids have and they want that too. They're not interested in the Glen way of life. You see ... there is too much emphasis on material wealth nowadays. If everybody was happy with enough to pay their accounts and have a bit of tobacco and a dram, things would be different. (SA 1992/44)

An extract from the *Third Statistical Account* bears this out:

> The old surnames are dying out. There are no Lindsays and no Christisons. A few Caithnesses and Stewarts are left, and a number of Davidsons. But most of

the other common surnames such as Littlejohn, Campbell, Strachan, Skene, Lowden, Guthrie, and Michie, have all appeared during the last century or anyhow since 1830.[2]

Sadly there are no longer Michies or Strachans in the Glen. Continuity of names relies on reviving the old naming tradition in the Glen where the eldest son adopts the father's name and the youngest son is given the mother's maiden name as a middle name. This was never strictly adhered to but, as in many instances in the Highlands, the tradition is gradually being influenced by external naming trends and fashions.

HOUSING

A survey of the properties in the Glen in 1992 revealed that there are 97 properties in Glenesk. Of those, 49 properties were under-used, 33 were holiday properties, five were used for seasonal employees, four were ruins and seven were empty properties. Holiday homes are causing grave concern in the Glen. Empty properties include the school-house (because the school teacher lives with her parents) and properties which are not quite in ruin but need extensive repairs and modernisation to make them habitable. Seasonal accommodation, such as bothies, is used for additional estate workers during the grouse season. The remaining 48 properties house the population of Glenesk and they fall into these categories: five owner/occupied houses, five rented from the estate for those in other employment, ten provided by the estate for retired employees, twelve tied cottages for estate employees, three Angus District Council houses for general allocation, two provided by Tayside Regional Council for employees of the Lochlee Water Scheme, and eleven tenant farmers. Of the five private houses, three are used as holiday homes and only two are permanently occupied by a family. The tied cottages are given rent free to gamekeepers, under keepers and shepherds employed by the estate. The tenant farmers are given a nineteen-year lease for the farm and the rent is reviewed every three years, calculated by the number of ewes, ranging from £4.50 to £6 per headage. Cattle are no longer part of the equation.

There are a few houses such as Woodhaugh, Muir Cottage and Druid's Knowe available for those who live in the Glen but do not work directly for the estates. The annual rent for these properties, also reviewed every three years, has recently increased from around £530 to around £800. The tenants are responsible for all care, maintenance and repairs and may even be penalised in the rent review if they attempt to improve the property.

---

[2] *Third Statistical Account of Scotland*, The County of Angus, Arbroath, 1967, 172.

The house and steading at Burnside, Arsallary. 1902. Glenesk Museum.

HOLIDAY HOMES

Holiday homes do not fall into the normal category of houses that are available on a weekly or fortnightly basis to casual visitors in the summer time. They form part of an arrangement whereby regular visitors to the Glen, generally retired people or those approaching that status, can come to an agreement with the estate to rent a cottage on a long lease. When they are not using the cottage themselves, they let it to other visitors, friends or family. Traditionally, those who lease holiday homes in the Glen come from nearby areas and have been coming there over a period. They have an affinity with the Glen and its people, joining in all the social events. This is changing now and very often the Glen people do not know the people who lease the holiday homes.

Residence	Name	Place of Origin
**Burnside	Dalhousie	
Glentennet	Morris	Chester
Shinfur	Legge	Oxford Street
St Drostan's Lodge	Episcopal Church	Brechin
Burnfoot	Keates	Glenesk
**Heatherbank	Dalhousie	
Tarfside Cottage	Black	Dundee
Skairhead Cottage	Bury	Dundee

*Cairncross	Milne	London
**Townhead	Millden	
Larg's Bungalow	Millar	Menmuir
Christie's Hut	Christie	St Andrews
Peep O'Keen	Cargill	Forfar
Smiddy	Brown	Wycombe
Ritchie's Hut	Ritchie	Dundee
Henderson's Hut	Henderson	Brechin
*Mangie	Orr	Edzell
*Manse	Forbes	Dundee
Keenie Cotagge	Main	Glenesk
Turnabrane Farm	Scott	Hillside
Mudloch Cottage	Davie	Dundee
Holmhead	Myles	Dalbog
Waggles	Dr Dally	Edzell
Greenburn Cottage	Coutts	Dundee
Jubilee Cottage	Youth Organ.	Brechin

* Bought Holiday Homes.
** Holiday cottages kept by the estates and let on a casual basis. There is no information on the following holiday homes, except that they are long term leases: Glenmark, Westbank, Whitehillocks, Blackness, East Migvie, Ivy Cottage, Milton Cottage, and Gleneffock Cottage.

Hilda Bury is such a visitor, and she reported that when she took over the lease of the Skairheid Cottage, Tarfside, in 1964, the rent was £17 per annum. In 1992 it was £300 per annum under review. With additional expenses such as the Community Charge and high maintenance costs, the real cost is nearer £1,000 per annum, and the cottage does not have piped mains water. The tenants are responsible for the financial outlay involved in care, maintenance, repairs and improvements during the tenancy (SA 1992/45). There has been an increase in the past five to ten years in the number of properties available as holiday homes in the Glen and there is bitter feeling about this. To add to the general unease, holiday properties such as Mangie cottage and The Manse, which were previously rented, were sold by Millden Estates to the current leaseholders. Ramsay Guthrie says that '... holiday homes will be the death of the Glen'.

Apart from houses supplied by Angus District Council for general allocation and by Tayside Regional Council for their own employees, only seven other properties in the Glen have central heating. This amounts to partial oil central heating and the tenants have arranged for its installation. None of the properties have double glazing. Peat is no longer cut in the Glen and there is no mains supply of gas to the Glen. The fuel used for cooking is generally electricity, or coal or wood stoves (QSA.1992). The houses generally date to around the middle of the nineteenth century, stone built, and of the three down / two up variety, occasionally with a dormer window upstairs. Some of the tenants complained of dampness, leaking roofs and the houses requiring fairly major repairs, but the estate management has adopted a 'make do and mend' attitude.

EMPLOYMENT

The estates either facilitate or create all the employment in the Glen. Although this has always been the case, there are fewer employment opportunities now than there used to be. There are several reasons for this. The last joiner and undertaker in the Glen was Jim Davidson and, when he retired in 1951, he was not replaced, since tradesmen come to the Glen from Edzell and Brechin to service the Glen area and funerals are generally organised by the Blacks of Brechin. Smaller farms are amalgamating with larger ones since any unit carrying fewer than 500 sheep is no longer considered financially viable. Hill farming is economical only if the work is done by the family so farmers do not employ extra help except in exceptional circumstances. Lambing time involves the whole family and sheep shearing is a communal activity. Opportunities for the younger generation to work in the Glen are scarcer now. Ramsay Guthrie was at Keenie as a young lad, helping on the farm and acting as caretaker until the eldest son in the family was of age to take over (SA1992/46).

Mechanisation has also affected the number of jobs available on the farm. The tractor can do the work of five men in half the time, yet the grazing lands which are increasingly under threat from bracken are inaccessible to it. Alistair Skene says the removal of bracken is labour intensive and the labour is no

The Campbell family resting while working in the fields. The men are wearing tackety boots. Note the four-pronged graip. From left to right: Andrew, Mary, John Campbell Snr, Jim (lying down), Lizzie, Jim Jnr. 1900s. G1/21/2A.

Clipping at Cairncross. Included are Joseph Dunbar (Kirn), Rob Jolly (the 'Loon'), and George Michie. Note the wooden tripods in the background, used for hay or grain stacks depending on the weather. 1908. Glenesk Museum.

longer available. Mrs Duffield has recently experimented with systematic helicopter spraying of vast areas of bracken on Millden Estate. This has been effective but it is too expensive for the hill farmers to use. The landrover has revolutionised the work of the gamekeeper and the shepherd alike. Fred Taylor spoke about when he was a young gamekeeper in the Glen and had to walk miles in the hills, 'often from seven in the morning until eight at night. Nowadays they take the landrover to the hills; 'they don't walk unless they're gathering sheep'. Fred also spoke about driving the grouse, which gave seasonal employment to young men in the Glen. Now, however, the grouse are becoming fewer and fewer. It means less income for the estate because the grouse shooting is becoming difficult to let (QSA 1992). In general, there is little diversity of employment in the Glen although this was not the case as recently as the mid-sixties.

> Apart from the farming community we have a resident minister, a teacher, two shopkeepers (one a post-mistress) a local postman, a gardener, two water attendants, a housekeeper, a museum curator and six elderly house-holders without definite occupation. The smithy was dismantled a year or two ago, for this is the age of the tractor and combine harvester. The last joiner retired about fourteen years ago and we rely on tradesmen from Edzell and Brechin.[3]

---

[3]   ibid, 167.

An early form of mechanisation, with a binder in operation at Milton. 1920s. Glenesk Museum.

The farming and gamekeeping community will be discussed later in this chapter. The minister is now based at Edzell and the manse has been sold by the church as a holiday home. There is still one teacher, two shopkeepers, three water attendants and a museum curator in the Glen. The local postman has been replaced by a Royal Mail delivery service from Brechin. The retired postman, Jimmy Caithness, does part-time gardening at Millden, and there are no trades-men in the Glen because the labour force for estate maintenance is centralised at Brechin. Another example of the negative effect of centralisation is the care and maintenance of the roads. According to Jimmy Caithness, there used to be a local 'road squad' employed by the former County, who kept the roadsides tidy, mended the stone dykes and kept the roads clear in winter: 'The roads were kept safe then. The worst is the damage caused by rabbits. They burrow all that gravel above the roadside and when it rains this falls down on to the road surface. There's been some nasty accidents when people try to brake on that kind of surface, especially visitors who maybe don't know' (SA 1992/48). Isobel Low spoke about the local 'road squad' organised by the keepers into road-clearing teams during heavy winter snows. They started at the top of the Glen and hoped to meet in the middle before more snow fell! 'We don't get snow like that any more' (SA 1992/44). Since regionalisation in 1975, this service is now adminis-tered by Tayside Regional Council. The Glen is included in a cyclical rota of maintenance when the Region men arrive in their yellow vans and do the roads. It is evident that this system does not work. The dykes are badly in need of repair in several places, the bracken at the roadside reduces visibility and makes driving hazardous and the damage caused by the prolific rabbit population is out of control. Angus Davidson shook his head: 'There are yellow vans with their lights on, whizzing about here when they're no needed. Someone in Arbroath decides that the Glen should have a snow plough that day and up they come. There may be no snow, but the very next day you could be inches deep in it and there's no sign of them' (SA 1992/44).

One of the 'road squads' formerly organised by the keepers to keep the roads clear during the winter snow falls. Possibly the 1940s. G1/16/28A.

Geordie Duncan, roadman at Tarfside, stone knapping for road metal. He lived in the westernmost part of 'Shorehead' (Tarfside Cottages). He has a clay pipe in is mouth. A wooden 'coggie' that belonged to him is in Glenesk Museum. c. 1920. Glenesk Museum.

FARMING

Amalgamation of land has been a feature linked with depopulation since Jervise was writing in 1853:

> The whole of the north-western part of the Glen (Glenesk) is also to be thrown into a deer forest, which will unite with the extensive preserves of his Royal Highness Prince Albert and the Earl of Airlie on the north and west, and with the Marquis of Huntly on the north-east.[4]

The concern in the nineteenth century was that such alterations would depopulate the Glen. There are similar fears in the twentieth century concerning amalgamation of farms. Writing in the 1960s, Greta Michie said that there were fifteen farms and one croft in Glenesk. Alistair Skene said that there were in fact seventeen farms in the parish of Lochlee, and five in the part of Edzell parish at the foot of the Glen. In Lochlee, in the 1960s, the farms were: Auchronie, Gleneffock, Dalbrack, Drumgreen, Buskhead, West Migvie, Tarfside, Milton, Baillies, Cairncross, Turnabrane, Cohairncross, Ardoch, Auchintoul, Keenie, Mill of Aucheen, Blackcraigs. In the Gannochy there were: Greenburn, Haugh, The Hillock, Colmeallie, Auchmull and Dalhestnie. In 1992 there are eleven farms in the parish of Lochlee, and two on the Gannochy. Dalhestnie and Greenburn Haugh on the Gannochy Estate remain as individual farms but they are incorporated with The Hillock, Colmeallie and Auchmull, and the houses are let separately.

A brief history of the amalgamation of farms on the Millden and Invermark Estates is as follows: Auchronie and Westbank, 1943; Gleneffock and West Migvie, 1978; Dalbrack Farm and East Migvie in 1984; Tarfside Farm and Milton Farm and the grazing at Ardoch in 1984 (Ardoch Cottage is now a Keeper's house); Cohairncross and Turnabrane, 1977; Keenie and Mill of Aucheen and arable land on Auchintoul and Greenburn Farm in 1990; Blackcraigs and Wester Aucheen, 1935; Greenburn Farm-Hill land to Mill of Aucheen, 1990. The Baillies makes the eleventh farm, and it is managed by Joe Menzies for Dalhousie Estates.

There is very little cropping done in the Glen. A few acres of grass are used for silage or hay, or as Alistair Skene describes the latest project, 'haylage'. Keenie and Dalhestnie do grow a few acres of fodder rape to feed small lambs, but this is still at the experimental stage. Since 1965, breeding cows have increased in number owing to the introduction of the hill cow subsidy, but the Dalhousie Estate does not want to encourage cows on the hill as it believes this interferes with grouse breeding. There are only two shepherds in the Glen now, Littlejohn at Dalbrack and the Haugh, and Menzies at the Baillies. Ramsay

---

[4] A. Jervise. *Land of the Lindsays*, Edinburgh, 1853, 93.

Guthrie says that in the 1920s and 1930s there were nine shepherds in the
Glen: two at Gleneffock; two at Keenie; one at Cairncross; one at Blackcraig;
one at Burnside; one at Dalbrack; one at Dalbog.

*Hoeing turnips at Auchintoul. Left to right are: Victor Strachan, Duncan Strachan, George S. Strachan, ?,
Bob Gibb, Jimmie ?. 1920s. Glenesk Museum.*

*The interior of Tarfside Smithy, now converted into a modern dwelling. Willie Fraser was the last black
smith in the Glen. His tools are in the Museum. 1930s. Glenesk Museum.*

EMPLOYMENT IN THE GLEN

Male		Female	
Farmer	11	Housewife	14
Headkeeper	3	Retreat	3
Under keeper	8	Teacher	1
Water Board	3	Nurse	2
Shepherd	1	Shopkeeper	2
Shopkeeper	1	Waitress	1
Student	6	Secretarial	2
Unemployed	1	Shepherd	2
Other	5	Housekeeper	2
Outwith	3	Guest House	1
Retired	11	Domestic Work	1
		Retired	9
Total	53	Total	41

There are 27 children. This Table shows that 56 per cent of the Glen population in 1992 is economically inactive. Apart from farming, shepherding and gamekeepering there is little opportunity for employment in the Glen. The major contributors to other employment are Tayside Regional Council who employ three people at the Lochlee Water Scheme on a permanent basis, and one teacher. Joan and Henry Gordon run the local shop and Post Office with part-time help from Fiona Korst; Isobel Low, Muriel McIntosh, Gilbert and Agnes Lowden run the Folk Museum, Tea-room and Gift Shop with help from local students. Bea Rawlinson runs the House of Mark as a boarding house catering for tourists and her husband Richard is a Reporter to the Children's Panel. There is the opportunity for seasonal domestic work at the lodges during the summer season but many of the women are choosing to work outside the Glen.

SOCIAL LIFE

COMMUNITY

Despite pessimism about depopulation there is a strong community spirit in the Glen. Several fund-raising events are held and every able-bodied person in the Glen contributes. There are three main institutions in the Glen which need regular funds – the Masonic Hall, the churches and the Retreat, and the funds are rotated on an annual basis. The Masonic Hall is used for the majority of social gatherings. If a dance or ceilidh is held the whole community turns out, but the format of these social events has changed drastically over the years.

The musical tradition in the Glen has disappeared and nowadays a band comes in from Brechin or Montrose to play at these dances, costing upward of £250. The Hall can hold only one hundred and fifty people so the evening is not financially viable. They also bring, according to Jimmy Caithness and Alistair Skene, 'a battery of amplifiers and sound equipment which is totally unsuitable for the Hall. You canna hear yersel speak'. In a scattered population like Glenesk the main function of these gatherings is to 'enjoy the crack' with friends and neighbours.

The fiddle played a large part in the musical tradition of the Glen, as it did in the north-east in general. At one time Rob Littlejohn made them in his own home. Ramsay Guthrie spoke about the time before and just after World War II when he played the fiddle in a local band which consisted of Ramsay, his brothers David and Joe, and Mrs Smith on the piano. Their band was only one of several in the Glen at the time – Ramsay mentioned that Rob Littlejohn and Jim Davidson also ran dance bands. They were often paid £1 to £1.10s (£1.50) plus taxi fares for an evening's entertainment.

He spoke about the time after the War when the band he played in had 'gigs' in areas round about Glenesk such as Brechin, Fettercairn, Montrose or Edzell, and they were only allowed to travel twelve miles in one journey. This regulation possibly had something to do with petrol rationing, but Ramsay was not too sure. They managed to circumvent it by travelling from Tarfside to the foot of the Glen, a distance of twelve miles, in a local taxi, and then take public transport or another taxi to the 'gig' depending on the distance (SA 1992/46). Isobel Low said her father, Jim Davidson, played at a bazaar and was given a packet of biscuits he was especially fond of as payment (SA 1992/44). Hilda Bury talked about the New Year celebrations in the Glen. The Keepers still 'shoot out the Auld Year' by going outside at midnight and firing shots and this signals the beginning of the celebrations. Another New Year tradition was the Clay Pigeon shoot organised by the Keepers on 2 January. Previous traditions included a curling match on New Year's Day and the White Hare shoot on the 2 January when 200–300 white hares were killed. Many Glen 'exiles' return to take part in these activities, although the participants are usually male. The women who are not curling organise the food for the party in the evening. This is a mobile feast and can occur anywhere in the Glen, usually around the Tarfside area. It was formerly a time for parties and community get-togethers but this is diminishing now (SA 1992/45).

It is curious that at a time when transport is more available and winters are milder there is increasingly less social activity around New Year. Marion Campbell said that there are too many alcohol-related events nowadays. 'Social life is not the same as it was when we first came to the Glen, when we could spend many happy evenings in each other's houses, playing cards and chatting, and then having a lovely cuppa with home baking. Drink was never consumed on these occasions unless it was a special event' (QSA 1992).

The local band playing at a dance held in the Masonic Lodge at Tarfside. 1930s. Per Greta Michie. G1/16/29A.

The first winners of the North and South Esk Province Trophy were Glenesk Curling Club. Left to right are: John Lowden, James Lowden, Andrew Campbell and James Stewart (Skipper). 1920s. G1/12/35A.

A clay pigeon shooting competition. One was traditionally held every 2 January, but was discontinued a number of years ago. Mr J.H. Davidson, Glen Prosen is about to shoot, while Mr G. Caithness and Mr H. Ferrier move into position for their second pigeon. 1960s. G1/12/23A.

Duncan Michie throwing the 'hammer' at the Tarfside Games. 1930s. G1/14/20A.

FREEMASONS

Freemasonry is a world-wide organisation, originally only admitting members of the Mason's Guild. It is accused of secrecy and maintaining certain rituals but Masons claim that the policy is '… not keeping a secret but not breaking your word'. The organisation is divorced from organised religion but members believe in a supreme being. The Lodges are now open to men of all ranks and members profess a mixed ideology. A recent Papal decree has allowed Roman Catholics to re-join the organisation.

The Lodge was constituted as St Andrews Lodge, Lochlee, No. 282 in June 1821, but, before that, possibly as far back as 1780, there was a Masonic meeting at Dykeneuk. It is said that a woman, curious to know what went on, hid inside the grandfather clock during a Mason's meeting at Dykeneuk and the Masons decided the only course of action open to them was to make her a fellow Mason.

The Masons, as they are called, have had an important function in the Glen although this is now diminishing. Alistair Skene, for example, joined the Masons in 1949, when he was nineteen years old. Although it is unusual to join before the age of twenty-one, Alistair was continuing a family tradition and exceptions are made in such cases. His grandfather joined in 1861, and his father was a Master Mason at the time Alistair joined. At that time it cost 7 guineas (£7.35) to join the Masons, the equivalent of three weeks' wages. Now it is £100.

Originally the Masons also had a financial function in the Glen, acting as a kind of bank and helping the poor of the parish. Alistair says that when he joined most of the young Glen lads joined and the Masons was a 'men's social club'. When the evening's business was concluded it was followed by an informal ceilidh where everyone joined in. The older Masons, such as Pat Caithness, had their own particular song which they were encouraged to sing. Fiddling and piping were also part of the entertainment (SA 1992/45).

This is less likely to happen nowadays. There are fewer members – only about eighty – and they come from as far away as Brechin to attend meetings. Not all the Lodge members live in the Glen. Alistair is a piper and has contributed his services to the Annual Church parade, leading the Masons from their hall at Tarfside to the Church of Scotland and back again after the service to a cup of tea with fellow Freemasons and friends. The Masons also organised Saturday night dances in Tarfside Hall when bands were 'about £5'. This has become difficult lately with the price of bands running at £200–280 (SA 1992/45).

The Masons in Glenesk claim to be the only Lodge in Scotland to have a monument on a hill top. The Mudloch Tower commemorates the establishment of the Lodge, but it was to have a practical function as well. An extract from the Minutes of October 1825 reads that the Tower was to be built ' ...with a small alcove with two stone benches facing South, with enough room to accommodate 2–3 persons'. In those days the Glen road passed over the Mudloch summit which rises to about 900 feet above sea level before descending to Auchintoul. It was a treacherous route in winter time and a number of tragedies had already occurred before the Tower was built. There is an annual inspection of the Mudloch Tower on St Andrew's day and when all is 'Marked Well' the Masons 'refresh themselves in the traditional manner belonging to a Tower visitation' (Document from Alistair Skene).

St Andrew's day is traditionally celebrated with the Masons' Ball. This used to be a grand affair and the Masons, their wives and invited guests in formal dress and full Masonic regalia sat down to dinner upstairs in the Tarfside Hall, waited on by the younger members of the Lodge. Jimmy Caithness said that if the girls in the Glen had not been invited to the Masons' Ball three months before the event they knew they wouldn't be asked that year. The dress is less formal now and outside caterers attend to the catering services, but the format remains the same. After the dinner there is an appeal for a particular charity – in 1992 it was Cystic Fibrosis. The Senior Office bearers and their partners start off the Grand March and the rest of the company join in, breaking into groups of four for the Foursome Reel. This completes the formal part of the evening.

CHURCH OF SCOTLAND WOMEN'S GUILD

The Women's Guild, or the Guild as it is known, is a national Christian association, affiliated to the Church of Scotland. The Guild welcomes members from other denominations but only members of the Church of Scotland can become office bearers. The members are not involved in the running of the church. The association promotes Christian fellowship and unity, bringing together women who are interested in issues which concern the Christian community. My informant on this occasion was Agnes Lowden who is the Guild President for 1992.

There never has been a large Guild membership in the Glen, and its future is in crisis at the moment. At present there are fifteen members, mostly from the older Glen population, and on average about nine attend meetings regularly. The young people are not church attenders and they see the Guild as being an extension of the church. There have been suggestions to make the Guild more secular, but, according to Agnes, this defeats the purpose: 'We are a Christian association'. The meetings are held on the first Wednesday of the month and the first meeting is always a Dedication Service, given by the minister, Mr Forbes from Edzell, or a representative of a Christian organisation.

The Guild year begins in July with a Coffee Evening and the 'Bring and Buy' Sale in Tarfside Hall, in aid of Guild funds.

For 1992 the topics introduced were:

Homelessness, by Captain Thomson, Salvation Army, Aberdeen
Homoeopathy, by a doctor from Brechin
The Christian Activity Centre, by Mr Ockendon
Lighthouses, by Mrs Keen, Arbroath Signals Museum
Craft Demonstration, by three Guild members
Women's World Day of Prayer, which is celebrated internationally in March.

The Women's Guild Project is decided annually at Headquarters at 121 George Street, Edinburgh. Last year's project was to raise funds to enable theology students to buy books, but the most successful project in recent years has been the fund-raising for the Centre in Leith which gives counselling to drug addicted prostitutes.

SCOTTISH WOMEN'S RURAL COMMITTEE

Because the Rural, as it is known, has been an integral part of the social life of the Glen since it was formed in 1924, a detailed look at this organisation is justified. The aim of the SWRI, which is written on an introductory leaflet and given to new and prospective members, is:

1. To provide social, educational and recreational opportunities for those who live and work in the country or enjoy county life.
2. To study domestic science and improve the amenities of the home.
3. To encourage the production of home grown food and to use them to the best advantage.
4. To encourage home and local industries, both individual and co-operative, and uphold high standards of craftmanship.
5. To consider family welfare and citizenship and any matter which affects the home and community.
6. To help to preserve the beauty and traditions of rural Scotland.
7. To work for international peace and understanding and goodwill.

This seems quite formidable but Mary Malin, who provided information, says she became a member of the SWRI when she was fourteen. The Glenesk branch is part of a structured national organisation, governed by the National Council of the SWRI in Edinburgh. The SWRI is non-denominational and does not enter into any political controversy.

Each local Institute is autonomous, organised within the guidelines issued from headquarters in Edinburgh. The Rural in Glenesk elects its committee by secret ballot, and the committee then chooses its president, an office which is held for three years. There are no founder members left in the Glen, but according to Mary Malin there are thirty members and the number of young women joining is increasing. According to the Minutes there were fifty-eight members in 1958. The Rural meets once a month, the third Thursday in this case, and the syllabus for the next twelve months is set by the committee.

The chosen night for the meetings in 1924, and for many years after that, was the night of the full moon. Members would start off from Craigoshina at the foot of the Glen and walk up to Tarfside, swelling in their numbers as they were joined by women from the various farms and cottages along the way. They came down from Inchgrundle, at the top of the Glen, in the same manner. Mary says that even after many of the members acquired bicycles, they still tended to arrive in large parties.

The 1924 syllabus had such items as: 'How to Bone a Fowl' and 'Making Gloves from Rabbit Skins'. Ella Ostler spoke about learning about cheese making at the Rural when she was first married in 1954. They brought their own milk (one gallon per lb or 500 gms of cheese) and their cheese presses, to the meeting. The milk was heated, the rennet added, the curds broken up and then strained through a cheesecloth. Salt was added, the cheese was pressed into moulds and left to set. The cheese was then released from the mould, wrapped in muslin and 'left to mature all winter with the hams in the store'.

The Entertainment's Committee Minutes relate that in January 1935 S. Cowieson's Band (Brechin) was to be paid 10s (50p) per three instruments plus motor hire, in payment for their appearance at the Burns' Night Supper at Tarfside. Admission to the Supper and Concert was 1/6 (7.5p) and the dance which followed was 1/- (5p) for non-members, and members paid 3d (-1p). For the same evening in January 1984, the band from Brechin cost £180, the admission fee for members was £2, non-members £2.50, and school children 50p each. In 1992, the admission fee for members was £4.50, non-members £3.00 and the band cost £200.

The syllabus for 1992 demonstrates how the Rural works in the Glen. It includes many lively topics, attempts to appeal to all age groups and also to keep within the aims of the national organisation. The year begins in July with a members' outing. This particular year they went tenpin bowling in Brechin and had a supper afterwards. In August they held a cheese and wine open night at Tarfside Hall in aid of funds. It was a busy evening attended by summer visitors who are 'weel kent' in the Glen, Glen residents and Institute members from Edzell.

In September the topic was a demonstration of exotic fruit and vegetables from Safeway Supermarkets and the competition was a fresh fruit salad. October's theme was photography and the competition was 'The Bonniest Glen View'. In preparation for Christmas, November's meeting dealt with making Christmas gifts and decorations. December is the highlight of the winter programme with the children's Christmas party in the Tarfside Hall. The fire is lit, the tree is decorated and Santa brings gifts for all the Glen children.

The children's Christmas party has been a tradition since the beginning of the Rural in the Glen. The 1939 Minutes say:

> Agreed not to have a tree because of all the extra expense which would be incurred because of all the evacuated children living in the Glen, mostly in the Waterside district. Fruit, sweets and crackers to be provided as usual.

In December 1941 there was no tree either, but crackers were provided and each child received 3d (-1p). Despite all these restraints the Rural Christmas party is fondly remembered by all those who grew up during World War II. Mary Malin's friend, Mary Fitzimmons, who grew up at Gleneffock but now lives in Nottingham, wrote in 1983 reflecting on her childhood in the Glen: ' ... I remember the children's Christmas party. It was one of the highlights of our year in the days of my childhood'.

The January meeting is a Burns' Supper. The members take responsibility for making the haggis in the stomach of a hind, traditionally donated by

The 'Burns' Supper' held at Tarfside in 1952. Left to right are: Alistair Skene (Blackcraigs), Mrs Dickson (Ardoch) and Mrs S. Michie (Cairncross). Per Greta Michie. G1/17/23A.

a keeper. At the Burns' Supper the haggis made by this original method is piped into the Hall and supplementary haggises are made in a bowl and served from the kitchen. The Supper is followed by an evening of Burns' music and song, the entertainment being provided by members and their friends.

February's meeting was a demonstration on reflexology given by Isobel Low's daughter Margaret. The founding of the Glen Rural is celebrated in March and on special occasions such as the Golden Anniversary (1974) and the Diamond (1984) there is a cake to mark the event. In March the members were given a talk on Alpine Gardening by a representative from Christie's Gardens. April is International Night with a talk and slide show on Denmark given by the mother of a Glen member who is Danish. April is also the time for the members' Bulb Show, and this always involves a children's competition. In 1992 it was an eggshell picture, and Mary remarked that the entries were 'ingenious'.

There is always a business meeting in May, and in 1992 it was followed by a demonstration of precious jewellery given by a member from another branch who is in the business. The competition was an edible necklace. In June there was a demonstration of glass engraving and the competition was a decorated light bulb. Because the Tarfside Hall was being refurbished this meeting was held in the Retreat, on the eve of the young President's wedding.

As well as being members of the local Rural the women are also encouraged to become delegates at Federation level and attend meetings in Angus District. They help to organise the Annual Handicraft show which is a mobile event, visiting Forfar, Kirriemuir and Arbroath. Brechin can no longer be considered because of traffic problems. The 1992 show was held in Forfar. Delegates from the Angus District Federation are elected to represent the district at national and international level. Mary Malin attended the meeting of the International Women's Institutes at The Hague in 1991.

YOUTH CLUB

The Youth Club was originally run by the Church of Scotland but is now organised by Richard Rawlinson and Ronnie Hepburn. The Youth Club meets every Friday evening at the Masonic Hall, and membership is open to children from ten to seventeen years. They organise a varied programme including physical activities, both indoor and outdoor, visiting lecturers on various topics and trips to places of interest in the locality.

COMMUNITY RESOURCES

EXTERNAL SERVICES

There is no outward evidence of social services in the Glen. For some time now there has been no resident Community Nurse and there never has been a resident doctor. The nearest medical services are based at Edzell and they visit the Glen on a regular basis. There are no social services such as home-helps – possibly because until now neighbours have been keeping an eye on the elderly in the community. This is referred to as: 'the Gaelic custom of neighbour helping neighbour' (TSA).

The nearest hospitals are Stracathro Hospital, which was built in 1940 as a military hospital, and Brechin Hospital. Public services are minimal. Angus District Council has provided a weekly refuse collection since 1981 and a monthly Mobile Library Service since 1983. Since David Stevens retired in 1972 there has been no minister in the Glen.

Until the late 1970s and the beginning of the 1980s Glenesk was served by mobile merchants who came up from nearby towns on a regular basis. Vans were plentiful. A grocer's van visited on Mondays, Wednesdays and Fridays, a butcher's on Thursdays and a fishmonger on Wednesday (TSA).

These vans no longer visit. As Hilda Bury remarks: 'The vans were expensive and unreliable'. Responses to a questionnaire show that most of the population shop for groceries once a week in Edzell, twice a month at Montrose or Brechin and daily at the local shop. The local shop and Post Office has been identified many times by informants as the single, most important recent development. A deep-freeze is not a luxury (in the Glen). Mail order is still used occasionally for specific items like hill gear (QSA 1992).

Ramsay Guthrie, Hilda Bury and Agnes Lowden expressed their concern for the diminishing woods in Glenesk. Wood has always been a popular fuel but recently there has been a trend towards installing wood burning stoves which has caused some concern. There used to be an annual allocation of wood for each household from the estate, supervised by the gardener, and this meant that tree cutting was selective: 'Between wood-burning stoves and the rabbits, there will be no trees left in the Glen. It'll be as bare as Glen Lethnot. It's these Bushman saws ... if they had to cut wood in the old fashioned way there would be less cut' (Ramsay Guthrie, interview, 1992). Coal is delivered by lorry from Brechin every fortnight, and a combination of coal and wood is used by most for heating.

Since 1980 there have been no dairy cattle in the Glen and now pasteurised milk is delivered weekly from Brechin. The mail-van arrives from Brechin to deliver Glen mail, daily at around 10.00 a.m. and collects all the outgoing mail in the Glen. There is no petrol outlet and no banking services – not even a visiting mobile bank – and the bank in Edzell is only open on certain after-noons. There are no off-licence premises, hotel or licensed public house, and no fast-food outlets.

The nearest Police station is at Edzell and recently there have been com-plaints about having to 'go through Brechin for the police'. Henry Gordon says: 'that there is a sense of loss of security in the Glen or perhaps a compla-cency engendered by living in the Glen' (QSA 1992). Burglaries, almost unheard of before 1989, are common-place now. Their shop has been broken into several times recently, as has the Folk Museum at the Retreat.

The Glen was linked into the North of Scotland Hydro Electric grid in 1957. Glenesk was the first Glen to receive this service because the power was needed for the Water Station: 'The Hydro Board came to the hall (Masonic Hall, Tarfside) with all this equipment. I think every household bought a cooker first' (interview with Gilbert Lowden, 1992). The tenants were respon-sible for the expense involved in having their houses wired and after the cooker the next most popular household items were an iron and a washing machine with wringer attached.

Water was piped into Tarfside village in 1939, and before that the main supply of water was the village well. The water tanks, which trapped the water from fast flowing burns above the village were installed by Lord Dalhousie. In 1944 the Rural Water Supplies and Sewerage Act stated that local authorities in Scotland were responsible for piped water supply and sewage purification in their own areas (document on History of Lochlee Water Scheme, from Gilbert Lowden).

In 1958 the first meeting of the Lochlee Water Board was held in Forfar, and by 1959 work had commenced on the Lochlee Water Filter Station. Until recently the water from the Lochlee Water Scheme was distributed as far south as Auchterarder in Perthshire, and none was available to householders in the Glen. Householders are now given a choice, either to be linked to the Lochlee Water Scheme or to continue to use water from the tanks in the hillside. At present, some properties in the Glen are served by the Lochlee Water Scheme and some are on the old system. There is an element of choice and those who obtain water from one system will claim that theirs is superior to the other (SA 1992/46).

TOURISM

The Scouts, Girl Guides and Boys' Brigade do not come in any great numbers to the Glen now. Isobel Low spoke of the times when every available camp site was occupied by children under canvas for the summer months, up until the early 1960s.

The woods around Tarfside are popular camping grounds for Scouts and Guides (TSA). The children were mainly town bred and were, perhaps for the first time, being introduced to the delights of country activities such as hill walking, climbing and pony trekking. Ramsay Guthrie spoke of how little some of these children knew about the countryside when they first arrived, being terrified of cattle and in some cases even sheep and dogs, and the delight they took in chasing hens. After two weeks they had gained in confidence and respect for the livestock.

Angus Davidson also spoke of a special summer camp for children who had been disruptive and come to the attention of the courts and how they gained enormously from their time in the Glen in the 1950s. Some of these 'children' still keep in touch with Glenners they came into contact with.

Another tradition which lasted throughout the 1930s to the 1950s was the summer flitting. Angus and Isobel recall how their family vacated the home and moved into Dykeneuk so that the house could be let to visitors: 'At that time everybody usually had another house they moved into, or a cottage or something, and you used to flit out in the summer and let the house to visitors. They were called the ludgers (lodgers) then, now people take guests' (SA 1992/44). Some families flitted to the barn, which had to be cleared out first. The temporary house was scrubbed clean, the family moved in, and then the home was given a spring clean. The houses had no piped water, no bathrooms and very few had electricity but they were spotlessly clean. The host family did not cater for the family except to sell them milk, eggs, cheese and butter. Angus Davidson says: 'It was to make ends meet because they were very hard up. Some of these visitors come back to the Glen, ... with children and grandchildren some of them ... to visit, not to stay' (SA 1992/44).

The only provision for tourism in the Glen is the Guest House at Invermark and Glenesk Caravan Park on the Gannochy. Most visitors to the Glen are mainly day trippers from nearby towns and cities who either bring a picnic with them or go into the Retreat for afternoon or high tea. The estates do not encourage extensive tourism. They are happy for people to walk in the hills providing they adhere to the prescribed routes and do not disturb the game.

TELEPHONE

The introduction of television is often blamed for the breakdown of community life but possibly the telephone, although it has its advantages, has replaced the need for personal, social communication in the Glen. Every house in the Glen, with the exception of some holiday homes, has a telephone. Jimmy Caithness says that when he was a lad there was only one telephone line, to the Post Office in the Glen. As Postie later, he transmitted all kinds of news and messages from one person to another ' ... births and deaths, someone needing a plumber or a joiner, lambing news and so on' (SA 1992/48).

Telephones were installed at Milden Lodge and Invermark Lodge in 1946. Ramsay Guthrie remembers a time when his brother Joe ran a taxi service in the Glen after World War II, and the butler from the Lodge would come down personally and give him details of visitors who had to be picked up at Montrose or Brechin railway stations. Nowadays it is so convenient to pick up a telephone and relay messages without any direct contact with anybody, and individuals in the community have become more isolated as a result. But, as a service, the Glenners would not be without the telephone. It is a vital link with emergency services when time can be of the utmost importance when such great distances are involved.

TRANSPORT

The private car has also played its part in the lack of communication in the community. Although it is now easier to travel to Brechin or Montrose to 'do a quick supermarket shop' it is also true to say that fewer and fewer people walk anywhere. They travel by car and wave to each other in the passing, occasionally stopping their vehicles to have a brief conversation.

In beautiful weather there is rarely anyone walking on the road. Jimmy Caithness speaks about a time in the Glen when 'no-one could hardly afford a push bike, and now nearly everyone has a car' (SA 1992/48). The private car, like the telephone, is a double-edged sword. Being without one in the Glen is a tremendous handicap because of its isolation, but driving does limit contact with fellow Glen dwellers.

There was never a railway system or public transport service in the Glen. Joe Guthrie's taxi ran a twice-weekly service from Tarfside to Brechin, on Wednesdays and Saturdays, leaving on Wednesdays after delivering the children to school and returning in time to collect them again in the afternoon. On Saturdays the car left at midday and returned about six o'clock. The charge for this service was initially 5s (25p) return and then latterly it increased to 7/6 (37.5p). The taxi service doubled as a parcel pick-up service, carrying 'anything from prescriptions to spare parts for farm machines'.

TELEVISION AND RADIO

Television has been mentioned and this feature of Glen life was introduced to the Glen in the late 1950s although reception was so poor that many areas did not receive proper transmission until the mid 1970s. In 1979, Mrs Susie Michie,

Cairncross, contacted a television dealer in Scone, Perthshire, who was prepared to install a receiver in the Glen and those who wished to use the service
paid £100 deposit plus £30 per annum for the maintenance of the line and a
television ariel. This system still operates.

Television does not play an important part in the lives of the adult Glenners,
although they do like to watch news, documentaries, especially those which
pertain to Glen life, such as wildlife series and farming news (QSA 1992). The
first programmes they remember watching on television include *Take the High
Road*, *What's My Line?* *Z-Cars*, *Six-Five Special* and the Oxbridge Boat Race.
The majority prefer to listen to radio, especially music programmes, and, even
more specifically, Scottish radio programmes.

The younger generation are interested in popular children's programmes
and the more recent soap operas, such as *Neighbours*. They listen to radio programmes relating to pop music but also show a strong preference for folk or
traditional music (QSC 1992). It is interesting to note that one family, (Elara
Browne) says they do not have, and never have had, television.

LANGUAGE

According to the QSA, the loss of local dialect is causing some concern:

> In ordinary speech, Scots is retained, the dialect more Aberdonian than Angus;
> but so many of the words formerly used have been forgotten ... English is used
> when we are on our dignity (TSA).

Perhaps the clue to the dilemma lies in the final statement. Henry Gordon
says: 'Those born after 1950 do not speak it and those born after 1970 do not
understand it' (QSA 1992). The older generation have retained a sprinkling of
Scots words. One of the questions in the children's survey asked: 'Do you
speak, or are you learning, any language except English?' and the response was
100 per cent: 'negative'. The children either do not identify Scots as a separate
language from English, or do not speak Scots.

INSTITUTIONS

EDUCATION

School provision in the Glen has had to adapt to the dwindling population. The children attend Tarfside Primary School and then they all go on
to Brechin High School for their secondary education. What was formerly
Edzell Junior Secondary School is now Edzell Primary School. The children

are taken by bus to Brechin every schoolday morning and return in the afternoon. Angus Davidson said that when he attended Brechin High School he cycled from Dykeneuk to Edzell (twelve miles) on Monday morning, took the bus to Brechin, and stayed in lodgings all week. On Fridays the journey was made in reverse. For one week during his time at Brechin School he did not have lodgings due to an administrative error and he made the journey daily (SA 1992/44). The decision to bus the children daily was taken for two reasons. It is more economical than providing lodgings for them in Brechin and they are able to spend their formative years in a home environment.

At the beginning of this century there were three schools in the Glen, at Waterside, Invermark and Tarfside. Invermark school took in pupils from the top of the Glen but closed down in 1930. Waterside school served the foot of the Glen and it closed down in 1965. This is an extract from information on Waterside School from a document prepared by Dennis Caithness:

> Waterside School was closed in 1965. It had been opened in 1876, following the Education Act of 1872. Between the parish schools of Lochlee and Edzell there were, in 1865, twelve miles with a school in the Hillocks area maintained by the parents. The site had varied. At one time it was at Bentyfaulds, now a ruin about 150 yards Northeast of Dalscampy where it was situated at the time of the Commissioner's Report (1865). It was described as a hovel and the need was stressed for the construction of a new school for a population of about 250. A school and schoolhouse were built and were in use by 1876. In the 1880s it was attended by 40–50 pupils.

This paragraph has been quoted in full because it demonstrates so many aspects of Glen life. Mary Malin's grandmother went to Bentyfaulds school, described as a hovel by the Commissioners. Mary told me that her grandmother wrote the most interesting and descriptive letters and in the most beautiful handwriting, to her daughter, (Mary's mother) in London when they lived there. The names Bentyfaulds and Dalscampie have almost dropped out of general usage now and Waterside School has been bought by Mr and Mrs Keats who have decided to retire there after spending many holidays in the Glen.

Tarfside Primary School is the only remaining school in the parish, with a roll of twelve pupils who commute daily from all parts of the Glen. The children who attend the school are intelligent and lively, very interested in farming topics, wildlife and local history as well the broader curriculum. Sandra Guthrie, the only teacher, is a Glenner, and is herself a product of the Miss Michie era.

When asked how education in the Glen had changed since her time, she said that some of the children now have to be encouraged to read, preferring to watch television instead. The children go to Brechin once a week for swimming lessons. There are also three computers in the school and the library has

been extended. The tradition of project-based education begun by Miss Michie
has been developed.

CHURCH

There are three churches in the Glen: the Maule-Memorial Church of Scotland, St Drostan's Scottish Episcopalian Church at Tarfside and Lochlee Parish
Church four miles further on at Lochlee. Lochlee Parish Church was originally
the United Free Church until it amalgamated with the Church of Scotland in
1932. Roman Catholics in the Glen attend mass either at Brechin or at the US
Naval Base at Edzell.

The area was traditionally Scottish Episcopalian although traditionally the
Dalhousies were active in the United Free Church of Scotland who were against
patronage. In 1845 the Episcopalian chapel in the parish was attended by
'about 113 individuals' (*New Statistical Account*) although there is no mention
of this church in the *Old Statistical Account*. Jimmy Caithness was brought up
in the Episcopalian Church, but joined the Church of Scotland at the time of
his marriage. The Episcopalian minister refused to marry them because his
intended wife was a member of the Church of Scotland and would not consent
to becoming a member of Episcopalian church. There is a weekly Sunday service
in the Scottish Episcopalian church during the summer (Easter–September) and
none in the winter.

There is a steady decline in church membership in all denominations. In
1848, 440 individuals attended Church of Scotland services and there were
250 communicants (*NSA*). Jimmy Caithness, who has been an elder for 30
years, says that ten years ago there were 100 members in the church, now
there are 71. He says this is another symptom of depopulation but it could
also be part of the national decline in church attendance. According to Jimmy
'in-aboot workers' do not join the church (SA 1992/48). The Rev. Forbes
holds a service in the Maule-Memorial Church every Sunday afternoon, for
three Sundays, and on the fourth Sunday there is a service at Lochlee Parish
Church.

The Church of Scotland is run by a Session and Board. Sandra Guthrie, who
was clerk to the Board, was elected as the first lady elder in the Glen. Curiously, members can be elders or on the Board but not be regular church
attenders. They undertake to be Acting Beadle for one month and have to
attend services during that period, but apart from attending Session meetings
this completes their obligation to the church. When asked about church
organisation and church attendance the retired Rev. David Stevens said that
he ' … didn't know anything about the church now. I'm retired. I don't go any
more'. The Sunday School has been discontinued.

LOCAL GOVERNMENT

Flow chart of local government processes

MEMBER OF PARLIAMENT, ANGUS EA
(Andrew Welsh, SNP)

TAYSIDE REGIONAL COUNCIL
(Hugh Arbuthnot)

KINCARDINE AND DEESIDE   **ANGUS DISTRICT COUNCIL**
DISTRICT COUNCIL   (David Myles)

INVERESK COMMUNITY COUNCIL
(Lethnot, Carrieston, Menmuir, Stracathro, Brechin Landward, Glenesk)

GLENESK COMMITTEE
Mary Malin, Marion McIntosh, Alistair Skene

Since the re-organisation of local government in 1975, Glenesk is served by Angus District Council, Kincardine and Deeside District Council and Tayside Regional Council. The District Councils are responsible for Housing and Finance, Environmental Health, Town and Country Planning, Licensing, Cemeteries, Leisure and Recreation (including Libraries and local Tourist Information) and Building Control. The Regional Council is responsible for Education, Social Work, Water Services, Police and Fire Services, Consumer Protection, Roads, Public Transport, Registration of Births, Deaths and Marriages, Valuation Assessments, Electoral Registration, Regional Tourism, and Strategic Planning.

The most important recent development in the Glen's participation in local government has been the setting up of the Community Council in 1975, which provided the community with the opportunity to express their views on local government through elected representatives. This is achieved by having a local committee of three people in Glenesk who hold meetings on an ad hoc basis once a month.

The people of Glenesk can come along to these meetings and present their views to the committee. The committee then take these views to the meeting of Inveresk Community Council, which meets in the different communities it represents on a rotating basis. This meeting is attended by the Regional Councillor, Mr Arbuthnot and the District Councillor, Mr Myles who are regular visitors to the Glen. The MP (in 1992 it was the SNP's Mr Welsh) is never seen in the Glen, not even at General Election time.

The system has worked very well so far, and this year the committee has raised issues such as rights of way which have been fenced off by absentee landlords, the litter problem in the Glen, excess water on the road and a request for a receptacle for depositing material for recycling, such as paper, glass and aluminium cans.

19

CONCLUSION

The object of the Glenesk book is to portray and preserve the past of this upland, rural community, mainly from the seventeenth century, although it has been possible to draw on much older sources and evidence which shed some light on the more distant past. While the book is a celebration of the people of Glenesk, their history and culture, it also charts the decline of the traditions, values and way of life of a thriving, rural community. Radical changes in land use, introduced by the estate as progressive, upset the age-old agricultural/ecological balance of the Glen. There is now far less integration between people's lives and their environment, as much grazing land has been given over to deer forest and grouse moor, forcing many people to leave. Industrialisation also played its part in the exodus from the Glen, as new technologies, combined with the reduction of farms, created a redundant work force. Local tradesman can no longer practise their age-old crafts.

The pattern of chronic decline and continuing emigration is established because there is no demand for the skills of those with professional or vocational qualifications. Lack of housing is a barrier to those wishing to live in the Glen and commute to urban centres. People's expectations are now higher, and they are more mobile, going to where the work and good money is to be found. People are not inclined to work on farms because of the decline in agriculture.

Glenesk was once a thriving community containing many small townships. The Glen was alive and it had a history. People had a sense of place and belonging as well as of something shared. It was not a romantic or idyllic way of life as people worked hard and suffered many deprivations in the past. Glenesk is a beautiful place, but as with many other areas of Highland Scotland, there is a tinge of sadness as one recalls that the empty landscape was once alive with the sound and movements of farm animals, people at work, children at play and of travellers using the hill passes of the Mounth. The sense of something lost is heightened as the eye lingers on the ruins of shieling huts, whisky bothies and dwelling places.

The people of Glenesk have given the Glen its history and they are its future. These pages record their lives, their story. They have contributed with their memories and anecdotes. This is their book.

APPENDIX

CLASSIFICATION OF SITES

A.	Houses permanently occupied.
B.	Houses occupied during weekends, summer holidays and on certain seasons or occasions.
C.	Empty houses.
D.	Farm buildings, stables, mills, waterworks, kennels, etc in present use.
E.	Ruinous sites, including houses, steadings, mills, kilns and stills.
F.	Ecclesiastical sites.
G.	Mines and quarries.
H.	Monuments.
I.	Prehistoric sites.
J.	Whisky stills.

GLENLEE AND INVERMARK.

C	The Stables of Lee
15E	A group of oval foundations, probably shieling sites, in the neighbourhood of the Lee Wood, not recorded in Roy's Map of 1775 as occupied dwellings.
C	Rebuilt shieling in the Lee Wood, of the same size as several of the above. Occupied by John Gordon until the mid-nineteenth century.
EJ	Whisky bothy at the back of Carlochy of Lee.
EE	Bridge of Lee (two houses).
EEE	Midtown of Glenlee (several houses).
E	Doughty.

273

E	Littlebridge.
C	Glen Lee.
EJ	Whisky bothy above Glen Lee.
ACD	Inchgrundle (double house, bothy, etc).
E	A ruin in Glen Lee at the base of Craig Maskeldie.
F	Old Lochlee Church and churchyard.
E	Old schoolhouse, etc.
EEE	Kirkton of Lochlee (several foundations), rising up the hill from between the present houses and the church to above a clump of trees, including unidentifiable site of former malt kiln.
AAAD	Present Kirkton of Lochlee (three houses in a row. Farm buildings).
AB	Two bothies at the kennels.
EEE	Invermark Castle, with foundations of former buildings around it.
A	Gardener's House, Invermark.
C	Former school (Invermark Side School until 1930 and later a bothy).
EEE	Foreside of Drum of Invermark (several foundations).
BABD	Invermark Lodge, including the Chalet and house at the stables.
AD	House of Mark (formerly the manse of Lochlee, with outhouses).
B	Cottage of Mark.
F	Present Lochlee Church and churchyard.
E	The Muirtown.
E	Damhead.
E	Several old buildings in the vicinty have still to be examined.
E	Mill of Auchronie.
E	Diddlin' Davie's house.
E	Jimmy Dhu's house.
AD	Auchronie and farm buildings.
E	East Auchronie.
EEEE	Cross Style (several houses and a smithy at the foot of Auchronie Road. Demolished in 1950).
C	Shiel of Branny.
C	Shiel of Saughs.
C	The Goat's house on the Slates.
C	Shiel of Logan.
EJ	Whisky bothy at Fashieloch.
C	Shiel of Mark.
C	Craig of Doune Shiel.
E	Bonnymune's Cave.
E	White's House.
EEE	A group of small ruins not far from White's House.
E	Glenmark Cottage, where Queen Victoria lunched in 1861. It stood slightly to the east of the present house and has practically disappeared.

B	Present Glenmark Cottage, for many years occupied by a deer-stalker, now let furnished by Dalhousie Estates.
H	Queen's Well.
E	Ruins of house on Glenmark side of the Drum.
EEE	Ruins (ovals and circles) in and around the Cowie-hillock planta-tion, including the I remains of a Bronze Age burial.
E	Ruins on the slope behind Cowie-hillock.
G	Disused lead mine on Gilfuman.
E	Rottenha', once an inn, half-way down Glenmark.

AUCHLOCHY AREA

EE	Auchlochy (several ruins).
EE	Glack (several ruins).
EE	Stilemouth of Auchlochy (two ruined houses at least).
E	School at Stilemouth.
EJ	Whisky bothy at Stilemouth.
EE	Turnagob.
B	Westbank (present site, also ruin behind it).
EEEE	Above the Glack are small foundations (ovals) and at least one Bronze Age Burial I Cairn.

GLENEFFOCK TO TARFSIDE

D	New Water Board buildings.
B	Whitehillocks.
AA	Two Water Board houses (Birchgrove) at Cock's Hillock.
AE	Haugh (also ruin beside present house).
E	Bellestrypes.
AD	Gleneffock.
B	Gleneffock Cottage.
C	Old Gleneffock Cottage.
D	Old Gleneffock Farmhouse at side of stream (now a shed).
E	There was also a shooting lodge at Gleneffock.
E	Whitehillocks in Gleneffock.
E	Scrabbie's.
E	Cochlie (an inn).
E	Fauldhead.
E	Bathie.
E	A ruin in the middle of the park near Gleneffock on the side of the bridge next the main road.

EEE	Broomknowe (three houses).
A	Blackness.
E	House at Brig Haughie ('Kindrochwood').
EJ	Whisky bothy at Clashinnie.
BBB	Dykeneuk (West Migvie), two houses and bothy together.
E	House on the west side of Dykeneuk among trees.
ADEEE	Migvie (five sites discernible, including the new house and old house).
E	Tillyroan (in the park east of Migvie).
A	East Migvie.
E	York Redoubt.
EE	Tirlybirly (house and smiddy).
AD	Woodhaugh.
C	Ivy Cottage.

ROWAN, HILL OF MILTON AND TARFSIDE

III	At least three large hut circles on the Rowan, ie excluding the Hill of Milton, two on the east side, one on the west side.
I	The Chief's Cairn on the Lang Howe. There is probably more unidentified material here.
EEEE	Foundations with rounded corners among the cairns on Lanf Howe and the higher slope of the Rowan.
H	The Rowan Tower.
III	At lest three hut circles on the Hill of Milton.
F	Site of former Episcopal Chapel (1723–1803).
EEEE	Foundation, near chapel, of ruins with rounded corners.
G	Kiln near chapel.
AD	Tarfside farm.
E	Treefaulds.
AD	The Parsonage.
EF	St Drostan's Chapel (1810–80).
F	St Drostan's Chapel (present building).
A	St Drostan's (former school and schoolhouse).
I	Bronze Age Burial on Glentennet road, near Tarfside.
A	Heatherbank with shop.
A	Post Office with shop and house.
B	Masonic Hall.
AD	Elm Cottage.
B	Tarfside Cottage 1.
B	Tarfside Cottage 2.

A	Tarfside School and Schoolhouse.
H	War Memorial.
B	Peep O' Keen.
I	Blue Cairn, and circle within School Wood.
E	Ruin of a house behind Schoolhouse, beyond fence.
C	Old Parish Council room.
A	Druid's Knowe.
AA	Two Dalhousie Cottages.
F	Maule Memorial.
E	Ruin of Beadle's house, on same side of road as church.
E	Foundation of a building opposite Cairncross steading, on brae.

CAIRNCROSS TO AUCHINTOUL AREA

AD	Cairncross (roughly on site of Balhangie Inn).
EEEE	Foundations of houses below and above Cairncross.
AA	Midtown of Cairncross, with Cairncross bothy behind.
D	Old smithy at Midtown. Foundation of Smith's house.
EEEE	Ewe Cottages, Burnside, Ardgieth. Unidentified foundation near the old Games Park.
EEE	Ruins inside Cairncross part of Ardoch Woods, including that of Tarry Inn, said to be the resort of the miners.
E	Foundation above Midtown, on road to hill gate.
E	Dykeneuk of Townhead.
AB	Townhead of Cairncross.
EE	Several ruined sites to east of present building.
E	Croft of Townhead.
EJ	Whisky bothy beyond Townhead, in Bothy Howe.
I	The Mile Cairn.
G	Lead and silver mines on Craig Soales.
BBB	Three summer huts below the main road, at Cairncross.
A	Smithy and house (now modernised dwelling house).
A	Manse of Glenesk.
A	Waterside Cottage.
B	Summer hut.
BE	Mangie.
AD	Ardoch.
B	Ardoch Cottage.
EEEE	Bankhead.
E	Foundation east of Retreat, on high bank.
ED	Cosie Howe (Birkenshaw or Wood Cottage).

AD	The Retreat (Gamekeeper's House).
A	The Retreat Lodge (Folk Museum, shop, tearoom, private house).
A	Cuttlehaugh.
EE	Two ruins at Cuttlehaugh, below main road.
E	Dryburn.
AD	Auchintoul.
B	East Auchintoul.
E	School at East Auchintoul.
BBB	Three summer huts.
H	St Andrew's Tower.

AUCHEEN AREA

CD	Mill of Aucheen.
AD	Mill of Aucheen farm.
A	Mill of Aucheen bothy.
A	Moor Cottage.
E	Damside Smiddy and Joinery.
AD	Blackcraig.
B	Blackhills.
E	Leywell.
EEE	The Shank (two houses – a tailor lived in one).
EJ	Whisky bothy up the Turret at Ladyholm.
EJ	Whisky bothy up the White Burn.
E	Spar Muir.
E	The Snob.
EE	Corhidlin and Corhidlin school.
B	West Aucheen.
E	Aucheen.
I	Several hut circles and short cist graves in this area.
E	Broomfauld.
EEE	Many small ruins, where miners were said to have lived in the eighteenth century, west of Broomfauld.

ARSALLERY, MILTON, BAILLIES AND GLENTENNET AREA

Arsallery

| BD | Betwixt the Burns, 'Tween the Burns or Burnside (there are many kilns in this area). |

E	Arsallery.
E	Arsallery (a school).
E	Badabae.
E	Whisky bothy at Badabae.
E	Kirny.
E	Stoneywell.
E	Garthead.
E	Dykefoot.
E	Greenesken (Green Erskine).
E	Tilliecoulter.
E	Blackhaugh.
E	Turnamuck.
E	Stripeside.
E	Shade.
E	Whitestane.

Milton

B	Milton Cottage.
E	Mill of Milton.
AD	Milton of Lochlee.
E	'Sarah's House', beside Milton of Lochlee.

Baillies

E	Breidless.
EEE	Boghead of Baillies (several ruins, including a smithy).
B	Burnfoot.
E	Burnfoot (once Free Church School and make-shift Church (1843–7)).
EE	Burnfoot (several ruins).
A	Baillies.
E	Old house at Baillies.
I	White Cairn.
EEEJ	Glen Cat. Several ruins, including an inn at Burn of Cat, plus a kiln and a whisky bothy.

Glentennet

E	Middleford.

BD	Midtown (now called Glentennet).
E	Shoggles.
D	Eastertown.
EE	Cawit or Cove.
EE	Several houses, some said to have been occupied at one time by weavers.
E	Unnamed ruin past the re-seeding.
B	Shinfur.
E	Burnfoot of Kedloch.
E	Kedloch (Inn and holding).
EJ	Whisky bothy.

SOUTH SIDE OF NORTHESK

EJ	Whisky bothy at the back of Garlet.
ABBD	Dalbrack (three houses).
E	Drumgreen (ruin).
AD	Kirn (two houses joined). Now described as Drumgreen.
EEEE	Tillibuchle (several ruins).
EE	Whigginton (two ruins).
EEEE	Leyhillock (several small ruins).
AD	Buskhead (new house beside remaining part of old house).
E	Ruin.
E	Birkenbrowl.
ABD	Turnabrane (three houses, one a shed).
B	East Turnabrane.
E	House in the hollow of the Lang Hillocks.
A	Corhairncross.
E	Cotlatericks.
BEE	Skelly (several small ruins and one standing house, once a school-house).
ACBDEE	Keenie (present house, old house, shepherd's house, bothy and unidentified ruins).

PARISH OF EDZELL

E	Keenie Mill (ruin).
E	Fauldheads.
E	The Skairs.
E	Boddam.

E	Berryhill.
E	Tillyoaram.
E	Faulds of Beck.
EJ	Whisky bothy on the Shank of Wirren.
E	John Cobb's hut.

PARISH OF LOCHLEE

E	Hillcroft.
B	Fernybank.
B	Millden Shooting Lodge.
A	Gamekeeper's house, Millden.
A	Under gamekeeper's house, Millden.

BIBLIOGRAPHY

Black, G F. *The Surnames of Scotland*, Edinburgh, 1993.

Burton, John H, ed. *Register of the Privy Council of Scotland*, (Second Series) X, Edinburgh, 1877–87.

Callander, R J. *A Pattern of Landownership in Scotland*, 1987.

Checkland, O. *Philanthropy in Victorian Scotland: Social welfare and the voluntary principle*, Edinburgh, 1980.

Colorado State Business Directory, Denver, Colorado, 1943.

Corr, H. An exploration into Scottish education. In W Hamish Fraser and R J Morris, eds, *People and Society in Scotland, Vol 2*, Edinburgh, 1990.

Cruickshank, E. *Navar and Lethnot*, Edinburgh, 1899.

Dobson, E B. Angus. In L Dudley Stamp, ed. *The Land of Britain*, London, 1946.

Donaldson, G. *Scotland. James V – James VIII*, Edinburgh, 1965.

Donaldson, G and Morpeth, R. *A Dictionary of Scottish History*, Edinburgh, 1977.

Donnachie, I and Hewitt, G. *A Companion to Scottish History from the Reformation to the Present*, London, 1989.

Duncan, A M. *Scotland. The Making of the Kingdom*, Edinburgh, 1975.

Edwards, D H. *Historical Guide to Edzell, Fettercairn and Glenesk*, Brechin, 1915.

Eeles, F C. Undescribed sculptured stones and crosses at Old Luce, Farnell, Edzell, Lochlee and Kirkmichael, with some late medieval monuments at Parton, Maryton and Wick, *Proceedings of the Society of Antiquaries of Scotland*, XLIV (1910–11).

Fenton, A. *Scottish Country Life*, (Edinburgh, 1976), revised edn East Linton, 1999.

Fenton, A. Coffee drinking in Scotland in the seventeenth – nineteenth centuries. In Daniela U, ed. Ball, *Coffee in the Context of European Drinking Habits*, Zürich, 1991.

Fenton, A, ed. *At Brechin with Stirks*, Edinburgh, 1994.

Fenton, A. Two Scottish day labourers' day books. In B Larsson, and J Myrdal, eds, *Peasant Diaries as a Source for the History of Mentality*, Stockholm, 1995.

Ferguson, W. *Scotland. 1689 to the Present*, Edinburgh, 1968.

Flinn, M, ed. *Scottish Population History from the Seventeenth Century to the 1930s*, Cambridge, 1977.

Fraser, D. *Discovering Angus and the Mearns*, Montrose, 1966.

Fraser, W. *History of the Carnegies, Earls of Southesk and their Kindred*, Edinburgh, 1867.

Graham, H G. *The Social Life of Scotland in the Eighteenth Century*, London, 1971.

Haldane, A R B. *The Drove Roads of Scotland*, Edinburgh, 1997.

Hunter, S Leslie. *The Scottish Educational System*, Oxford, 1971.

Innes, C, ed. *Acts of the Parliaments of Scotland*, VI, Part One (1643–7), London, 1850.

Innes, C. ed., *Acts of the Parliaments of Scotland*, VI, Part Two (1648–60), London, 1850.

Innes, C and Chalmers, P, eds. *Registrum Abbacie de Aberbrothoc*, Edinburgh, 1848.

Jervise, A. *The Land of the Lindsays*, Edinburgh, 1853.

Jessop, J C. *Education in Angus*, London, 1931.

Kyd, J G, ed. *Scottish Population Statistics*, Edinburgh, 1952.

Lawrie, A C. *Early Scottish Charters*, Glasgow, 1905.

Lindsay, Lord. *The Lives of the Lindsays*, London, 1849.

Maidment, J, ed. J, Ochterlony, *Account of the Shyre of Forfar*, 2 Vols, Edinburgh, 1845.
Marker, Willis B. Scottish teachers. In H Holmes, ed., *Institutions of Scotland: Education* (Scottish Life and Society. A compendium of Scottish ethnology IX), East Linton, 2000.
Michie, M F and Lenman, B. The Miners of Glenesk, *Scots Magazine,* 98 (November) 1972.
Michie, M F. *Studies in the History of Glenesk: Glen Folk*, Book 2, Glenesk Museum.
Michie, M F. *Studies in the History of Glenesk: The Parish of Lochlee*, Book 1, Glenesk Museum.
Michie, M F. *Studies in the History of Glenesk: Arsallary, Milton, Baillies, Glentennet*, Book 4, Glenesk Museum.
Michie, M F. *Studies in the History of Glenesk: The Dalhousie Family*, Glenesk Museum.
Michie, M F. *Studies in the History of Glenesk: Church and School*, Book 5, Glenesk Museum.
Michie, M F. *Studies in the History of Glenesk: Sport*, Book 3, Glenesk Museum.
Mitchell, Sir A, ed. MacFarlane, *Geographical Collections*, Edinburgh, 1907.
Munro, R. Notes on a set of five jet buttons found on a hill in Forfarshire, *Proceedings of the Society of Antiquaries of Scotland*, XII (1901–2).
Murray, D. *The York Buildings Company*, Edinburgh, 1973.
Myers, D. Scottish Schoolmasters in the Nineteenth Century. In W Humes and H Paterson, eds, *Scottish Culture and Education 1800–1900*, Edinburgh, 1983.
New Statistical Account of Scotland (second edition): Forfar and Kincardineshire, 11, Edinburgh, 1865.
Nicholson, R. *Scotland. The Later Middle Ages*, Edinburgh, 1993.
Nicolaisen, W F H. *Scottish Place-Names*, London, 1976.
Old (First) The Statistical Account of Scotland 1791–99, XIII (Angus), Wakefield, 1976.
Oram, R. *Angus and the Mearns. A Historical Guide*, Edinburgh, 1996.
Paul, Rev. J. *Up Glenesk*, Brechin, 1894.
Paton, H, ed. *Register of the Privy Council of Scotland* (Third series), X (1684–5), Edinburgh, 1927.
Roger, Rev. *General View of the Agriculture of Angus or Forfar Drawn up under the Direction of George Dempster of Dunnichen for the Consideration of the Board of Agriculture and Internal Improvement*, Edinburgh, 1794.
Scotland, J. *The History of Scottish Education*, London, 1969.
Sherriff, J R. *The Archaeological Sites and Monuments of Scotland. Central Angus*, 18, Edinburgh, 1983.
Simpson, J B. The late glacial re-advance moraines of the Highland border west of the River Tay, *Transactions of the Royal Society of Edinburgh*, LVII (1933).
Simpson, W Douglas. Edzell Castle, *Proceedings of the Society of Antiquaries of Scotland*, (1930–1).
Simpson, W Douglas. Invermark Castle, *Proceedings of the Society of Antiquaries of Scotland*, VIII (1933–4).
Stuart, J, ed. *Registrum de Panmure* (compiled by Harry Maule of Kelly, 1733), Edinburgh, 1874.
Synge, F M. The glaciation of north-east Scotland, *Scottish Geographic Magazine*, 72 (1956).
Third Statistical Account of Scotland:The County of Angus, Edinburgh, 1977.
Thompson, J Maitland, ed. *Registrum Magni Sigilli Regnum Scotorum 1546–80*, Nos 822 and 1579, Edinburgh, 1886.
Thomson, P. *Take One Glen:Recipes from Glenesk*, Montrose, 1973.
Thomson, T, ed. *Acts of the Parliaments of Scotland*, V (1625–41), London, 1817.
Thomson, T, ed. *Acts of the Parliaments of Scotland*, VI (1643–51), London, 1819.
Warden, A J. *Angus or Forfarshire. The Land and the People*, Dundee, 1880.
Watson, A and Allan, E. *The Place-Names of Upper Deeside*, Aberdeen, 1984.
Wightman, A. *Who Owns Scotland*, Edinburgh, 1996.
Wood, S. *The Shaping of Nineteenth Century Aberdeenshire*, Stevenage, 1985.

PUBLIC RECORDS

National Archives of Scotland (NAS), GD45/16/117, Dalhousie Muniments.
NAS, Forfeited Estate Papers, 5, Panmure.

NAS, GD45/18/1790, Dalhousie Muniments (Barony of Lochlee Money Rents, Martinmass 1875).

NAS, GD45/18/2353, Dalhousie Muniments (Extract Petition, The Right Honourable Wm Maule against Dukes and others).

NAS, GD45/18/1788, Dalhousie Muniments (Account charge and discharge of the intromissions of Robert Stocks, Factor to the Earl of Dalhousie, 1 September 1874 – 31 December 1874).

NAS, 237, Crawford Papers Vol 2.

NEWSPAPERS

Dundee Courier and Advertiser

CHURCH RECORDS

Brechin Presbytery Records

UNPUBLISHED THESES

Collins, Kenneth D. 'A Thesis on the Parishes of Lochlee and Edzell', PhD, University of Glasgow, 1963.

Mackenzie, C J. 'Glenesk. An ethnological study of a community in Angus', Honours Dissertation, School of Scottish Studies, University of Edinburgh, 1992. The 'SA' references are to tapes in the Sound Archive of the School of Scottish Studies.

INDEX